Hillary Clinton's Race for the White House

HILLARY CLINTON'S RACE FOR THE WHITE HOUSE

Gender Politics and the Media on the Campaign Trail

Regina G. Lawrence
Melody Rose

LYNNE
RIENNER
PUBLISHERS

BOULDER
LONDON

Published in the United States of America in 2010 by
Lynne Rienner Publishers, Inc.
1800 30th Street, Boulder, Colorado 80301
www.rienner.com

and in the United Kingdom by
Lynne Rienner Publishers, Inc.
3 Henrietta Street, Covent Garden, London WC2E 8LU

Library of Congress Cataloging-in-Publication Data
Lawrence, Regina G., 1961–
  Hillary Clinton's race for the White House : gender politics and the media
on the campaign trail / by Regina G. Lawrence and Melody Rose.
       p. cm.
  Includes bibliographical references and index.
  ISBN 978-1-58826-670-5 (hardcover : alk. paper)
  ISBN 978-1-58826-695-8 (pbk. : alk. paper)
  1. Political campaigns—United States—History—21st century. 2. Clinton,
Hillary Rodham. 3. Clinton, Hillary Rodham—Relations with journalists. 4. Women
presidential candidates—Press coverage—United States—History—21st
century. 5. Press and politics—United States—History—21st century. 6. Presidents—
United States—Election—2008. I. Rose, Melody. II. Title.
  JK2281.L39 2009
  324.973'0931—dc22
                                                                    2009026973

British Cataloguing in Publication Data
A Cataloguing in Publication record for this book
is available from the British Library.

Printed and bound in the United States of America

  ∞   The paper used in this publication meets the requirements
      of the American National Standard for Permanence of
      Paper for Printed Library Materials Z39.48-1992.

  5   4   3   2   1

Contents

Preface

This book began in the fall of 2007 with a phone call. "It looks like Hillary Clinton may become the Democratic nominee," Melody said to Regina. At that point it seemed clear that the 2008 presidential contest would be a historic one. With the first truly viable female candidate in the mix—possibly producing the first female US president—we saw the potential for the election to take on epic proportions. We could not have anticipated, however, the many additional ways in which the election would mark profound electoral and social change. Among the many history-making aspects of the 2008 election were, most obviously, the election of the nation's first African American president. The election also featured historically high voter turnout, a healthy showing by young and new voters, unprecedented fundraising by the major candidates, and the longest presidential primary in US history.

This book focuses on the role played by gender and the media in the first presidential nomination contest in which a woman was actually predicted (at least initially) to win. We argue that gender took on both predictable and unforeseeable dimensions in 2008. Blatant in some arenas, insidious in others, gender discrimination seemed at some times intractable and at others surprisingly nonexistent—or at least vigorously contested. Importantly, factors other than gender contributed to the outcome of this epic primary process, leaving us with the complex and challenging task of teasing out gender bias from other variables.

Though it seemed at the time of our initial phone conversation that Hillary Clinton was well positioned to win the nomination, we were also fairly sure that if she did not win, a prime target of blame (in perception and perhaps in fact) would be the media. We could not have known how true our prediction would be, as a firestorm of outrage broke out among

Clinton supporters and feminists over what many perceived as media mistreatment of the first woman with a good shot at the White House. As we waded into that controversy, we found a much richer topic than we had anticipated. As we explain in this book, gender bias and media coverage were certainly key factors in this campaign, but a larger framework of interlocking factors was at work in Clinton's successes and in her defeat, from the deeply gendered notions of the presidency that prevail in US political culture, to the media routines that structure presidential election coverage every four years, to the party rules that shaped the terms of competition in 2008, to the specific profiles of Hillary Clinton herself and her main competitor, Barack Obama. This complicated context shaped the "gender strategy" Hillary Clinton deployed in her quest for the White House.

In writing this book, we each bring to the project our own scholarly backgrounds and interests as well as distinct personal and political inclinations. The possibility of a successful female presidential candidate piqued Melody's interest due to her training in elections, the presidency, and gender politics. The Clinton campaign offered Regina, as a scholar of media and politics, a fascinating test of standard theories of how the media cover elections in a new and historic context. Melody, a stalwart Clinton supporter from the beginning, is engaged with state Democratic Party politics and gave donations to the Clinton campaign before work on this book began in earnest. Her children peppered the lawn with Clinton signs and watched every primary contest with her. For her part, Regina was more ambivalent about Clinton's campaign: proud that her daughter could see a powerful woman in the news striving for the highest political office, but troubled by many of Clinton's political choices. Having recently relocated, Regina did not participate in her new state's primary contest, thereby casting a vote neither for Clinton nor for any of her competitors.

For two female scholars with such different outlooks on the campaign, this project has challenged our thinking in surprising and rewarding ways. We watched with keen interest as some, such as *New York Times* columnist Maureen Dowd, claimed that charges of sexism in the campaign were trumped up and disingenuous. "For months," Dowd argued, "Hillary has been trying to emasculate Obama with the sort of words and themes she has chosen, stirring up feminist anger by promoting the idea that the men were unfairly taking it away from the women, and covering up her own campaign mistakes with cries of sexism" (Dowd 2008c). Similarly, the *Huffington Post*'s Hilary Rosen argued, "I don't really buy into this notion of the campaign is faltering because

Hillary is a victim of sexism. I may part company with some of the Hillary sisterhood on this point. There has been lots of sexism in this race, but this campaign is losing because of choices and strategies of it's [*sic*] own making" (Rosen 2008).

We debated this ourselves as we watched the campaign unfold. Was Clinton being unfairly pilloried for actions that would have been accepted or excused in a male candidate? Did she and her staff overstep the bounds of acceptable political campaigning with references to her "hard-working . . . white" supporters and her own "testicular fortitude" (MSNBC 2008a; Pearson 2008)? Ultimately, Regina's mixed feelings about Senator Clinton intensified, though she developed a greater respect for Clinton's trailblazing accomplishments and her determination and persistence in the face of near-certain defeat. Melody found herself alternately impressed with Clinton as she waged her historic campaign and concerned over what appeared to be serious campaign missteps. Perhaps that is the irony of Hillary Clinton, that she can produce quite contradictory responses, sometimes in the same breath. Indeed, writing about so enigmatic a subject is daunting, given what one journalist has described as "the lack of an Archimedean point from which to judge Hillary Clinton" (Green 2006). Yet, we both agree with Kathleen Jamieson that in "the complex interplay between Hillary Rodham Clinton and the labels through which she [is] viewed by reporters, columnists, supporters, and antagonists . . . we see the residues of the complex and sometimes contradictory expectations we carry into our encounters with women" (1995, 23).

Our differences in perspective, opinion, and training added immeasurably to the rigor with which we approached the book. As steadfast friends, we engaged in lively debates about methods and interpretive challenges. Our many lengthy work sessions over the past year and a half have enhanced our mutual regard as well as our thinking—we have each tested the assumptions and interpretations of the other, to the great benefit of this book.

Many people helped us to navigate this challenging topic and formulate a more coherent argument. Regina's colleagues at Louisiana State University (LSU) offered sharp, insightful comments on our work; we thank all of them, especially Kathleen Bratton, Johanna Dunaway, Kirby Goidel, Heather Ondercin, Leonard Ray, and Michael Xenos. The faculty and students at Tulane University's Newcombe College Center for Research on Women and the Department of Communications offered invaluable reactions to an early version of our manuscript (thanks especially to Mauro Porto), as did the faculty and students at Portland State

University (PSU) who attended a Faculty Favorite presentation in spring 2008. The University of Washington's Center for Communication and Civic Engagement provided an additional opportunity to sharpen our thinking (special thanks to Lance Bennett and Christine Di Stefano). We also appreciate Terri Bimes and Amy Gurowitz for inviting Melody to the Institute of Governmental Studies at the University of California, Berkeley; and Jack Levy and Lisa L. Miller of the Department of Political Science at Rutgers University, who, with the School of Communications, Information, and Library Studies, invited Regina to present our research. Special thanks go to Dianne Bystrom and Kim Fridkin, who reviewed the manuscript in its penultimate version, and to Mel Gurtov, Melody's colleague at PSU, for introducing us to Lynne Rienner Publishers.

We are thankful for the support of our endeavors offered by the Manship School of Mass Communication, the Reilly Center for Media and Public Affairs, and Adrienne Moore at LSU. We owe a particular debt to graduate assistant Amy Ladley, who gathered and helped analyze much of the data presented here and provided invaluable insights; we also thank our other assistants, Drew Thompson, Erica Taylor, Christopher McCollough, and Christopher Branch at LSU, and Suzanne LaBerge and Tyler Browne at PSU. We are especially grateful to Senator Clinton's policy adviser, Neera Tanden, who met with us during a very busy time in the election, along with others who agreed to speak with us about the campaign, including Charlie Cook, Howard Kurtz, Anne Kornblut, and Joe Trippi. We also thank the Catt Center at Iowa State University for awarding us Honorable Mention in the 2008 Carrie Chapman Catt Prize for Research on Women and Politics. And we thank Leanne Anderson at Lynne Rienner Publishers for seeing this project through.

Finally, we recognize our families. Melody wishes to thank her husband, Eric, and their children, Isabella, Cloe, Madison, and Simone, for their love and support during this project. Regina owes a special debt to Steve for countless hours of extra child care and unwavering support, and to Mackenzie and Henry for "keeping out of Mommy's hair" just long enough for the book to be completed.

1

Introduction:
Gender, the Media,
and Hillary Clinton

Nobody knew how to run a woman as leader of the free world.
—Gail Sheehy, *Vanity Fair*, August 2008

A s Senator Hillary Rodham Clinton suspended her campaign for the Democratic nomination in June 2008, bringing her historic effort to a close, *CBS Evening News* anchor Katie Couric received an award in the name of feminist icon Alice Paul. Couric marked the occasion by observing, "However you feel about her politics, I feel that Senator Clinton received some of the most unfair, hostile coverage I've ever seen." From her vantage point within broadcast news, Couric argued that Clinton's defeat was rooted in sexism (*Fishbowl.com* 2008). Couric followed these remarks with a video commentary posted on the CBS News website, in which she claimed, "Like her or not, one of the great lessons of Hillary Clinton's campaign is the continued—and accepted—sexism in American life . . . particularly in the media" (Couric 2008).

Couric's perceptions were shared by a large number of feminists, Clinton supporters, and others. The Women's Media Center, for example, posted a video "illustrating the pervasive nature of sexism in the media's coverage" of Clinton's campaign and an online petition campaign urging television viewers to "call on the national broadcast news outlets (CNN, FNC, MSNBC, and NBC) to stop treating women as a joke; to stop using inherently gendered language as an insult or criticism; and to ensure that women's voices are present and accounted for in the national political dialogue" (Women's Media Center 2008). The National Organization for Women (NOW) assembled an online "Media Hall of Shame," a video collection of "the most outrageous moments of

1

sexism from mainstream media's coverage of the 2008 elections," accompanied by a "Misogyny Meter" so viewers could rate each one (National Organization for Women 2008).

Most of Couric's colleagues in the mainstream media denied sexist bias in their coverage of Clinton's campaign, with varying degrees of thoughtfulness. CNN political reporter Candy Crowley claimed that while she saw some sexism in cable news commentary, she hadn't seen it in regular broadcast news coverage. Crowley also noted that it was "hard to know if these attacks [by cable commentators] were being made because [Clinton] was a woman or because she was *this* woman or because, for a long time, she was the front-runner" (Seelye and Bosman 2008, emphasis added). Long-time CBS political correspondent Jeff Greenfield argued that, "Throughout this campaign, people's perception of the press has been in line with what they wanted to happen politically. . . . If my person lost, the press did a bad job" (quoted in ibid.). Taking his remarks one step further, MSNBC commentator Keith Olbermann (himself a frequent target of charges of bias against Clinton), added Couric to his "worst people in the world" list, calling it outright "nonsense that Senator Clinton was a victim of pronounced sexism."[1] At the same time, some in the media wondered aloud if perceptions of media bias actually helped Clinton rather than hurt her, particularly among women voters. Some even charged the Clinton campaign with drumming up sexism talk in order to win more votes. Senior vice president of NBC News Phil Griffin, in response to questions about media sexism, charged the Clinton campaign with creating the controversy for political ends: "They were trying to rally a certain demographic, and women were behind it," Griffin contended (Seelye and Bosman 2008).

Ultimately, our argument reflects each of these perspectives to some degree. There is little question that as Clinton's chances of winning the nomination became increasingly remote, her campaign began to talk openly about what it saw as media sexism, and that many Clinton supporters (mostly if not exclusively women) were galvanized by what they saw as unfair treatment of Clinton by national reporters and pundits. Unlike Griffin, though, we maintain that these perceptions were not groundless.

We seek to document in this book the variety of ways that gender stereotypes shaded coverage of Clinton's presidential bid and perhaps wounded her campaign. Our findings lend some credence to charges against the media, particularly to the perspective expressed by Allida M. Black, the director of the Eleanor Roosevelt Papers at George Washington University, who believes that the media "compounded the missteps" made by Clinton's campaign (Seelye and Bosman 2008). But we also illuminate the complexity that Crowley attempts to describe: Much of what Senator Clinton faced from the media was driven by standard news media routines for covering presidential elections, and any effort to indentify "bias" against her must grapple with the fact that those routines have long been applied to other (male) presidential candidates. Media critics must also grapple with Clinton's own troubled history with the US public and the press.

We also push beyond the question of media treatment of Hillary Clinton's candidacy to the larger question concerning what her campaign can teach us about women in presidential politics. There have been so very few women on the US presidential stage that Hillary Clinton's near-win of the Democratic primary poses a fascinating case study for testing the observations and predictions of the women and politics literature. We find many ways in which that literature was confirmed, but also many ways in which it fell short of predicting the twists and turns of the Clinton campaign—in large part because the "small n" problem of limited cases to study has left large gaps in what we know about how women presidential candidates might present themselves to and be received by the media and the public. Rather than simply explain how Clinton lost her bid for the presidency, this book is an effort to build a more complete theory of women, media, and strategy in presidential politics—an effort that begins by sketching a fuller picture of the many factors that formed the context for Hillary Clinton's presidential bid.

Understanding Clinton's Context: Three Interlocking Variables

We contend that the story of how Senator Clinton nearly won but ultimately lost the Democratic nomination is not a simple story of media bias or sexism (terms that, we argue below, must be thoughtfully defined), though both may have played roles in her defeat. In the end, the story of her campaign must be understood in terms of three interlocking factors: the role of gender in presidential politics (and therefore the conundrum of running for a masculinized office as a woman), contemporary media norms and routines, and the individual candidate and her particular political context (see Figure 1.1). It is at the interstices of this figurative Venn diagram that Hillary Clinton waged her battle for the presidency, and these three dimensions together create the dynamics within which any woman who would be president must compete. Considering these three sets of interlocking factors allows us to appreci-

**Figure 1.1 Three Interlocking Variables
for Analyzing Female Presidential Candidacies**

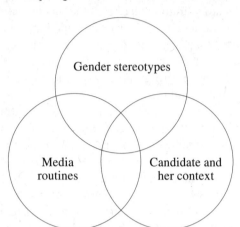

ate both the unique institutional and personal characteristics of the 2008 nomination contest as well as more enduring forces in presidential politics and US political culture.

Gender Stereotypes and the Presidency

In significant ways, deeply entrenched cultural attitudes that associate the presidency with masculinity (what scholars of women and politics refer to as "androcentrist" attitudes) indelibly and unavoidably shaped the terrain upon which Clinton forged her campaign. Deeply rooted attitudes about women's inherent attributes collide with long-held beliefs about the US presidency. For instance, a recent study of news coverage of women presidential candidates that was published shortly before the 2008 primaries began reminds us that "the assumptions that women are emotional and men rational is part of conventional stereotyping," according to which "natural sexual differences" include "the irrationality of women and the rationality of men" (Falk 2008, 55).[2] Given the public's presumed preference for a rational president, this stereotype and others act as a powerful barrier to would-be female presidents.

Sex stereotypes are not immutable barriers to political advancement for women. Noting the strong patterns of support for female candidates expressed in public opinion polls, Falk also argues that "actual polling about women and the presidency indicates that should a woman run for the presidency her sex is unlikely to keep her from office, even though the press tends to cover women as losers" (Falk 2008, 158). Critics of societal and media sexism sometimes fail to note that although she ultimately fell short of gaining her party's nomination, Hillary Clinton won more votes than any Democratic presidential contender in US history,[3] and that she lost the 2008 primary by a narrow margin.

Yet Clinton's successes do not negate the power of gender in politics. The backdrop of gender stereotypes creates for women politicians a challenging set of "double binds" in which they must simultaneously defend alternating standards of femininity and credibility in leadership (Jamieson 1995). In presidential politics in particular, these binds tighten, leaving women candidates with a narrowed range of options for how to present themselves to the public. We theorize that a fundamental task of the female presidential hopeful is to design a "gender strategy" that can navigate this troubled terrain.

Media Routines

In presidential elections in particular, the media have become the central conduit connecting voters with the candidates, and media coverage is one of three essential factors (along with money and organization) that shapes the fate of presidential campaigns (Aldrich 1992; Patterson 1994). Clinton's path toward the White House, like that of every other candidate since at least the 1960s, ran through the newsroom, and she found that path cluttered with media scripts and frames that emphasized her negatives at the expense of her positives—just as many other aspirants to the White House have discovered. In many ways, the media operated according to their own established routines for covering presidential elections, thus treating Hillary Clinton just like one of the boys. In other more subtle respects, however, media coverage drew upon gendered stereotypes, and in some ways held Clinton to a different set of standards than her male counterparts. Thus, in running for president, Hillary Clinton experienced some (though as we will show, not all) of the media "biases" observed in research on media coverage of other women candidates in addition to virtually all of the biases experienced by most male presidential candidates—and some additional media bias owing to her own particular communicative style and troubled history with the press. The resulting negative coverage does not necessarily make the media responsible for Clinton's loss, but it does raise questions about how different coverage might have affected the outcome of a close nomination contest. Clinton's media treatment thus underscores the critical task faced by all presidential candidates—and, arguably, female candidates in particular—of effectively shaping the news about their campaigns.

Research shows patterns of media coverage since at least the late 1960s that have undermined many presidential candidacies (not just those of women). The media's routine "horse race" and "character" based coverage, often markedly negative in tone, was in full display in 2008, and because Hillary Clinton entered the race as the presumed front-runner she received the full brunt of this kind of coverage. While confirming these patterns, our study also illustrates unique hurdles for women who enter the presidential election arena. In particular, while scholars have bemoaned the decline of substantive, issue-oriented coverage and the predominance of horse-race coverage of presidential elections, our study shows how this coverage may be especially tough on female candidacies due to the intertwining of negative horse-race narratives with pointedly gendered themes and expectations.

The Candidate and Her Context

By separating out this third set of variables, we call attention to the unique assets and liabilities with which Clinton approached her run for the presidency and the particular institutional and political factors that shaped her campaign. Hillary Clinton's run for the White House was unique—not just in the obvious fact that she was the most viable female presidential candidate in US history, but in the fact that she was a *particular* female candidate with a particular political history who faced a particular political context. We maintain that though any female presidential candidate will contend with media hurdles and the androcentric expectations of the presidency, each individual female candidate will bring a unique constellation of attributes to that interaction. Hillary Clinton was an unusually well-known and controversial political figure by the time she sought the nation's highest office—and a woman who had already occupied the White House in the role of First Lady. To a certain extent, therefore, Clinton's challenges were not just those faced by women politicians in general, but very specific to Clinton's own personal and political history—challenges exacerbated by strategic and tactical missteps Clinton made throughout her campaign. This reality further complicates any effort to pin Clinton's demise on a single factor.

Moreover, Hillary Clinton faced a political context in 2008 that posed unique challenges to her candidacy, the most obvious of which was the talent, historic qualities, and meteoric rise of her chief rival, Senate colleague Barack Obama (D-IL). It is difficult to overstate the importance of the Obama candidacy for any conclusions we might draw about women and politics from the 2008 election; had he not entered the 2008 contest, it is quite possible that this book would be exploring the reasons for Hillary Clinton's success in gaining her party's nomination— maybe even the presidency. Indeed, at the beginning of the campaign season in 2007, Obama was a long shot, and Hillary Clinton the one to beat. Delving into the many reasons for Obama's success would take us beyond the scope of this book, so we limit our observation to the simple fact of Obama's enormous personal appeal and his team's considerable political skills. Among other things, as one recent account puts it, "the Obama delegate operation ran circles around the Clinton campaign" (Todd and Gawiser 2009, 15). Not only did the Obama camp out-strategize the Clinton team in terms of winning delegates, they proved masterful at exploiting the fundraising possibilities of the Internet (while effectively tapping into old-fashioned large donations as well [see Green 2008a]). While the Clinton team had raised a formidable early war chest, the money was poorly managed. Indeed, "when Super Tuesday came and went, the Clinton campaign was broke and behind. The Obama campaign was just getting started" (Todd and Gawiser 2009, 15).

Another crucial aspect of Hillary Clinton's context in 2008 was the Democratic Party's nomination rules. As with all elections, the rules of the game profoundly shaped the way the race was won—and lost. Rules are so essential, in fact, that we refer readers who want to better understand the dynamics of the 2008 campaign to the Appendix at the back of the book. For our purpose here, we note several rules that mattered mightily in 2008, including the party's decision to punish Florida and Michigan (states in which Clinton polled well) for holding its primaries early; the Democratic primary calendar that, among other things, lumped an unusually large number of contests together on February 5; and, perhaps most significantly, the party's use of proportional representation for awarding delegates. These rules in effect (if not in intent) worked against Clinton—and her campaign often strategized poorly in response to them—leading more than one observer to note that had the party rules been different, Clinton may have been the 2008 Democratic nominee.

These basic political realities loomed so large in 2008 that it was tempting to dismiss the role of gender in the election altogether, as many a pundit did. But we maintain that gender stereotypes and media routines for covering elections must be taken into account along with these contextual factors when analyzing how Clinton ran and how she lost. These variables are woven together in ways that create an analytical challenge to the scholar—and presented a significant political challenge for Senator Clinton.

Overview of the Book

The book opens by exploring the three fundamental sets of variables presented above: gendered presidential politics, media routines for covreing presidential elections, and the unique characteristics and context of candidate Clinton. Chapter 2 delves into the institutional and cultural structuring of presidential politics—the fundamental terrain that Clinton (as well as her predecessors and successors) must navigate. We document how the traditional pathways to the presidency have not been occupied by women, making Hillary Clinton a truly unique contender, and how gender stereotypes and masculinized images of the presidency continue to shape women's paths to power, particularly by shaping the unspoken "qualifications" for the presidency and a deeply rooted "cult of true womanhood" that limits women's public role. Here we lay out a framework for understanding the gender strategy employed by candidate Clinton and the strategies to be employed by future female presidential candidates as well.

Chapter 3 documents the difficulties that virtually all presidential candidates face—male or female—in gaining and maintaining positive media coverage, and also reviews the literature on media coverage of female candidates for the presidency and other offices. Here we identify three media routines for covering presidential elections that can seriously disadvantage many candidates: the focus on "defining moments," particularly candidate missteps and gaffes; the focus on the "horse race" and the "game" of elections; and the tendency to write stories conforming to a preestablished "script" for each candidate. Each of these, we will argue, proved decisive to Clinton's campaign, operating on their own and in tandem with gender stereotypes to powerfully shape the public image of her campaign. We also consider the particular media disadvantages faced by female candidates.

Chapter 4 explores the unique personal attributes—or perceived attributes—of Hillary Clinton that have indelibly marked her relationship with the public and the press. Not least among these are widely held perceptions of Clinton as inordinately ambitious and duplicitous, attributes that draw from gendered societal attitudes in general and have stuck (fairly or unfairly) to Hillary Clinton particularly strongly. While political ambition is expected and even desired among male presidential candidates, ambition in women violates our cultural understanding of "true womanhood" defined by selflessness and service on behalf of others. Female ambition, an attribute that Senator Clinton seems to have plenty of, is therefore culturally problematic. We also explore in this chapter two of the "binds" that have shaped and constrained Clinton's career: the femininity/competence bind that makes it difficult for women to simultaneously seem leader-like and womanly, and the more Clinton-specific bind of independence/dependence, in which Clinton has struggled with perceptions that she is simultaneously too independent and yet, ultimately, too dependent upon others (her husband in particular) in her quest for power. Finally, we examine her troubled relationship with the national press corps, stemming back to her years as First Lady, and her communicative and press management style, which has hindered her ability to reframe her image with the public.

The next section of the book builds upon the framework presented in the first section, presenting empirical evidence gathered from Clinton campaign materials and interviews with staffers and others, as well as from media coverage of the campaign. Chapter 5 closely examines Hillary Clinton's messaging to reveal a gender strategy that attempted to negotiate the femininity/competence and equality/difference double binds. On its surface, the campaign emphasized a putatively gender-neutral appeal that Senator Clinton was simply the best person for the job. But, based on the key advisers' internal predictions of a wave of female voter support, the campaign also deployed gender: first in a sometimes coded appeal to female solidarity, and later in the campaign season, running strongly on a contradictory message of masculine toughness. We also analyze in this chapter the experience/change bind specific to candidate Clinton and the political context of 2008.

In Chapter 6, we analyze media coverage of Clinton's campaign to assess to what degree she was subject to the biases documented in coverage of other presidential campaigns. Here we present empirical data that provide only limited support to charges of pervasive sexist media treatment of Clinton. Indeed, we find that Clinton avoided the most basic kind of media "bias" by achieving parity in the amount of news coverage she received in comparison to her main Democratic opponent; we also find little evidence of overt and systematic sexist treatment of Clinton in mainstream media coverage. But we also find a clear pattern of greater negativity in coverage of Clinton versus two of her main male competitors, Senator Obama and Senator John McCain (R-AZ); just as consequentially, we find relatively favorable treatment of Senator Obama. We conclude that while explicitly sexist bias was not necessarily widespread in traditional news outlets' coverage, outright sexism was more common in the online world, which also served as an echo chamber in which instances of sexist speech reverberated and took on a life of their own.

If Hillary Clinton overcame some of the media obstacles that have stymied other female candidacies, however, there is evidence of more subtle gendering in coverage of her campaign, little of it helpful to her quest. In Chapter 7, we show that standard media routines for covering presidential elections served candidate Clinton particularly poorly. Most notably, Clinton's decision to remain in the fight until the last primary vote was cast operated against media expectations of quick closure to the primary season. When played out against a background expectation that the nomination "should" be decided early in the campaign season (an expectation that Clinton herself had stoked), her long losing fight against Obama became a consuming focus of campaign coverage, playing perfectly into the media's obsession with the "horse race." Moreover, drawing upon established scripts for covering Hillary Clinton as well as upon deeply rooted notions of proper femininity, the media often portrayed her quest as unsettling and unseemly. Overall, this chapter illustrates the subtly gendered playing field upon which Hillary Clinton had to stage her run for the White House—an analysis we extend in the final chapter, where we consider the lessons learned from the Clinton campaign for the future of women in presidential politics.

Theorizing Hillary Clinton

Theorizing about presidential politics has always been somewhat limited by the simple but daunting "small n" problem: With so few available cases to analyze (particularly if one focuses on the contemporary presidency), robust theory that can stand up to statistical and logical testing is difficult to build. That problem is significantly compounded for those who study women in presidential politics. With so very few women ever attempting to enter the US presidential stage, the analyst runs the risk of investing particular, idiosyncratic events arising in a few female candidates' experiences with a deeper theoretical meaning than they may really have. Even Susan J. Carroll, veteran scholar of women and politics, doubted at first the scholarly potency of the Clinton race: "After all, she was a single case of a very exceptional woman with an idiosyncratic background as a former first lady" (2009, 2).

The flip side of that problem is to dismiss the theoretical potential offered by what are necessarily limited and somewhat idiosyncratic events, and to conclude that there is little to learn from an *n* of one. As we wrote this book, we attempted to avoid the former problem, yet sometimes met with skepticism based in the second. "Hillary Clinton is a bad case for theory-testing," the argument would go. "Her case is too unique to base any conclusions on; Hillary Clinton is sui generis." We agree, in the sense that treating one female candidate's experience as evidence of larger trends must be handled very carefully (and we attempt to mitigate that problem by comparing her experience against that of her main male competitors). But we disagree that there is little to learn from Clinton's quest for the White House, or that she is so unique that no other woman can walk her path. By definition, *any* woman to have reached the milestones of the Clinton candidacy in terms of fame, fundraising, and votes won would have been "too unique." The problem is not simply a Hillary Clinton problem—it is an indelible fact of US presidential politics, and the next woman to reach and surpass those milestones may well face the same theoretical objections. In the meantime, Clinton's experiences and those of a handful of other women are the cases that political scientists have to work with.

The small *n*/unique case problem is intensified in the case of Hillary Clinton because of the quite visceral reactions she seems to evoke. We suspect that for at least some of our skeptics, it was *this* Hillary Clinton problem that made her case seem "too unique": A woman who has been so reviled for so long by a sector of the public, and treated with milder disdain or bemusement by many more, would seem to be a distorted prism through which to view the general category of women in politics. (The opposite position is passionately argued by some Hillary supporters and women and politics scholars: that her vilification is a quintessential example of what happens to smart, strong women who refuse to fit the cultural mold.) Indeed, along her way toward amassing the formidable political networks and resources that made her historic run for the presidency possible, Hillary Clinton has also made mistakes, and some enemies. To what degree the intense dislike of Hillary Clinton is based on tangible positions she has taken or mistakes she has made, versus personality traits she exhibits (or that are attributed to her), and to what degree it reflects deeper cultural discomfort with ambitious women attaining power, we cannot say. There is perhaps no modern public figure who has evoked more contradictory responses from the public. As analysts, however, we are left with the fact that it is *this* woman who ran for the presidency in 2008 and, in nearly winning it, may have challenged or confirmed existing theories of women and politics.

We therefore argue for the need to build the particularities of individual women's candidacies into a more nuanced theory of women in presidential politics. A woman running for the US presidency, we contend, will face a constellation of challenges (and opportunities) based not only on gender norms and stereotypes and on media routines for covering presidential politics, but also on her own particular set of attributes, assets, and liabilities.

Notes on Language

As with any academic enterprise, this one includes some careful choices regarding language. The first was about "firsts." We became increasingly wary of the uses of the "first female" language so often employed to describe the candidacy of Hillary Rodham Clinton. In point of fact, she isn't the first, but rather the latest in a long effort by women to ascend to the presidency. What is more, as previous research reminds us (Falk 2008; Heldman, Carroll, and Olson 2005), "first" is often code for "unusual" and thus "not normal." So in this book, when we refer to Clinton's campaign in this regard, we do so fully aware of the problems inherent in the label "first"—problems we try to address with additional adjectives, such as "the first truly viable female candidate for the presidency," or simply by placing the term "first" in quotation marks.

We have thought carefully, too, about how to name our subject. The public and punditry often refer to Hillary Clinton simply by her first name, or in relation to her husband as "Mrs." Clinton. As we explore in later chapters, for Clinton herself there have been strategic advantages and disadvantages to these variations in her name. President Bill Clinton's former press secretary Dee Dee Myers argues that calling her "Hillary" is

> breezy and familiar and warms that cool exterior just a touch. It also makes it easier to distinguish her from a former president with the same surname. But at the same time, it does undermine her authority ever so slightly. After all, "Hillary" sounds less formidable than "Senator McCain" or "Governor Romney" or "Mayor Giuliani." (Myers 2008, 46)

For our part, we alternate (for variety's sake) between two primary ways of designating our subject: by her official title (at the time) of "Senator," or simply by her (first and) last name. We also opt at times for the use of "Ms.," because to our contemporary ears, it is a more neutral term than "Mrs."; very occasionally, we employ her first name only.

Other key terms that will show up repeatedly in this book also require some contextualization, including "media," "media bias," and "sexism." *Sexism* is defined by "the way in which American society systematically overvalues men and undervalues women" (Falk 2008, 155). For our purposes, gender, as opposed to sex, is "the socially constructed meaning given to biological sex, especially sex difference" (Duerst-Lahti and Kelly 1995, 13); it is not biological, but rather a practice of socialization. Gender is a "coherent set of beliefs about what constitutes masculine or feminine" (Ibid., 17). Sexism would be present in media coverage and public discourse whenever candidates are over- or undervalued in accordance with their sex.

In many instances, media coverage of female candidates is not sexist per se, but rather, reflects a reification of gender stereotypes, which "attribute to men and women different tendencies, characteristics, and areas of competence" (Ibid.). The gendering of media discourse is evident whenever we see media criticism of a candidate's gender attributes—when a candidate is criticized for behaving in a way that is "unfitting" of her sex, or when she (or he) is criticized for behavior that is insufficiently "masculine" for the presidency. Because our culture expects that female = feminine (and analogously, male = masculine), and femininity implies a certain set of assumptions, gender bias is present when the media draw critical attention to a candidate for having either confirmed gender stereotypes ("Clinton is overly emotional") or having strayed too far from gender norms ("Clinton is aggressive"). Feminism is the systematic effort to debunk sexist practices and gender assumptions.

When we refer to the "media," we will be talking primarily about the major news outlets, often called the "mainstream media" ("MSM"), which form the core conduit of campaign communications with the public. This includes the nation's leading print media, such as the *New York Times* and *Washington Post,* and the leading broadcast and cable television news programs, from NBC's *Evening News*, with its nightly audience of 7 to 9 million, to CNN's *Situation Room* or MSNBC's *Hardball*, which garner a far smaller audience. But we will also dip into the fast-paced world of the "new" media, looking for clues as to how the campaign unfolded in the Wild West of the Internet. We are mindful that in the 2008 campaign, more than any election year before, the new media played a central role,[4] and we identify some of the key themes and moments from the campaign that took on added significance because of how they reverberated in new media venues; in particular, the much greater range of "acceptable" speech online fueled the fires of anti–Hillary Clinton vitriol and provided Clinton supporters with a wealth of ugly examples of egregious sexism. The Internet therefore figures in our analysis of the images and discourse surrounding Hillary Clinton, while blogs and other Internet sources also helped to drive the mainstream media's focus on particular "key moments" from the campaign that we analyze closely. But we keep our focus in this book mainly on the MSM because they command the largest audiences, because the campaigns themselves still focus primarily on mainstream media venues (press conferences; television, radio, and newspaper interviews; and talk shows, as well as television ads), and because much online content actually derives from the mainstream media.

Media "bias" is a particularly tricky concept, not least because humans are prone to perceive bias in information they disagree with more than in information they agree with (Vallone, Ross, and Lepper 1985; Dalton, Beck, and Huckfeldt 1998). (Research suggests that CBS's Jeff Greenfield, quoted earlier in this chapter as saying "people's perception of the press has been in line with what they wanted to happen politically," is correct about this general tendency, though one suspects that such claims are also a convenient fig leaf for media coverage that *is* biased). Media bias can also be a moving target because "the media" includes so many individuals and organizations across print, broadcast, cable, and the Internet. Moreover, media bias could take several forms: (1) individual news stories or commentators could exhibit sexism or other forms of prejudice; (2) individual news outlets could exhibit a pervasive pattern of prejudice not evident in other news outlets; or (3) pervasive patterns of sexism or other prejudice could be evident across all (or most) news outlets. The third would of course be the most damaging to female candidates, and most disturbing from the point of view of democratic ideals of equal opportunities for all. It is also the least likely to be found, if one assumes at least some diversity of viewpoints among journalists and media commentators. The second and particularly the first pattern, while not welcome from the perspective of feminists, do not necessarily violate democratic norms. If an individual network or newspaper or columnist or commentator makes sexist remarks on a regular basis, those comments may well be balanced out, even overshadowed, by a larger number of feminist comments. And unless a commentator's remarks are particularly hateful, even sexist comments may be defended on freedom of speech grounds.

Biases of the first and second type are also the patterns most likely to be found through casual observation of the media. In an election marked by the historic entrance of a woman onto the stage of presidential politics, it is probably inevitable that some sexist or otherwise inappropriate comments would be made by some commentators some of the time. But to qualify as "media bias," something more pervasive must be demonstrated than occasional tasteless or hurtful remarks. To be persuasive, the charge of media bias must rest on evidence more substantial than anecdote: *pervasive* patterns in a *significant portion* of overall media coverage. While we respect the sensitivities of organizations such as the Women's Media Center, NOW, and others who led the charge against what they perceived as sexist media bias against Hillary Clinton, we aim to provide a more comprehensive view of the treatment Clinton received from the national media.

A Note on Methodology

The original research presented in this book derives from a number of sources. We collected thousands of pages of documents during the 2008 primary campaign, including news coverage in newspapers, magazines, and television programs; postings in a number of political blogs and other websites; and television and Internet-based advertisements and other campaign communications produced by the Clinton campaign, including her campaign website and regular e-mails to supporters.

Unless otherwise noted, all of the analyses of mainstream news coverage throughout the book are based upon searches of the Nexis news database of coverage appearing in six top news outlets: the *New York Times*, *Los Angeles Times*, and *Washington Post*—among the nation's leading newspapers for political coverage—and the evening news programs of ABC, CBS, and NBC. Focusing primarily on these leading outlets, selected for their regional diversity, audience size, and agenda-setting power with political elites and with other media outlets, allows us to understand how the mainstream media generally covered the campaign (though, as we note below, there were sometimes important differences in coverage across particular news outlets). For the extensive analysis of coverage of Clinton's campaign featured in Chapters 6 and 7, we constructed a systematic random sample of front-page and prime-time news stories from these six outlets. We also conducted additional news searches on specific moments from the campaign that appear throughout Chapters 5 through 7, in these cases often extending our searches into the realms of cable television and the Internet; specific information about those searches is provided in those chapters.

We also monitored the Internet and blogosphere during the campaign. The sheer size of the blogosphere makes random sampling impracticable; moreover, we wanted to closely monitor how discourse about Clinton's campaign played out on some of the most heavily trafficked political blogs. So, throughout the campaign, we monitored a set of eleven sites on which discourse about Clinton was likely to be particularly pointed—the conservative blogs we monitored clearly opposed Clinton; the liberal blogs were divided, with some like Daily Kos strongly opposing her, and others like MediaMatters generally supportive; and the feminist blogs were generally very supportive—thereby putting our fingers in some sense on the pulse of heated opinions throughout Clinton's campaign. Given the hyperlinked nature of the Internet, monitoring these blogs (and the online versions of major news organizations such as the *New York Times*) quickly led us to additional online material, and we occasionally include examples from these additional sources throughout the book. Finally, in order to assess how Clinton's campaign presented itself to its supporters and potential supporters, we took cataloged screen shots of the home page www.hillaryclinton.com from the middle of December through Clinton's suspension speech in early June.[5] We coded the content in terms of the issues mentioned, and looked for changes in the content of the site over time. We describe in further detail in the appropriate chapters the specific methods used to analyze these various sources.

We also wanted to capture a sense of the campaign as it unfolded in real time, looking in particular for key turning points and defining moments for Clinton and her main competitors. We therefore kept voluminous notes on happenings in the campaign, beginning in the fall of 2007 and carrying through the Democratic convention in August 2008. We then matched our notes against the weekly reports produced by the Project for Excellence in Journalism (journalism.org), which are based upon extensive content analysis of the week's news across a large number of news organizations, and the more occasional reports by the Pew Research Center for the People and the Press (pewresearch.org). These reports allowed us to verify whether our experiential sense of "key moments" in the campaign was born out by objective data on the main topics and themes of news coverage each week. The key moments that arose from this analysis, highlighted in each chapter that follows, serve as a focal point for our qualitative analysis of the campaign.

Finally, we did our best to check our hypotheses about the strategic choices made by the Clinton campaign against the testimony of her campaign staff and others from the world of politics. In many cases personal interviews were not possible, but fortunately, several in-depth profiles of her campaign, based on interviews with her key staff and advisers, were published in the weeks leading up to and following her exit from the race; we cite from these pieces extensively. We also conducted some personal interviews that contributed significantly to our understanding of this campaign; these interview data are referenced along with all other research materials in the chapters that follow.

The Legacy of the Clinton Campaign and the Future Female Presidency

To summarize, the core argument developed in this book is that Hillary Clinton's bid for the presidency embodied the many challenges that face virtually all would-be female presidents—the troubled landscape of gendered stereotypes in media coverage and political culture, along with the competing pulls of various gendered double binds—as well as challenges faced by virtually all presidential candidates stemming from standard media routines for covering presidential elections. In addition, she faced challenges uniquely her own, stemming from, among other things, her own public history, her long and troubled relationship with the press, and the unique candidacy of Barack Obama.[6] This tangled web of variables has made it difficult for many observers to isolate the impact of sexism versus other factors on Clinton's failed nomination campaign, and has made public discussion of her campaign fraught with confusion and, in some cases, high emotion.

This book to some degree challenges assumptions of the women and politics literature. Women and politics scholars have tended to agree with Falk that

> given that women candidates are rare, that society tends to look through a gendered lens, and that news norms put a premium on novelty, it is very likely that when a reporter or assignment editor approaches a race in which there is a woman candidate . . . [they] are likely to view any woman candidate *qua woman*. (2008, 74, emphasis added)

While this is arguably true, it is also likely that experienced national reporters would subject a female presidential hopeful (particularly one as formidable as Clinton) to the same coverage they bring to all candidates—coverage focused on the candidates' standing in the polls, coverage focused on the candidates' gaffes and missteps and personalities more than their policy proposals, coverage decisively framed by notions of which candidates are likely to win and lose. We find that in many respects, Clinton was covered not just "qua woman" but also "qua *front-runner*"—an advantage she held going in to the election that rather quickly became a disadvantage in terms of the tone of her coverage, particularly as she performed less well in many early primaries than it was assumed she would. Moreover, media coverage approached Clinton very much as a *particular* woman, an individual with a well-established (and not always positive) public image. Indeed, Hillary Clinton's highly unusual combination of professional bona fides with a long and controversial history in the public eye made her quite unlike the women candidates imagined in much of the women and politics literature, and subjected her to her own unique double binds.

Moreover, the women and politics literature may not fully account for Hillary Clinton's specific case because it did not contemplate the implications of a female "first" who was also a former First Lady, and because it could not have imagined that the first woman to come near the presidency would have to battle against the most viable and talented African American candidate in history. The consequence of these contextual features was great, not just for Clinton's fortunes, but for theorizing about women and politics. For example, Clinton's decision to forgo the explicit mantle of running as a woman was in part as a response to Barack Obama's sudden surge early in the election season, on the assumption that race would trump gender in the public imagination (Green 2008a). Our analysis suggests that this intuition (if not necessarily the response) was correct, for the media treated issues of race and gender at times very differently, in ways that fundamentally disadvantaged Clinton and, it must be said, advantaged Senator Obama.

Ultimately, however, the lessons learned here are not necessarily "bad" ones for students of women and politics. From Hillary Clinton's run for the White House, we learn a great deal about the possibilities as well as the constraints on women's political advancement. As Clinton biographer Gail Collins (2008d) wrote the day after Clinton suspended her campaign,

> Over the past months, Clinton has seemed haunted by the image of the "nice girl" who gives up the fight because she's afraid the boys will be angry if they don't get their way. She told people she would never, ever say: "I'm the girl, I give up." She would never let her daughter, or anybody else's daughter, think that she quit because things got too tough.
> And she never did. Nobody is ever again going to question whether it's possible for a woman to go toe-to-toe with the toughest male candidate in a race for president of the United States. Or whether a woman could be strong enough to serve as commander in chief.

Her campaign didn't resolve whether a woman who seems tough enough to run the military can also seem likable enough to get elected. But she helped pave the way. . . . By the end of those 54 primaries and caucuses, Hillary had made a woman running for president seem normal.

Notes

1. See "Olberman Names Katie Couric as 'Worst Person in the World,'" at www.youtube.com/watch?v=QWmizWPFqc (viewed June 13, 2009).

2. We are mindful that the lingering vestiges of these deeply rooted attitudes do not monopolize contemporary US political culture. Rather, women strive for professional and political gains on terrain shaped by both vestigial sexism and the contemporary gains of feminism. Falk contends that despite many changes in politics and culture over the past 130 years, "for the most part . . . our traditional assumptions about women and men are still very much a part of our culture" (2008, 55). However, she also contends that there may be "a movement toward a more complex cognitive structure of gender roles, in which women in traditionally men's fields are associated with different stereotypes. More androgynous archetypes may be developing in the culture, which ultimately could help women appear more competent in the political sphere" (Ibid., 73). In addition to expecting that the media and the public will rely upon and reinforce traditional gender stereotypes, we should also look for signs of these "more complex cognitive structures."

3. As Clinton famously claimed in her concession speech in June of 2008, her candidacy had put "18 million cracks in the highest, hardest glass ceiling." Her claim of winning that number of votes, disputed by the Obama camp, rests on the full inclusion of her votes in Florida, where Obama had not campaigned, and Michigan, where Obama was not even on the ballot.

4. There is little doubt that new media are one of the key ways that young voters in particular interacted with this election, both in how they accessed mainstream media content such as candidate speeches and interviews, and in how they accessed the campaigns via social networking sites like Facebook (see for example Pew Research Center for the People and the Press 2008a; Stelter 2008a).

5. The Clinton website has since been cleansed of its campaign content, and so throughout the book, where we cite a specific Clinton website link, we note the date we accessed it.

6. No book can do everything, however, and this one is no exception. This is not, for example, an in-depth examination of the prospects for Republican versus Democratic women who may seek the presidency. Though there may be important lessons in the Clinton campaign for the role of partisanship in female presidential bids, that effort is beyond our scope, and we assume that future studies will look directly at the role party played in this process.

2

Women and
Presidential Politics

Women are never front-runners.
— Gloria Steinem, *New York Times,* January 2008

ate in 2007, Senator Hillary Rodham Clinton was interviewed on the
CBS Evening News about the upcoming caucuses and primaries. In
that interview, Katie Couric peppered Clinton with questions about
her plans for the campaign and her decisions regarding the tone of the
campaign. While Clinton stated repeatedly that she took "nothing for
granted" in campaigning for the presidency, Couric pressed on, asking
Senator Clinton about whether she intended to lower expectations
because of rival Barack Obama's increased momentum. "I never raised
them," Clinton claimed. While Senator Clinton focused her answers on
her preparedness and her respect for her opponents, media coverage
after the interview focused on one phrase. When Couric asked Clinton
how disappointed she would be if she were not the nominee after the
February 5 "Super Tuesday" contests, Clinton replied decisively, "Well,
it will be me." And though she went on to say she would support the
Democratic nominee if she lost to another contestant, pundits and political observers focused on what sounded like Clinton's assertion of
inevitability—an assertion many pundits interpreted as a denial of her
own shortcomings, or arrogance, or both (Kurtz 2008c; Rich 2008a).

The moment was stunning, but not for the reasons the pundits suggested: For the first time in US history, a female candidate could plausi-
bly claim "frontrunner" status in a presidential election. Though it may
be difficult for some readers of this book to recall, in the fall of 2007,
virtually all bets were on Clinton to win the 2008 Democratic Party
nomination because of her considerable name recognition, association

with a popular former president, formidable financial resources, and experienced campaign team.

Months later, when Senator Clinton suspended her bid for the presidency, many pundits drew the lesson from her closely fought campaign that the era of exclusion of women from presidential politics was over. Following the lead of women leaders like Speaker of the House Nancy Pelosi (D-CA), some argued that Clinton's "near success, as Pelosi has noted, makes it easier for future women candidates" (Hunt 2008). Surely, many argued, if a woman could gain so many votes (Clinton actually won the popular vote in three out of the six ways of tallying the votes)[1] and come within striking distance of the Oval Office, more female contenders and the first female chief executive could not be far behind. But this reassuring analysis did not seem to acknowledge the considerable hurdles that women candidates have faced and will probably continue to face. Those hurdles and the strategies women employ in response to them, which form the essential context for understanding Hillary Clinton's 2008 campaign, are the subject of this chapter.

Women in Presidential Politics—US Style

Across the globe, women compete ardently and often successfully to serve as president or prime minister of their nations. Yet the United States lags behind, one of the last democratic nations that has yet to produce a woman chief executive. Clinton's status as the presumed frontrunner at the start of the 2008 election season belies the fact that, with 43 male presidents and not a single female, the barriers to women candidates in the United States are daunting.

To some degree, our understanding of the constraints and opportunities for women seeking the presidency is limited by the fact that there has never been a woman president: without a single successful case to analyze, our understanding of the barriers specific to the presidency is by definition limited. As a consequence, our knowledge about these barriers stems not from case studies of the successful women who have occupied the oval office, but rather, from the failed attempts to do so. Fortunately, scholars of women and politics have also produced a voluminous record about the constraints faced by women who serve in or seek other offices, women in the "pipeline" positions for the White House. Much of the literature that informs our theoretical framework in this book is grounded in research that analyzes women's races for the US Senate and governorships—typical launching positions for would-be presidents.

This literature can tell us much about what we might expect from the "first" viable female presidential candidate. Senators and governors represent statewide populations, providing us with studies of how women fare with larger constituencies. Additionally, these works explain how dominant political issues shape women's political chances. For example, typically, US senators deal with foreign policy while governors are concerned with domestic issues, and these issue expectations are likely to shape media interpretation of candidates and voter assessment of their viability.

This chapter surveys this literature and discusses the sometimes surprising ways it intersects with Senator Clinton's campaign. According to this literature, being a woman generally helps candidates when the stereotypical expectations for women coincide with the expectations of the office (as in governorships, county commissions, and school boards), but hurts when the expectations for women conflict with expectations of the job. This latter dynamic plays out in races for the Senate and the presidency, particularly when the major issues of a campaign shift from "female" concerns like health care to "male" concerns like national security. Against this backdrop, Clinton's emergence as the first viable female presidential contender conforms to predictions in the gender and politics literature regarding the experience and attributes the first woman president would likely present. Clinton is one of only a handful of US women who have the resume for the job and therefore has risen through the small but growing pipeline of women with the proper credentials to make a presidential bid. The credentials and context required for a female candidate highlight both the opportunity and challenges that exist for contemporary female politicians whose sights are set on 1600 Pennsylvania Avenue.

Why No Woman President? Structural Barriers

In the twenty-first century, women chief executives can be seen around the globe, from Argentina to Liberia (Hoogensen and Solheim 2006). Most US women have had the vote since 1920 and have voted in numbers greater than men since 1980. So how is it that US citizens, who pride themselves on democratic principles, have never elected a woman to serve in the West Wing? Increasingly, scholars are asking whether "gender inequality is a deep-seated feature of the American political system and whether liberal political structures will ever provide equal rights and recognition for women" (Ritter 2008, 12).

The barriers to women candidates broadly fall within two categories: structural and attitudinal (Heldman 2007). Structural barriers include those hurdles that are built into the political institutions and the "rules of the game." In some instances around the globe, women have ascended to the chief executive post because their countries are *not* democratic societies, allowing women to achieve executive success through family succession or even divine right. In the United States, where those pathways are not open, structural barriers include the power of incumbency, which extends to sitting (male) elected officials a plethora of electoral advantages,[2] and the political party system, which appears to recruit and mentor men for political advancement more deliberately (Freeman 2000; Lawless and Fox 2005; Sanbonmatsu 2005, 2006), though Barbara Burrell has argued that parties can be a help to women (1994, 2006).

Other structural barriers to women candidates in the United States include the US system of single-member congressional districts. Countries that have a high proportion of women in their legislative bodies are likely to have multimember congressional districts, allowing women candidates to draw support from a wider region and often requiring a smaller percentage of the vote to win office. In the US system, in contrast, the successful legislative candidate must win the most votes in a given district to win election. Furthermore, the presidential system itself appears to place a limit on female advancement (Jalalzai 2008). Many women serving in chief executive posts around the world come to office through prime ministerial systems, which allow them to be elected from among their legislative peers, where they have built coalitions and demonstrated policy acumen. The US presidential system forces "entrepreneurial" candidates to stand for public election, and as a consequence, media and image—and thus, as we will discuss below, political attitudes and culture—become more significant predictors of success (Iyengar and McGrady 2006).

Pathways to the Presidency

We find, in recent decades, four predictable paths to the White House that apparently provide presidential hopefuls with the credentials and resources necessary for a successful campaign. Recent presidents have come to the Oval Office through the military, the vice presidency, a governorship, or Congress (usually service in the Senate or both chambers) (see Table 2.1 below).

Two of these four pathways disqualify all contemporary female candidates. Though two women (Geraldine Ferraro [D] in 1984; Sarah Palin

Table 2.1   Paths to the White House, 1952–2009

President	Path to White House
Dwight D. Eisenhower	Five-Star General
John F. Kennedy	US House and Senate
Lyndon B. Johnson	US House and Senate, Vice President
Richard M. Nixon	US House and Senate, Vice President
Gerald R. Ford	US House, Vice President
Jimmy Carter	Governor
Ronald Reagan	Governor
George H. W. Bush	US House, Vice President
Bill Clinton	Governor
George W. Bush	Governor
Barack H. Obama	US Senate

[R] in 2008) have been nominated for vice president of a major party, no woman has yet been vice president (except in the movies). Given the propensity of vice presidents to seek the higher office, this barrier is significant. And, given the historical reality of presidents dying in or stepping down from office, occupancy of the vice presidency becomes an even more likely pathway for promotion. Table 2.2 reminds us of the instances where a presidential passing has resulted in the vice president assuming the presidency. While this list only includes those whose deaths have resulted in a transition of power, other circumstances, like the threat of impeachment in the case of President Nixon and his subsequent resignation, have also elevated a vice president to the chief executive.

Although it is not a common contemporary route to the White

Table 2.2   Presidents Who Have Died in Office

President	Year(s) Elected
William Henry Harrison	1840
Zachary Taylor	1848
Abraham Lincoln	1860, 1864
James A. Garfield	1880
William McKinley	1896, 1900
Warren G. Harding	1920
Franklin D. Roosevelt	1932, 1936, 1940, 1944
John F. Kennedy	1960

House, a few have advanced through military service. Caroline Heldman (2007) explains that the very office of the president is infused with the notion of the "citizen soldier," linking military service symbolically as a route to the commander-in-chief position. Yet federal law limits women from serving in traditional combat roles, and because the rank of four-star general has historically relied upon combat experience, women are effectively excluded from acquiring full-general status.[3] Moreover, one has only to recall the investigations into the Tailhook scandal and numerous charges of sexual harassment in the military to understand why women today still find credentials in the military difficult to acquire. While President Dwight D. Eisenhower advanced in this manner, the fact that there has never been a woman five-star general is a distinctly gendered barrier.

Table 2.1 reveals additional underlying barriers for women candidates. It appears that coming from a governor's mansion is the most common political pathway for contemporary presidents (the 2008 election year notwithstanding), particularly serving as the governor of a large state such as California or Texas, or a southern state, where increases in population have given those states a greater role in presidential elections. But few women have achieved this status, narrowing considerably the number of women in the pipeline. Only 31 women have served as governors in 23 states (19 Democrats, 12 Republicans). The largest number ever serving at one time was 9 (in 2004 and again in 2007). Of the 31, only 20 were elected in their own right; many were elected to fill out the term of a family member. Governor Ella Grasso (D-CT) was the first woman elected to a governor's mansion in her own right in 1975. Interestingly, only one state (Arizona) has elected two successive women. Perhaps most important for the purposes of electoral vote counting in the general election, only one of the six largest electoral states has had a woman governor (Texas), but that woman, Ann Richards, has since passed away. The other five big states (California, New York, Florida, Illinois, and Pennsylvania) have never elected a woman governor, greatly restricting this pathway to the presidency. Table 2.3 reviews the female occupants of governorships in the United States. Given how few women have achieved this status, and the fact that four of the past five US presidents have come from governorships, women face a clear challenge of numbers in ascending to the White House.

This leaves us with one final, typical path to the White House: Congress. One need only to glance down Pennsylvania Avenue to see that women have made small but steady strides there in recent years. In 1920, when women gained national suffrage, there had only been one

Table 2.3   US Women Governors

Name	Party-State	Dates Served
Nellie Tayloe Ross	D-WY	1925–1927
Miriam Ferguson	D-TX	1925–1927, 1933–1935
Lurleen Wallace	D-AL	1967–1968
Ella Grasso	D-CT	1975–1980
Dixy Lee Ray	D-WA	1977–1981
Vesta Roy	R-NH	1982–1983
Martha Layne Collins	D-KY	1984–1987
Madeleine Kunin	D-VT	1985–1991
Kay Orr	R-NE	1987–1991
Rose Mofford	D-AZ	1988–1991
Joan Finney	D-KS	1991–1995
Ann Richards	D-TX	1991–1995
Barbara Roberts	D-OR	1991–1995
Christine Todd Whitman	R-NJ	1994–2001
Jeanne Shaheen	D-NH	1997–2003
Jane Dee Hull	R-AZ	1997–2003
Nancy Hollister	R-OH	1998–1999
Jane Swift	R-MA	2001–2003
Judy Martz	R-MT	2001–2005
Olene Walker	R-UT	2003–2005
Ruth Ann Minner	D-DE	2001–2009
Jennifer M. Granholm	D-MI	2003–present
Linda Lingle	R-HI	2002–present
Janet Napolitano	D-AZ	2003–2009
Kathleen Sebelius	D-KS	2003–2009
Kathleen Blanco	D-LA	2004–2008
M. Jodi Rell	R-CT	2004–present
Christine Gregoire	D-WA	2004–present
Sarah Palin	R-AK	2007–2009
Jan Brewer	R-AZ	2009–present
Beverly Perdue	D-NC	2009–present

woman to serve in Congress. By 1975, as a result of the women's movement, there were 19 women. Change has been steady, but modest. By 2009 (the 111th Congress), a total of 90 women served in both chambers (69D, 21R), occupying only 17 percent of all congressional seats. Of those, 73 were in the House (56D, 17R), and 17 in the Senate (13D, 4R). Since the founding of the United States, only 2 percent of all members of Congress have been women.

The proportion of women in the US Senate is of particular importance. When looking at Table 2.1 above, we find that not all congressional paths are equal. No president in recent memory has come to the White House directly from the House of Representatives; even Gerald Ford and George H. W. Bush, who did serve there, ascended to the presidency via the vice presidency, not directly from the House. Rather, the US Senate appears to be the more likely stepping stone. In part, this is explained by the fact that senators are elected statewide, which exposes them to a wider range of constituent views and tests their appeal against a wider swath of public opinion. Moreover, the Senate is considered the "upper chamber" and is more fundamentally connected to the White House in numerous ways. US senators, not members of the House, confirm presidential nominees, including cabinet members and all federal judicial nominees.

Thus, service in the US Senate would seem of critical importance to women with presidential ambitions. In total, only 38 women have ever served in the upper chamber (25D, 13R); many of those are deceased or have since retired from politics (see Table 2.4). Given that presidential hopefuls who have served in both chambers have fared relatively well in modern elections, it is significant to note that only eight women have ever served in both the House and Senate; seven of those are serving in the Senate today. Because the other avenues to the presidency are so restricted, we might reasonably anticipate that the first US woman president would rise from the Senate.

Because women have not occupied the pathways to the presidency in great numbers, it is easier to understand why no woman has succeeded in obtaining that position; in fact, some scholars argue that the pipeline to the presidency is too thin to imagine a woman president any time soon (Watson and Gordon 2003). Of course, some have tried. Table 2.5 documents the women who have been serious, major party candidates for the presidency. While a number of women have pursued the presidency in recent decades, there remain considerable barriers to success.[4]

Beyond Structure: Attitudinal Barriers to the Presidency

The most common paths to the White House reviewed here indicate unstated qualifications for that office. The fact that no men have been elected president outside those four pathways in modern times strongly suggests that vital political resources, connections, and qualifications are acquired on those paths that are in some way essential to achieving that office. Still, the thin "pipeline" by itself does not account for the full range of barriers to the presidency. Indeed, the attitudinal hurdles

Table 2.4   US Women Senators

Name	State	Party Affiliation	Years
Rebecca Latimer Felton	GA	Democrat	1922
Hattie Wyatt Caraway	AR	Democrat	1931–1945
Rose McConnell Long	LA	Democrat	1936–1937
Dixie Bibb Graves	AL	Democrat	1937–1938
Gladys Pyle	SD	Republican	1938–1939
Vera Cahalan Bushfield	SD	Republican	1948
Margaret Chase Smith[a]	ME	Republican	1949–1973
Eva Kelly Bowring	NE	Republican	1954
Hazel Hempel Abel	NE	Republican	1954
Maurine Brown Neuberger	OR	Democrat	1960–1967
Elaine Schwartzenburg Edwards	LA	Democrat	1972
Muriel Buck Humphrey	MN	Democrat	1978
Maryon Pittman Allen	AL	Democrat	1978
Nancy Landon Kassenbaum	KS	Republican	1978–1997
Paula Hawkins	FL	Republican	1981–1987
Barbara Ann Mikulski[a]	MD	Democrat	1986–present
Jocelyn Birch Burdick	ND	Democrat	1992
Dianne Feinstein	CA	Democrat	1992–present
Barbara Boxer[a]	CA	Democrat	1993–present
Carol Moseley Braun	IL	Democrat	1993–1999
Patty Murray	WA	Democrat	1993–present
Kay Bailey Hutchinson	TX	Republican	1993–present
Olympia Snowe[a]	ME	Republican	1995–present
Sheila Frahm	KS	Republican	1996
Susan Collins	ME	Republican	1997–present
Mary Landrieu	LA	Democrat	1997–present
Blanche Lincoln[a]	AR	Democrat	1999–present
Maria Cantwell[a]	WA	Democrat	2001–present
Jean Carnahan	MO	Democrat	2001–2002
Hillary Rodham Clinton	NY	Democrat	2001–2009
Debbie Stabenow[a]	MI	Democrat	2001–present
Lisa Murkowski	AK	Republican	2002–present
Elizabeth Dole	NC	Republican	2003–2009
Amy Klobuchar	MN	Democrat	2007–present
Claire McCaskill	MO	Democrat	2007–present
Kay Hagan	NC	Democrat	2009–present
Jeanne Shaheen	NH	Democrat	2009–present
Kirsten Gillibrand[a]	NY	Democrat	2009–present

Note: a. Also served in the US House of Representatives.

Table 2.5   Women Who Have Run for President: Major Party Candidates

Name	Year	Party
Victoria Claflin Woodhull	1872	Equal Rights
Belva Lockwood	1884, 1888	Equal Rights
Margaret Chase Smith	1964	Republican
Shirley Chisholm	1972	Democratic
Patsy Takamoto Mink	1972	Democratic
Ellen McCormack	1976	Democratic
Patricia Schroeder	1988	Democratic
Elizabeth Dole	2000	Republican
Carol Moseley Braun	2004	Democratic
Hillary Rodham Clinton	2008	Democratic

found among voters, the media, and candidates themselves may be more powerful ceilings to women's advancement.

The constitutional qualifications for the presidency are few. Article II of the US Constitution states that one must be a natural-born US citizen, be a 14-year resident of the United States, and be at least 35 years old. In 1951, the 22nd Amendment also disqualified those who have served two terms as president from running again for that office. These stated qualifications do not on their face exclude women, suggesting that the barriers to women's service must reach well beyond structural considerations.

Historical Legacies

The attitudinal barriers to a female president stretch far back into Western history. Christianity itself has produced some of the most effective strictures against women's public service. 1 Corinthians 14:34 tells us, "Let your women keep silence in the churches: for it is not permitted unto them to speak; but they are commanded to be under obedience as also saith the law" (King James Version). Based in part on this passage, the founders excluded US women from not just the suffrage and other trappings of citizenship (jury service, military service), but also the rights of property and bodily integrity, creating a system of "coverture" that "transferred a woman's civic identity to her husband at marriage" (Kerber 1998, 11–12).

It was Abigail Adams, wife of founder and future president John Adams, who famously implored her husband "to remember the ladies" at Liberty Hall. Such pleas fell on deaf ears; in lieu of civil status, early

US women were subjected to the "Cult of True Womanhood," a nineteenth century standard of female virtue that emphasized "piety, purity, submissiveness and domesticity" (Welter 1966, 152). The True Womanhood ideal, with its exacting class, race, and behavioral expectations, effectively argued that the virtuous woman was one untouched by both private vices and public life. The true woman would eschew worldly pleasures, and find her salvation by using her "purifying passionless love [to] bring . . . an erring man back to Christ" (Welter 1966, 153); "men could be counted on to be grateful when women thus saved them from themselves" (156). This ideology grew out of the industrialization period of our nation's history, when men took up paid positions in inner-city factories, and women tended the home, creating the "separate spheres" doctrine that dominated twentieth-century norms about family structure. Woman's service to society would be manifest in her creation of a warm and loving home, a respite for her husband after a hard day in the coarse world of public life, creating a tidy division between the private (female) sphere and the public (male) sphere.

Thus, any woman entering the public realm would sully her good name and invite social stigma, and during Puritan times, possible excoriation and excommunication. Against this backdrop, it is no wonder that US women for so long did not succeed in their suffrage quest, officially begun in 1848 with the Declaration of Sentiments at Seneca Falls, New York. This history serves as a poignant reminder of the deeply rooted strictures against women in the public sphere. Even today, Harvard leadership expert Barbara Kellerman finds that in leadership roles, men are expected to dominate and women to defer (1984). Though notions of womanhood have in some ways changed dramatically in the intervening decades, any woman running for the White House today is still running with hundreds of years of ideological baggage strapped to her ankles. Is it any wonder that she might trip?

Where Are the Candidates?

When women run for lower offices, they often win (Burrell 1994, 2005; Fox 2006; Dolan 2008; Sanbonmatsu 2006). But political scientists Jennifer Lawless and Richard Fox have shown that fewer women run for office than men (2005). The reasons women run in fewer numbers, they explain, are complicated, varied, and insidious. Not only are women less likely than men to see themselves as qualified, they exhibit lower degrees of political ambition, and may be recruited less often than men when positions become available. This candidate gap helps explain the significant lack of women in the presidential pipeline and points to the deeply rooted barriers to women seeking the presidency: women themselves may have internalized masculinized definitions of political leadership identified by Kellerman.

Voter Attitudes and Candidate "Qualifications"

Gender clearly is not an immutable barrier to holding public office, and evidence of gender bias in electoral politics is offset to some degree by evidence of substantial support for female candidacies in some contexts (Burrell 1994, 2005; Dolan 2004, 2008; Falk and Kenski 2006; Fox 2006; Sanbonmatsu 2006; Smith and Fox 2001). Yet enduring public prejudices form key attitudinal barriers to female *presidential* candidates in the United States; though there has been enormous progress, gendered attitudes show stubborn resistance to change as well.

On the one hand, a solid majority of Americans supports the abstract notion of a woman president. Voters have been asked, since 1937, "Would you vote for a woman for president if she were qualified in every other respect?" (Gallup 2000, 235).[5] The General Social Survey (GSS) asked a similar question from 1972 to 1998. Over time, a growing number of US survey takers have reported that they are comfortable with voting for a qualified woman candidate (Dolan 2004). In fact, an October 2007 survey found that "one factor that may be helping [Hillary] Clinton is the view held by some Americans that it would be a good thing to elect a woman to be president. While a solid majority of Americans (55 percent) say they do not think the gender of the president matters, 33 percent say it would be a good thing to elect a woman as president, while just 9 percent believe it would be a bad thing" (Pew Research Center 2007b).

On the other hand, fewer people in the United States report that they think the country is "ready" for a woman president; early in the 2008 campaign, the percentage who said the country was ready to elect a woman hovered at around 55 percent, and those who said most people they knew would be willing to vote for a woman ranged between 34 and 40 percent (Gallup Poll, January 9–12, 2008). Moreover, because many surveys do not ask respondents about particular female candidates, but rather about the nebulous concept of electing a nameless woman, they may not be reliable measures of voters' actual willingness to put a woman—or a particular woman—in the White House (Falk and Kenski 2006). In addition, the GSS is problematic because it emphasizes party nomination; certainly, some voters might have discomfort about a female candidate running for their own party's nomination, but that discomfort might be trumped by their greater discomfort with voting for a male candidate of the opposing party.

Recent scholarship has also focused on the "social desirability effects" of such survey results: as it becomes socially less acceptable to admit bias toward women, do respondents lie on such surveys in order to hide their bias? One study has employed a unique method called a "list experiment" to reveal the extent of the social desirability effect on these prior survey results. That study found a full 26 percent of all respondents admitted feeling "angry or upset" by a list of political issues that included the possibility of a woman president, a significant increase in emotional reactions compared to a list not including that item (Streb et al. 2008; but see Falk and Kenski 2006, 414).[6]

Overall, the public opinion data reveal a striking and significant dilemma: People in the United States report favorably that they would vote for a woman, *if she were qualified* for the job. What do these responses mean? The very fact that pollsters have phrased the question in this way for decades reveals a presumption that most women are not qualified. Clearly, more is at stake in the mind of the pollster and the voter than the basic constitutional requirements of the job.

Women and politics scholars have examined closely this notion of being "qualified" and argue that the unspoken requirements of the job are defined in masculine terms. As Erika Falk contends in her book *Women for President,* "a female candidate stereotyped as a typical *feminine* candidate would most certainly lose electoral support because she would be seen to lack typical male traits and expertise in policy areas thought most necessary for effective national leadership" (Falk, quoting Huddy [1994], 2008, 54). Indeed, one study that measured perceptions of the credentials for the presidency of well-known, real-world candidates (including Elizabeth Dole, Hillary Clinton, John McCain, John Edwards, Rudolph Giuliani) found that the female contenders were perceived as less qualified than the males, even those with similar actual credentials (Paul and Smith 2008). These findings may echo a similar belief among the political class. Even Senator Bob Dole (R-KS) revealed his unease with his wife Elizabeth's presidential candidacy in 2000, telling one reporter that he "wanted to contribute to the [rival] campaign of Senator John McCain." During the same interview, he demonstrated little confidence in his wife's campaign, even indicating he was "a little bit concerned" that her candidacy had progressed slowly (Berke 1999).

More fundamentally, other studies have revealed a basic gender preference among voters for male political leaders (Sanbonmatsu 2002), particularly for higher political offices (Huddy and Terkildsen 1993). Deeply rooted gender stereotypes hold women as more compassionate, honest, and emotionally warm than men, and men as more competent, decisive, able to handle crises (Dolan 2004, p. 8)—in other words, more "presidential." A 1999 survey bolsters this point: "the majority of voters associated men, rather than women, with the top image characteristics they desire in a president—leading the nation during a crisis" (Bystrom 2003, 100). A 2000 survey, in fact, revealed that one-third of respondents believed "there are general characteristics about women that make them less qualified to serve as president"; 51 percent in this study believed that a man would do a superior job in a time of crisis (Deloitte & Touche 2000, cited in Falk and Kenski 2006; see also Pew Research Center for the People and the Press 2008b).

Female Strategies for the Androcentric Presidency

As recently as 2007, one scholarly volume called *Rethinking Madam President* asked in its subtitle, *Are We Ready for a Woman in the White House?* The general conclusion of this literature is that although social attitudes have changed significantly over the past several decades, citizens of the United States retain a view of the presidency that is steeped in masculinity, creating a host of special challenges for any woman seeking the job. The road to the White House is always a challenging one, and the obstacles are distinctly gendered.

The data documenting the experience of women running for Senate and gubernatorial seats illuminate these obstacles and some of the strategies women may employ to overcome them. One crucial element of those strategies is for the female candidate, as much as possible, to fit her public image to the expectations of the office she seeks. For example, as Kim Fridkin Kahn concludes (1996), there is a widespread tendency of US voters to perceive women as more qualified for the office of governor than senator. Although gubernatorial and US Senate candidates run in the same district (statewide), our public perception about those two jobs is distinct. While most people in the United States associate the governor's role with domestic policy, we are more inclined to rank foreign policy credentials highly for US Senate candidates.

These policy arenas carry gendered expectations. Women are thought to be experienced in domestic policy areas like education and health care (Witt, Paget, and Matthews 1994) and thus fare better in their bids for governorships than for the Senate. In one early study, a floor speech delivered by Senator Howard Baker was used in a natural experiment; half the participants were told the author was "John," the other half were told the speech was delivered by "Joan." The participants reading "Joan's" speech were far more likely to give the senator high marks for "improving the education system," "maintaining honesty and integrity in government," and "dealing with health issues," though the speech dealt with none of those issues (Sapiro 1982). Conversely, foreign policy acumen is generally ascribed to men, whether or not their records actually indicate such expertise: the same study indicated more respondents found "John" more competent in dealing with foreign policy matters than "Joan," though the speech was not about foreign policy (Ibid.).

With this in mind, Kahn advises that, "In campaigns for statewide office, women candidates should stress 'male' traits; they should also demonstrate their ability to deal with 'male' issues when those issues dominate the electoral landscape" (Kahn 1996, 137). Indeed, the "resonance" model of voting (Iyengar et al. 1997) holds that women candidates are generally perceived as more credible on issues stereotypically associated with women's competence in caring, such as education, health care, and protecting the environment. The resonance model predicts that women candidates will fare best when they stick to these issues rather than venturing into "male" turf of national security, crime, and economics (Iyengar et al. 1997). The resonance model also presents a double-edged sword: "A woman who calls for educational reform or for stricter enforcement of gender discrimination laws will be taken more seriously than a woman who calls for the death penalty or more aggressive monitoring of terrorist groups" (Iyengar et al., 1997, 97). In other words, the strong lesson of this research is that women should stick to "their" turf—something a woman running for the White House, especially during a time of war and terrorism, simply cannot do.[7]

Though they have an easier time with domestic policy, establishing expertise in general is a challenge for women candidates. The media and voters typically ascribe greater expertise to men than to women, even when the record says otherwise (Falk 2008; Falk and Kenski 2006), and the media tend to cover policy issues less than other aspects of elections and to give substantive coverage of female candidates even shorter shrift (Falk 2008; Kahn 1996). Media coverage of women's campaigns is also more likely to contain references to appearance, clothing, and hair, and other physical attributes unrelated to public service, and is also more likely to play up any emotionalism on the part of the candidate, fulfilling the public's stereotype of women as more emotional (patterns discussed further in Chapter 3). These findings lead Kahn (1996) to advise the female candidate to focus doggedly on policy issues in order to influence the news agenda and build a public image of policy expertise, and to carefully avoid fulfilling gendered stereotypes with displays of emotion or calling attention to her sex.

These challenges to women candidates in establishing credibility may account for why men and women candidates employ distinctive messaging styles (as observed by Bystrom et al. 2004). For example, while they feature similar verbal content in their advertising, men and women candidates employ very different nonverbal cues. Men are more likely to feature their families in their advertisements, while women tend to instead include other people's children. This decision is gendered, of course: the female candidate is attempting to show that while she relates to children, as a woman "should," she is more than a wife and mother. Both male and female candidates prefer to use male narrators in their ads, thus lending male gravitas to their message, yet women candidates are also more likely to speak directly into the camera in order to establish their own credibility. Most tellingly, the authors find, women dress more formally than men, thereby establishing credibility, but are also more often shown smiling—an expression of proper femininity.

Therefore, the research suggests that the challenge for female candidates lies in fitting the policy issues and duties associated with various political offices with deeply held gender stereotypes (Kahn 1996), and to establish "gender issue ownership," using voters' dispositions toward gender as an asset rather than a liability (Herrnson, Lay, and Stokes 2003; Jalazai 2006). Yet as one recent experimental study finds, gender traits "guide voter perceptions and choice" in presidential politics to such a degree that "when the person running for president is *not* a man, the role and the candidate are incongruent, and this mismatch produces gender-bias" (Smith, Paul, and Paul 2007, 226). This challenge may be compounded by the heavy emphasis on national security issues associated with the presidency. Jennifer Lawless (2004) found that in the post-9/11 environment, gender stereotyping may be particularly harmful to female candidates who must establish their credentials in a new era of national security concerns, though Susan Hansen and Laura Otero contend that some of the post-9/11 electoral climate has abated (2006).

Double Binds and Gender Strategy in Presidential Politics

In crafting her campaign strategy, the female presidential candidate also faces a series of what Kathleen Hall Jamieson (1995) calls "double binds" that force women to choose between nonchoices. As Jamieson explains, public women face a series of choices in which "both alternatives . . . carry clear penalties," creating pressure to "abandon whatever goal has aroused the . . . debate" (1995, 14). Any female candidate who enters presidential politics will be presented with tactical choices that either stabilize or topple her balance between competing gravitational pulls: demonstrating proper "femininity" along with the required "toughness" for the Oval Office, and striking a balance between claims of gender-neutral "equality" versus gender-conscious "difference."

Femininity vs. Toughness

The first familiar bind to political women is what Jamieson calls the femininity/competence bind (1995), in which the female candidate must choose between showing proper femininity and burnishing her credentials as a "competent" candidate. The danger lies not just in being "too strident and abrasive or not aggressive or tough enough," but also in "deviat[ing] from the female norm of femininity while exceeding or falling short of the masculine norm of competence" (Jamieson 1995, 121). Lori Cox Han and Caroline Heldman explain the bind this way: "Women may wear masculinist ideology, but they cannot embody it because masculinity is an exclusively male prerogative" (2007, 21). In trying to achieve a leadership role within a masculine institution, women must perform a delicate balancing act, conveying a degree of femininity acceptable to the voting public, while credibly assuming a mantle of masculinity in order to be perceived as qualified for the job. A woman candidate must prove herself "tough enough" for the Oval Office, yet a woman who demonstrates her toughness is very likely to be criticized (explicitly or implicitly) on the grounds that she is unwomanly. Journalists Eleanor Clift and Tom Brazaitis argue the point in a more essentialist vein: "For women, the key to winning is demonstrating toughness while not surrendering their inborn empathy" (2003, 72). Bystrom calls this the "tough but caring" message (2003, 105).

Whether one believes women's empathy is inborn or socialized, the first woman to achieve the presidency will have to strategize within the confines of this double bind. The literature predicts that in order to be successful, a female candidate would need to emphasize masculine traits and themes because, as Duerst-Lahti puts it bluntly, "Women are expected to be feminine, but presidential candidates are judged by the quality of their masculinity" (2007, 91). But exactly how masculine should she appear, and in what settings? The female candidate must choose how far to move along a continuum of gendered messaging, when and where to move from the territory of androgynous appeals rooted in competence into the masculinized territory of tough talk and aggressive attacks—a particularly tricky decision, since the news media are likely to exaggerate female candidates' attacks on opponents (Gidengil and Everitt 2003). Determining when and how far to move the campaign's messages along this continuum constitutes an important strategic choice in presidential politics.

As Clinton's race for the presidency has revealed, she was not immune from this bind, despite her demonstrable toughness. For example, while many detractors mocked Clinton when she occasionally showed emotion on the campaign trail, some commentators were just as likely to brand her a "castrator" or "ball-buster," revealing the deeply ingrained sense that any woman who holds power emasculates men. While our cultural expectations around masculinity assume self-assuredness and competitiveness, assumptions about femininity are rooted in modesty, decorum, and selflessness. By running for the presidency—the quintessential "public" position—Hillary Clinton challenged the very norms of our gendered society. By running aggressively, confidently, and determinedly, even after her frontrunner status evaporated and her chances of winning the nomination became increasingly remote, she challenged the definition of femininity, and her own grasp on womanhood.

Equality vs. Difference

Candidate Clinton also faced a decision familiar to many political women between asserting competence on equal terms with her male competitors and claiming her equal qualifications for the presidential office, or emphasizing her "difference" as a female candidate and treating her feminine gender as a unique and positive qualification for the office. The "equality-versus-difference" debate has framed many questions regarding women's status for much of our nation's history, and constitutes two poles in feminist theory.[8]

Equality feminism has roots in traditional liberal political philosophy and is characterized by arguments that "sexual difference ought to be an irrelevant consideration in schools, employment, the courts, and the legislature" (Scott 1988, 167). The roots of equality (sometimes simply called "liberal") feminism date back to the Declaration of Sentiments (1848) and John Stuart Mill's "The Subjection of Women" (1869). In a nutshell, equality feminism proposes that women simply be added into our existing modes of governing: if overt legal barriers to equality such as sex-based hiring practices are removed, women can use their individual rationality to succeed in the "race of life" (Kramnick 1977). In this vein, some of the critical legislative and judicial achievements of the 20th century (Title VII, Title IX, etc.) provided women with opportunities for equality by simply throwing open the doors to their inclusion. This form of feminism has been widely criticized for its "add women and stir" mentality, and for its reliance on the individual woman to achieve her own success in place of more rigorous attention to systemic obstacles that block women's way. Many also critique equality feminism for relying on an unstated premise of women's "sameness": in this view, arguing women's equality to men leaves in place the assumption that the male is the original or true form of humankind. Nevertheless, in a liberal society, claims of equality are powerful symbolic weapons, and choosing the equality path allows the female candidate to avoid calling overt attention to her sex.

In contrast, difference feminism insists that "appeals on behalf of women ought to be made in terms of the needs, interests, and characteristics common to women as a group" (Scott 1996, 614), and its achievements date back to the protective legislation of the early twentieth century. Today, scholars such as Carol Gilligan propose that women, by virtue of their social training and/or biology, operate in more relational capacity than men, and as a consequence, see the world differently than their male counterparts (1982). In an electoral context, gender strategies based in difference feminism claim that unique feminine attributes bring added value to the candidate's capacity to govern. Difference strategies seek to turn gender from a liability into an asset in winning office by claiming and deploying positively framed sex stereotypes, such as women's allegedly greater honesty and compassion. These claims often operate in tandem with claims of outsider status, such as some suffrage arguments that claimed women could clean up government, just as they cleaned up their homes and communities.

Claims of feminine difference have worked successfully for some women in the United States and beyond to win elective office, particularly because of widely shared notions that women are more honest and less arrogant, stubborn, and corrupt than men (Valdini 2007; Pew Research Center 2008c). Women congressional candidates in the 1990s, for example, benefited from public dissatisfaction with "gridlock" in government, promising (either explicitly or implicitly) more cooperative and compassionate policymaking (Jamieson 1995, 115–116). "Running as a woman" (Witt, Paget, and Matthews 1994) has sometimes offered political openings for female politicians and offers women the possibility to argue that "difference" is a virtue in elective office (rather than attempting to fit the masculine mold). But this tack is fraught with risk in the androcentric politics of the presidency. Indeed, even men who do not prove themselves adequately "tough" for the job rarely win the White House. (Recall *New York Times* columnist Maureen Dowd's questioning of Vice President Al Gore's masculinity during his presidential campaign, once claiming that "Al Gore is so feminized and diversified and ecologically correct, he's practically lactating" [Dowd 1999].)

Moreover, emphasizing claims of difference risks overemphasizing the female presidential candidate as a historical "first." Falk's (2008) analysis of press coverage of eight women's presidential campaigns across three centuries reveals a startlingly consistent tendency of the press to report on the novelty of women's bids for power. Falk finds, in fact, that *every* woman who had run for the presidency before Hillary Clinton was dubbed a "first." Not only was the observation usually not factually true, but terms like "first" and "historic," she contends, send a subtle message that the candidate is breaking a norm and that a woman's place is elsewhere, while signaling to the voter that women candidates have little real chance of success.

Alternatively, however, a female candidate who embraces equality feminism and asserts her equitable qualification for the job potentially sacrifices her very womanhood by establishing her ability to fill a masculinized role. Just as a man who seems unmanly may not be able to attain the presidency, a female candidate who seems unwomanly may be profoundly disconcerting to a public still influenced by deeply rooted notions of the qualities each gender "should" display.

Historically, the woman candidate has generally tipped her hand toward one or the other competing pull, either emphasizing her feminine qualities (and thus implicitly seeking to redefine the office) or by employing symbolic strategies that "out-maled the men" (Duerst-Lahti and Kelly 1995, 27). Much of the popular debate about women's roles in traditionally male-dominated venues such as politics turn on this question of whether women should opt to "play like the boys," or, alternatively, speak "in a different voice." Georgia Duerst-Lahti and Rita Mae Kelly explain the dilemma this way:

> Even if we set aside the problem women face being recognized as leaders at all, women can successfully enter masculine leadership roles but face two unhappy options. . . . Either women must conform to artificially heightened gender differentiation as a leader and agree that feminine leaders' styles exist, thereby perpetuating gender dif-

ferentiation in the process, or women leaders can "do masculine leadership"; they can perform their leadership tasks in a way more masculine than men.

> Neither option alters extant gender power. (1995, 31)

This dilemma lies at the heart of this double bind, for neither the path of difference nor the path of equality seems entirely politically tenable. Emphasizing either entails political costs. As we explore further below, candidate Clinton largely (though not entirely) avoided the symbolism and rhetoric of "difference" and instead staked her claim to the presidency in straightforward "equality" terms—leaving open the question of whether running more explicitly "as a woman" might have proven successful.

Clinton's Unique Binds: Experience vs. Change and Independence vs. Dependence

We also find in our research at least two ways in which these well-known binds were extended in the case of Hillary Clinton. A third bind arose from the tension Clinton faced between establishing her experience (a necessity for women candidates) and asserting her credentials as a change agent. Focused as she was upon an equality-based claim to the presidency, Clinton's strategy initially relied heavily on the notion of her "experience" for the job—that she would be "ready on Day One." But the 2008 political climate and her main opponent's messaging forced Clinton to assert that she had the "experience to make the change," an idea that did not take hold in news coverage or in the public imagination.

A fourth bind also noticeable in the particular case of Clinton was the bind of independence/dependence. Independence, self-direction, and autonomy are desirable traits in a political leader—traits subtly coded as masculine. A tension emerged in media coverage and public discourse around the true extent of Senator Clinton's independence, largely as a result of her relationship to Bill Clinton. This narrative raised questions about the source of her power and the cause of her successes—was she really "her own woman"?—and the implications of Bill Clinton's potential reinstatement in the White House—a "dynasty" narrative that did not work to Hillary Clinton's advantage. This bind, we contend, emerged because Clinton's particular path to the White House included her tenure as First Lady, a path few future presidential hopefuls may tread, but one that reveals even more deeply how gender stereotypes may shape women's bids for power.

Hillary Clinton's Presidential Strategies

We can evaluate Senator Clinton's choices leading up to and during her presidential campaign in light of gendered expectations of the presidency. Indeed, the women and politics literature predicts very well many aspects of her presidential strategy. Understanding the gendered nature of "qualification" for the presidency—an office that generally requires a balance of both domestic and foreign policy expertise—we would expect a female presidential hopeful to strengthen her foreign policy credentials in anticipation of the gendered bias in public attitudes. Given that very few pathways to the presidency open to women provide foreign policy experience, we would expect female hopefuls to gain foreign policy expertise through State Department service, CIA work, and committee placement in Congress. Senator Clinton's desire to serve on the Senate Committee on Armed Services makes sense within this context: service there gives a senator a unique role in the foreign policy process, as well as opportunities for foreign travel in the investigative phases of policy development, thereby offering invaluable foreign policy credentials.

This need to mold oneself to fit gendered expectations of the office while overcoming gendered attitudes about which sex is better suited to serve as commander in chief also explains much from Hillary Clinton's campaign that we explore in subsequent chapters. For example, on the campaign trail, Clinton often emphasized her foreign travel as First Lady. Though she came under criticism because some saw those activities as more symbolic than substantive (and because on several occasions she misrepresented the circumstances of her foreign visits),[9] her consistent efforts to portray herself as the most experienced foreign policy expert among the Democratic nomination contenders speaks to the importance of women candidates addressing the gendered bias head-on.

In the arena of domestic policy, on the other hand, the literature suggests that women candidates can benefit from the public presumption that women are naturally well qualified to deal with issues such as health care, child care, poverty, and so on. Perhaps because of these expectations in general as well as Clinton's own efforts on behalf of health-care reform during her husband's presidency, voters (particularly Democrats) consistently rated her highly in terms of her expertise on this issue.[10] On the campaign trail, Senator Clinton spoke knowledgeably and often on the state of the economy, the domestic mortgage crisis, and problems in health care and education, leaving her male opponents no opportunity to claim superior policy knowledge.

If voters are predisposed to see male candidates as more qualified on presidential policy issues, and female candidates as less, then women running for the presidency arguably have no option but to run on a theme of "experience." Indeed, the literature predicts (and counsels) a message strategy emphasizing qualifications and issue positions first and foremost—both because gender stereotypes will likely cloud the public's appreciation of the female candidate's political abilities, and because the press will likely overlook issues and qualifications unless the female candidate emphasizes them. Again, we see confirmation in Clinton's campaign strategies. Senator Clinton's consistently intoned campaign theme "Ready on Day One" attempted to firmly establish in voters' minds the notion that she was better experienced than her rivals to occupy the White House. Though pundits would later criticize Clinton for repeating this theme ad nauseum in a political season dominated by a public restive for change, the research on gender attitudes strongly suggests that any serious female contender may have seen little choice.

The alternative to an experience-based campaign is one rooted in ideas, freshness, and an "outside the beltway" theme, as Sarah Palin, the 2008 Republican vice presidential candidate did with her "just your average hockey mom" refrain.[11] Indeed, in some election cycles, "outsider" status lends advantage when incumbents are viewed as incompetent and government institutions suffer from low approval ratings. This option has been successful for some women: Senator Patty Murray (D-WA), was first elected to the Senate during such a climate in 1992 by running on the campaign slogan that she was "just a mom in tennis shoes." Indeed, one recent study suggests that women executives around the world have risen to power primarily as political outsiders (Tripp 2008).

Whether that strategy could allow a woman to win the White House is another question. Jimmy Carter rode outsider status to victory in 1976, and Barack Obama very effectively used the "change" theme to indicate his freedom from the political establishment. However, with women candidates, "change" may well equal "inexperience" or "incompetence" in voters' minds, and may implicitly call attention to their gender "mismatch" for the office. (Indeed, it was not until the mantra of "change" swept campaign discourse that Clinton began to comment that electing her would, like electing the nation's first African American president, represent change). Though not an impossible strategy, the research suggests that because no woman has ever held the position, most women presidential hopefuls would rely instead on themes of experience and qualifications for the job, precisely as Hillary Clinton did.

The literature also counsels against running as a "first"; as Falk's (2008) historical research shows, the notion of being the "first" woman to run for the presidency often becomes an implicit or explicit way of treating the female candidate as an interesting novelty rather than a serious contender. The literature would also seem to recommend that the female presidential contender "de-sex" herself and devise a gender strategy that carefully avoids overt displays of femininity or drawing attention to her sex; if gendered language and imagery are deployed, the literature seems to advise, they should lean toward the masculine rather than the feminine (Falk 2008; Huddy and Terkildsen 1993). The Clinton campaign largely followed this advice, embracing an equality argument and largely (though not entirely) eschewing the positively framed femininity granted in difference feminism. Put more simply, Hillary Clinton did not run "as a woman," nor did she emphasize the historic nature of her candidacy. Rather, she consistently emphasized experience and policy issues and presented herself much more as a capable and ready commander in chief than as US history's first viable *female* presidential candidate. Specifically, her campaign first attempted an ostensibly gender-neutral campaign grounded in her "experience" and her extensive policy knowledge and proposals (with some rather subtle feminine cues layered on top), followed by a much more aggressive, masculinized strategy of tough talk and "outmanning" her opponent.

Apparently, for a significant number of voters these strategies worked. But these strategies also carried risks that undermined her campaign. For example, the "experience" theme so emphasized by Clinton's campaign was fraught with landmines for a former First Lady, especially one who was perhaps best remembered for leading a highly ambitious and failed effort at health-care reform. It was also a nonstarter in terms of media coverage; indeed, her policy expertise was rarely highlighted in the news. Meanwhile, the campaign's shifts in and out of masculine tough talk fueled criticisms of Clinton that amplified preexisting, negatively framed aspects of her public image, leaving her more vulnerable to media scripts portraying her as duplicitous, inordinately ambitious, and willing to "do anything" to get elected. And, either because they followed the (lack of) cues from the Clinton campaign or because the story of the nation's most successful female candidacy did not seem newsworthy, the media largely overlooked the unique history-making aspects of Clinton's campaign—in a year filled with discussion of the historic nature of Senator Barack Obama's bid for the presidency.

Conclusion: How the "First" Ran

Though some have gone before her, Hillary Clinton represents the most successful female presidential bid to date. Her path was clearly marked by many of the gendered hurdles outlined above. She has made decisions about her career and her campaign in keeping with our knowledge about the traditional pipeline to the presidency and the unwritten androcentric qualifications for the job, and her campaign strategies in many respects faithfully followed the counsel of the women and politics literature. In fact, in some respects Clinton took this masculinized strategy to lengths not necessarily predicted in the literature, not so subtly presenting herself as the "real man" in the campaign. Yet at the same time, Clinton did not always stick to the androcentric gender script. Some of the most notable and controversial moments from her campaign occurred when Clinton explicitly brandished her support among female voters or made public comments about her experiences as the only woman in the field of Democratic candidates. It was at these moments that controversy over "the gender card" entered into the campaign.

Notes

1. Given the unusual closeness of the voting in the 2008 primaries and the disputed role of votes from Florida and Michigan due to Democratic Party rules for scheduling primaries (see Appendix A), vote tallies became closely watched and controversial. The website Real Clear Politics maintained six ongoing tallies both including and not including the Michigan and Florida results and other contested features of the vote count (see http://www .realclearpolitics.com/epolls/2008/president/democratic_vote_count.html).

2. Incumbency appears to benefit women as it does men (Dolan 2004; Fox 2006), though fewer women enjoy incumbent status.

3. In addition, only eleven active-duty four-star generals are permitted at any given time, making that designation a rarity. In 2008, President George W. Bush overlooked the combat requirement to nominate Ann E. Dunwoody for four-star status. The Senate confirmed Ms. Dunwoody in July 2008, making her the highest-ranking woman in US military history.

4. Jo Freeman has produced an exhaustive list of all women known to have sought (or seriously contemplated seeking) the US presidency. Her list contains those who pursued minor and major party nominations. See Freeman (2008).

5. The wording has changed slightly over the years, though it has always included the concept of women's qualifications.

6. Interestingly, given the relatively recent timing of this study and the fact of Hillary Clinton's wide name recognition, many respondents in this experiment were likely thinking of Clinton even though her name was not explicitly mentioned.

7. Recent research has begun to challenge assumptions about "male" and "female" issues. Dianne Bystrom, for instance, finds that "a 1999 study of spot ads from the 1996 mixed-gender US Senate and gubernatorial races found a new trend emerging: females stressed male traits such as toughness even more than male candidates, ran more negative ads, and actually stressed warmth and compassion less than male candidates" (2003, 102).

8. Recent feminist scholarship has shown the limitations of both theoretical traditions and has proposed alternative feminist frameworks. Despite their theoretical limitations, these modes of feminism still arguably constitute the predominant ways of thinking about how women should advance themselves in public life, at least among those in the political world.

9. As we explore further in Chapter 3, Senator Clinton made a number of references on the campaign trail to her visit to Bosnia as First Lady in March of 1996, seemingly in response to charges by her rival Barack Obama that being First Lady had not given Clinton real foreign policy experience.

10. See, for example, the *Wall Street Journal* poll from March of 2008, in which 50 percent of Democratic voters said Clinton would be "better" than Barack Obama in dealing with health care, while only 23 percent said Obama would be better at handling health care (Hart/McInturff 2008).

11. For our early analysis of how Governor Palin's messaging strategy may differ from Senator Clinton's, see Chapter 7 and see Rose (2008).

3

The Media and the
Path to the White House

We are at war. Is this how she'll talk to Kim Jong-il?
—Male reporter at the *New York Times,* according to *Times*
columnist Maureen Dowd, January 9, 2008

It was not that Senator Hillary Rodham Clinton teared up. It was all
the times she did not.
—Jodi Kantor, *New York Times,* January 9, 2008

On January 7, 2008, one day before the New Hampshire primary, Hillary Clinton cried. More accurately, Clinton's eyes appeared to well with tears and her voice to break. The moment occurred after a woman attending a breakfast campaign event at a diner with the candidate asked about her grueling schedule. "My question is very personal: how do you do it?" the woman queried. "It's not easy," Clinton replied. Resting her chin in her hand, she said softly, "I have so many opportunities from this country. I just don't want to see us fall backwards." As the attendees applauded and Clinton's voice dropped further and sounded choked, she continued, "You know, this is very personal for me. It's not just political, it's not just public. I see what's happening. And we have to reverse it. And some people think elections are a game. They think it's like who's up or who's down." Shaking her head, Clinton said, "It's about our country. It's about our kids' futures. And it's really about all of us, together." Observing that "some of us put ourselves out there and do this against some pretty difficult odds," Clinton continued, "But some of us are right and some of us are wrong. Some of us are ready and some of us are not. Some of us know what we will do on day one, and some of us really haven't thought that through enough." Clinton concluded her comment, her voice resuming its normal tone, by observing the potential of the country's troubles "spinning out of control," saying, "This is one of the most important elections America has ever faced."[1]

Some initial media coverage of the Portsmouth moment wondered aloud if, by appearing to cry in public, Clinton had just committed a major campaign gaffe. (So did the Clinton campaign staff).[2] According to journalist Gwen Ifill, the "first round of thought" among reporters watching the footage was that "this is going to be a Pat Schroeder moment" (National Public Radio, January 10, 2008). The reference was to former congresswoman Pat Schroeder, who cried when she bowed out of the race for the 1988 Democratic nomination—tears that became the focus of press coverage of her announcement. Other observers saw Clinton's moment as a calculated campaign stunt, a perspective captured neatly by a *New York Times* column headlined, "Can Hillary Cry Her Way Back to the White House?" (Dowd 2008a). Others quickly chimed in, some wondering "if she is breaking down now, before winning her party's nomination, then how would she act under pressure as president?"—a sentiment that feminist author Katha Pollitt called "the oldest, dumbest canard about women: they're too emotional to hold power" (quoted in Kantor 2008b).

Yet when it became clear that Clinton had won the New Hampshire primary, her teary moment was credited with helping to bring about her victory. According to the *New York Times*, for example, "Several New Hampshire women, some of them undecided until Tuesday, said that a galvanizing moment for them had been Mrs. Clinton's unusual display of emotion on Monday as she described the pressures of the race and her goals for the nation—a moment Mrs. Clinton herself acknowledged as a breakthrough" (Healy and Cooper 2008). NBC political analyst Chuck Todd called the New Hampshire moment "the tears felt round the world," observing, "whether she actually cried or just got choked up, the important thing was Hillary showed a pulse and New Hampshire voters, particularly women, were smitten" (Todd and Gawiser 2009, 13).

Meanwhile, many observers reacted to Clinton's victory in New Hampshire with surprise. Polls taken in the days leading up to the vote had shown her main competitor, Senator Barack Obama, gaining ground and even pulling into the lead. Despite this being only the second contest in the 2008 primary season, the press had been poised to write Clinton's electoral obituary. Indeed, some news stories about Clinton's New Hampshire victory rally opened with funereal imagery, casting a metaphorical pall over her win. "It was to have been Hillary Rodham Clinton's political funeral Tuesday night," one reporter observed, "and her podium stood three feet high in the middle of the room, draped in black cloth like a catafalque." "For a dead woman," the reporter continued, her victory "was no small accomplishment" (Milbank 2008a). Thus, even as she allegedly rode "a wave of female support" to victory (Healy and Cooper 2008), Hillary Clinton's campaign was painted in dark tones by the press.

Clinton's teary-eyed moment in Portsmouth illustrates the double binds faced by women in public life. By appearing to cry in public—even if no actual tears were shed—she risked confirming negative stereotypes about female emotionalism and raising questions about her readiness for the White House. Indeed, her competitor Senator John Edwards (D-NC) was quick to make that inference, telling reporters, "I think what we need in a commander-in-chief is strength and resolve, and presidential campaigns are tough business, but being president of the United States is also tough business" (ABC News 2008). Clinton's tears were taken by some pundits and voters as evidence that she was "weak" and unfit to be president, even while the moment highlighted for others that Clinton was indeed a feeling human being. Thus, the reaction also illustrates the particular attitudes stirred up by Senator Clinton herself, who has long been seen as calculating and emotionally distant. Some people praised the moment as a window into Clinton's normally walled-off inner life that bridged the gap between Clinton's usual public persona and societal expectations of feminine emotionality and warmth (one *Washington Post* headline read, "A Chink in the Steely Face").

The teary-eyed moment also serves as a revealing window on the ways in which contemporary campaigns are structured for voters by the news media. In this chapter we explore what decades of scholarly research have revealed about patterns of news coverage of elections—patterns that arise from the constraints and incentives of the news business and the profession of journalism as it is currently practiced in the United States, and from the unique role the media play in US politics. Three patterns that apply to virtually all presidential candidates, male or female, are crucial for understanding how Hillary Clinton's presidential campaign was portrayed in the media: (1) the tendency of the media to focus on key campaign moments, such as gaffes, missteps, and reversals in fortune; (2) the media's heavy emphasis on "horse-race" coverage, often with a negative tone; and (3) the "master narrative" that underlies media coverage of the candidates in each presidential race.

Understanding these media routines puts into larger context the findings of the women and politics literature, reviewed below, documenting explicit gender biases in news coverage of female candidates.

Interestingly, the political communication literature has not fully considered the impact of these news routines on coverage of female presidential candidates. As in other areas of literature on the presidency, and similar to some mainstream medical research in which men's bodies become the basis for conclusions about women's health (Jamieson 1995), the attention to male candidate news coverage has sometimes obscured the role that gender stereotypes and gendered attitudes may play when a woman runs. At the same time, a well-established literature shows how women candidates are portrayed in the news, but with a few exceptions, these studies focus on nonpresidential electoral contests (primarily congressional and gubernatorial races). Arguably, the dynamics are different when a female candidate enters *presidential* politics; not only are the stakes higher, but the volume and type of news coverage will be different than for lower-level elections, as may be the particular routines of the elite reporters and news organizations that cover national politics. Moreover, the women and politics literature sometimes too readily attributes to gender bias news patterns that may also be explainable in terms of standard (though not unproblematic) media routines for covering presidential elections. This chapter bridges these two literatures, bringing what is known about how the national media cover presidential politics together with what is known about how women candidates for all offices are typically treated in the media, and applying these to the study of Hillary Clinton's presidential bid.

We argue here that each of these media routines for covering presidential races—the focus on defining moments, horse-race coverage, and candidate master narratives—has created difficulties for the main presidential contenders in recent decades, all of whom until Hillary Clinton were male. But these routines may also particularly disadvantage female presidential candidates; as played out in the 2008 campaign, each took on a subtle but distinct gendering that favors masculinity. Overall, this chapter shows that the challenges of gaining and maintaining positive news coverage that virtually all presidential candidates face become particularly serious hurdles for female presidential hopefuls. In addition to the double binds faced by women candidates in general, Hillary Clinton in 2008 faced a double whammy of explicitly gendered plus putatively nongendered news routines—none of which were helpful to her campaign.

Defining Moments

In 1972, three weeks before that year's New Hampshire primary, Democratic contender Edmund Muskie had been crowned by the press as the presumed front-runner, based on polls predicting he would get two-thirds of the Democratic vote in that state and a plurality of votes in many other states. Then, the Manchester *Union-Leader* published a story alleging that Muskie's wife was a problem drinker. At a speech in front of the newspaper's offices, while Muskie defended his wife, he dabbed at his cheeks. Though it was never entirely clear if Muskie was wiping away tears or melting snowflakes, the moment was quickly labeled by the media as a "crying" incident and questions immediately arose about his emotional stability. Though Muskie won New Hampshire, negative news coverage of him increased; within weeks, Muskie had lost the Florida primary and had dropped out of the race.

That Muskie's allegedly teary-eyed moment in New Hampshire could raise questions in the news about his "readiness" for the White House illustrates the gendered expectations that structure presidential politics. Muskie's critics contended that his show of emotion betrayed an underlying emotionalism that nearly automatically disqualifies any contender from filling a job that is defined in quintessentially masculine terms (Heldman 2007).

But the fact that this single moment came to define and derail Muskie's bid for the White House also illustrates a pattern that has prevailed in news coverage of presidential campaigns since the early 1970s, even in contexts not centered on gender stereotypes. In 1976, incumbent Republican president Gerald Ford inadvertently stated during the second presidential debate of the season that there was "no Soviet dominance of Eastern Europe." Though a rational observer could have safely assumed that the president, who was no newcomer to the international stage, had simply mangled his words, and although polls taken immediately after the debate showed Ford to be the winner in more viewers' estimation, the media pounced on the moment and turned it into a major news story. Within a day, the poll numbers reversed, with more people suddenly agreeing that Ford had actually "lost" the debate.

A different example was found in the 1980 race for the White House candidate Ronald Reagan's early lead in the New Hampshire polls faded and he was widely predicted to lose there. But in a bit of widely publicized debate theatrics in which he unexpectedly invited other Republican contenders onto the stage for what was supposed to be a one-on-one debate with George H. W. Bush, and then roared "I'm paying for this microphone!" when the moderator threatened to cut the mic, Reagan salvaged his lead and later won handily over Bush (Patterson 1994).[3] In a more recent example, a moment of theatrical exuberance may have cost Democratic candidate Howard Dean his bid for the 2004 Democratic nomination. Dean's relentlessly replayed scream at a rally just after he came in third in the Iowa caucuses was interpreted by the press as prima facie evidence of Dean's instability and unreadiness for the presidency, though observers on the scene reported that Dean's enthusiasm simply played to that of the crowd. According to reporters, the "Dean Scream" revealed that the candidate was ill-prepared for the requirements of a nationally visible campaign ("Campaign Essentials: Unraveling of a Candidate" 2004).

The story of many presidential campaigns is condensed to a string of these kinds of highly publicized moments that are interpreted by the media as more than simple "gaffes," but as incidents that reveal the underlying character of the candidate—sometimes for the better, as in Ronald Reagan's case, but often to the candidate's detriment. It is the narrative cobbled together from these moments, rather than a steady examination of the candidate's policy positions and qualifications, that defines much contemporary media coverage of presidential campaigns.[4]

Defining Moments as Information Shortcuts

Writing in defense of this kind of coverage, commentator Madison Powers argues, "Through a look at gaffes that might sink a campaign voters get to see a candidate's moral blind spots. Debate performances, stump speeches, and victory and concession speeches over time reveal patterns of behavior that voters can use to decide whether they like or dislike a candidate" (Powers 2008). There seems little question that for the voter who takes only passing interest in the campaign and lacks much background information, these allegedly revealing moments become key bits of information as they form their impressions of the candidates. To the extent that such moments come to dominate news coverage, even better-informed voters are likely to be influenced by these key moments simply because they tune into the news more often; the saturation of the Internet with video clips of these moments makes their potential influence over larger numbers of voters greater.

To some extent, media coverage that focuses on key "moments" from the campaign may not be problematic and fits well with a standard way that many voters reason about politics. For most people, the perceived value of voting is not great enough to inspire extensive research on all the candidates and issues at play in any one election (Downs 1957). When deciding how to vote, many people therefore rely upon what scholars call "information shortcuts" (also known as "heuristics").[5] Lacking the incentive to become fully informed about every candidate's policy positions, and uncertain about what a candidate will actually do once in office, many voters rely on cues about the candidates' personality and character to "project" how those candidates will behave in the future (Glass 1985; Popkin 1992, 1994).[6] Observing how candidates manage difficult moments on the campaign trail—or how well they carry off successful moments—thus becomes an important source of shortcuts that lower the informational costs of voting.[7]

While Powers may be correct that gaffes reveal the innate characteristics of the candidates, it may also be true that, focused through the laser-beam prism of the media, these campaign moments take on a significance that far outweighs their informational value. That possibility seems even more likely in this Internet-saturated era. As media-scholar Kathleen Hall Jamieson notes, "People aren't watching thirty minutes of NBC or CBS or ABC anymore. There's a whole part of the electorate that is watching a segment of it, it gets what it needs of politics, and it starts to channel surf to get other political information" (Jamieson 2008). This way of interacting with campaign information potentially increases the power of "info bits" and defining moments in shaping voter perceptions—and reporters' perceptions as well.[8]

News coverage that emphasizes allegedly revealing campaign moments may also be deeply problematic because it encourages the illusion that the television (or computer) screen offers a window into politicians' souls (Graber 1976; Hart 1998; Keeter 1987). Focusing on such moments plays right into voters' illusion that they can predict how the candidates will act in office because they have, through television, seen into the candidates' essential selves (Hart 1998); "viewers believe they have 'seen for themselves,' and their visual impressions suggest to them the 'real' personal qualities of the familiar face" (Lang and Lang 1968, 210, quoted in Keeter 1987). Event-driven news coverage may also lead campaigns to become more volatile and the bases for voter choice less stable. "The nominating phase is especially volatile," Thomas Patterson argues; "with relatively small changes in luck, timing, or circumstance, several nominating races [since the 1970s] might have turned out differently" (Patterson 1994, 42).

Indeed, for the average voter, the campaign season may become little more than a series of highly publicized "moments" that seemingly define the candidates. Which raises the question, how does the press recognize these allegedly revealing moments? To some degree, such moments may arise randomly because each candidate and each campaign season are unique. Some candidates commit more gaffes, while some are more media-savvy; some face more or less difficult campaign circumstances than their competitors. But research has revealed that the press's choice of key campaign moments is not entirely random. Aside from the obvious (but not very helpful) observation that such moments are "newsworthy," two factors seem to play an especially important role: the way such moments fit into the media's overarching horse-race perspective on elections, and the way such moments fit into the election-specific narratives journalists construct around the particular candidates in each election. As we will see below and particularly in later chapters, many of the key moments from Hillary Clinton's campaign drew their significance in the news from these underlying journalistic routines.

The Horse Race and the Game: The Master Campaign Frame

Perhaps the best-documented pattern in media coverage of elections over the past three decades has been the prevalence of what is often called "horse-race" coverage. By this we mean coverage that focuses on who is winning and who is losing—the "process" of the campaign—rather than focusing on policy issues. Research shows a consistent pattern: a significant portion of news coverage of presidential elections—up to one-third or more, depending upon the medium and the phase of the election—is focused on horse-race stories more than the issues.[9]

For example, a thorough study of national network news, local TV news, and newspaper coverage of the 1992 campaign across four locales found that "issue coverage gets shorter shrift . . . when the horse race is most exciting (in the early primaries and the last month of the campaign)." It also found that "all three kinds of media put the greatest emphasis on candidates' personal qualities and their chances for election; issue positions come in third" (Just et al. 1996, 99–101). In fact, roughly one-third of the "personality" stories were focused on the candidates' abilities as campaigners, further skewing media coverage toward the "process" of getting elected. Moreover, "the low points for issue coverage were unfortunately in March and October, when the [outcome of the] nominations and election were most in doubt, and many citizens were becoming attentive to the campaign" (Ibid., 113).

More recently, a 2000 study by the Committee of Concerned Journalists found that less than 1 percent of campaign stories from that year's primary season focused primarily on the candidates' public records and policy positions, while a whopping 80 percent focused on "matters that affect the campaigns or the political parties (i.e. changes in tactics, fundraising strategies, and internal organizational problems)." Similarly, 7 out of every 10 news stories on the October presidential debates focused on the candidates' performance or strategies, while less than 1 in 10 focused on the candidates' policy differences (Kovach and Rosenstiel 2001).[10]

This pattern is so engrained in news coverage that some scholars and even journalists themselves have identified an underlying "game frame" that structures much news coverage of campaigns. Journalists organize the potentially numbing tide of campaign events and developments with an organizing "schema"[11] focusing on how each event helps one candidate to win or threatens others with losing. "Newsworthy" events are those that contribute to electoral wins and losses. Patterson's research shows a dramatic increase in this game-oriented coverage in the modern television age. In 1960, 1964, and 1968, front-page *New York Times* election stories were about evenly split between substantive and game-focused stories, but since 1976, coverage has been heavily skewed toward the game of electoral politics (see also Lawrence 2000; Vinson and Moore 2007).

The media's heavy emphasis on the game frame when covering elections marginalizes substantive discussion of policy issues. From the perspective of the game frame, policy issues are not unimportant, but they matter only insofar as they help or hurt candidates' electoral chances. This media routine may significantly impact women candidates, since other research (reviewed later in this chapter) shows that women candidates tend to win even less substantive news coverage than men. That most presidential election news is short on issues thus presents a particularly daunting dilemma for female candidates, since the women and politics literature counsels them to emphasize policy issues in order to establish credibility and expertise.

Game-framing also contributes to the media's well-documented focus on "winnowing" the field of candidates (Matthews 1978). News organizations face considerable challenges at the beginning of an election season when the field may be crowded with potential candidates. Reporters therefore look for signals about the various candidates' viability. Those candidates lagging in fundraising or in public opinion polls tend to be written out of the campaign coverage (Meyrowitz 1992)—thus creating an insurmountably vicious circle in which their lack of media coverage hurts their chances at fundraising, which further reduces their media coverage and thus their name recognition with the public. Again, this media routine seems to disproportionately affect female candidates, who often face more questions about their "viability."

Moreover, research has shown that along with this game-framed coverage goes a generally negative tone. As the study of election coverage in four locales described above found, "When news focused on what the candidates were like as people, the stories tended to be unfavorable" (Just et al. 1996, 111). Summarizing the research, Patterson says simply, "Candidates receive a high level of criticism from the press, and many of them get more bad coverage than good" (1994, 7), an observation borne out in his subsequent research as well (Patterson 2000). Underlying this negativity is a commonly shared perception among political reporters that politicians are manipulative and dishonest. According to Patterson, "reporters have a variety of bad news messages, but none is more prevalent than the suggestion that the candidates cannot be trusted" (Patterson 1994, 7–8).[12] As we shall see, this media script was applied with particular vehemence to Hillary Clinton's campaign, in part because reporters perceived her campaign team as particularly manipulative, and in part because the media's preset script for covering Hillary Clinton emphasized the notion of Clinton's unbridled ambition.

Moreover, the game frame so prominent in electoral politics is rife with masculinized imagery from the world of sports: "knock outs," "touchdowns," and "final rounds" abound in campaign reporting. (Exhibit A: a CNN ad in the *New York Times* before the 2008 Nevada Democratic debate blared, "Live from Las Vegas: They've warmed up— tonight, the gloves come off"). At the least, this trope may be unhelpful to women candidates (particularly those who wish to emphasize feminine difference) by forcing them to compete on implicitly masculinized terrain; it is also unhelpful to women voters and would-be political leaders, since "depictions of politics as a 'man's game' seem to lead women to disengage, resulting in men's continued dominance of politics" (Shames and Just 2008).

Interestingly, for a while during the 2008 campaign, Hillary Clinton turned this frame to her advantage, bolstering her "fighter" image as she refused to bow out of the race, thus gaining a kind of political street credibility. This illustrates that to the extent that presidential politics is treated like a high-stakes athletic event, complete with metaphors from football and boxing, any female presidential candidate enters into an arena defined by gendered double binds—what Georgia Duerst-Lahti (2006) calls the "gendered space" of presidential elections. If she competes aggressively, as the game demands, she risks violating public expectations of appropriate, "polite" feminine behavior. If she does not, chances are she will not be taken seriously as a contender. This double bind pervaded news coverage of Hillary Clinton as the Democratic nominating contest dragged on long past the expected final bell on Super

Tuesday. By late March of 2008, with Senators Clinton and Obama fighting a close battle for every delegate, pundits and commentators repeatedly called on Clinton to bow out of the race. As we will see, while these calls were usually couched in terms of the continuing battle being bad for the Democratic Party, the gendered subtext was hard to miss.

Portraying "Characters": Journalistic Narratives of the Candidates

As noted earlier, in recent presidential elections, a great deal of media coverage has focused on the horse race, with a much smaller fraction focusing on policy issues. The remainder is typically focused on the candidate's "character": her personal background and behavior, her upbringing and family life, her values and struggles—and especially, her personal shortcomings. These character stories reflect what former *Washington Post* reporter Paul Taylor once described as "a journalistic master narrative built around two principle story lines: the search for the candidates' character flaws, and the depiction of the campaign as a horserace . . ." (quoted in Rosen 2003).

Just as we cannot know whether fateful campaign moments would have proven as fateful to candidates had the media not magnified them, it can be hard to disentangle the "real" candidates from the media's presentation of their character. Certainly, reporters (particularly those assigned to travel with a particular candidate while he or she campaigns) have a unique opportunity to watch candidates closely in a variety of settings, to see them not only at their best, but also when they are the most tired, stressed, and challenged. So, in a very real sense, reporters are the eyes and ears of a public that cannot follow the candidates nearly as closely (both literally and figuratively) as the press can.

But reporters do not approach the candidates as a blank slate. Just as the horse race and game frame structure their approach to covering the election, reporters often bring a "script" to their coverage of particular candidates in particular elections. Just as the game frame helps reporters to recognize what is significant as daily campaign events unfold, this script guides reporters toward certain aspects of each "character." According to long-time journalists Bill Kovach and Tom Rosenstiel, "journalists have begun to rely on story-telling themes as a way of organizing the campaign in an engaging manner. They use story lines such as: Bush is a different kind of conservative. Bush is a natural politician. Bush is dumb. . . . Gore is a stiff. Gore is a liar. Gore is a political carnivore. We call these story lines the meta-narrative" (Kovach and Rosenstiel 2001). These scripts take on a life of their own the more they are repeated among reporters. "The more often journalists hear similar thoughts expressed by . . . other news outlets, the more likely their own thoughts will run along [similar] lines, with the result that the news they produce will feature [similar] words and visuals" (Entman 2003, 9).

Elizabeth Edwards, wife of Democratic candidate Senator John Edwards, noticed this media habit in the 2008 election and wrote about it in the *New York Times*:

> Watching the campaign unfold, I saw how the press gravitated toward a narrative template for the campaign, searching out characters as if for a novel: on one side, a self-described 9/11 hero with a colorful personal life, a former senator who had played a president in the movies, a genuine war hero with a stunning wife and an intriguing temperament, and a handsome governor with a beautiful family and a high school sweetheart as his bride. And on the other side, a senator who had been First Lady, a young African-American senator with an Ivy League diploma, a Hispanic governor with a self-deprecating sense of humor and even a former senator from the South standing loyally beside his ill wife. Issues that could make a difference in the lives of Americans didn't fit into the narrative template and, therefore, took a back seat to these superficialities. (Edwards 2008)

When character scripts organize campaign reporting, facts that don't fit the meta-narrative may not get reported prominently, and important aspects of the candidates' character may remain murky. Kovach and Rosenstiel (2001) offer this example:

> How does one write a story in which Bush is a good debater when the conventional wisdom holds that he is not? Ann Richards, the one politician who had been up against Bush in debates, warned reporters not to underestimate him, but her hard-earned wisdom was seldom reported. An initial faulty performance early in the [2000] primaries set the meta-narrative that Bush could not hold his own, and he benefited from this enormously in the general election.

Similarly, reporters often echoed the common wisdom that Al Gore was sullied by the scandals of the Clinton administration in which he had served as vice president, and that he was a "serial exaggerator." A report by the Committee of Concerned Journalists found that "the most common theme of the campaign was that Gore was scandal-tainted. This accounted for 42 percent of all the assertions about Gore's character. The second most common assertion about Gore was that he was a liar.

These accounted for 34 percent of stories about him. The least common of the major themes, accounting for 14 percent of assertions, was that he was competent, experienced, and knowledgeable" (Kovach and Rosenstiel 2001).

As these examples suggest, the point is not that reporters' scripts are completely wrong, but rather that they are simplistic. Political reporting often reduces complex, multidimensional human beings into two-dimensional characters who would be recognizable in a standard made-for-TV movie. Even more troubling, according to Kovach and Rosenstiel, such scripts make it "difficult for an individual reporter to write a story that differs from the popular meta-narratives" (Ibid.)

As the Bush and Gore examples illustrate, these meta-narratives exist for both Republican and Democratic candidates.[13] What has been less explored is how these narratives are applied to female versus male candidates. The media's focus on "personal" characteristics and campaign gaffes is particularly fertile ground for sex stereotyping. So is the media's resort to oversimplified narratives of the campaign's "characters": notice that common themes include the notion that "Bush is a liar" and "Gore is a stiff," but that Hillary is "a bitch."[14]

Thus, we return to where we began this chapter, for the media are likely to highlight those key moments from the campaign that fit—or offer a new twist on—the script reporters have developed for covering that campaign. Gerald Ford's erroneous comment that there was "no Soviet domination" of Eastern Europe not only threatened to hurt him in the polls (or so journalists thought as they quickly amplified the moment), but also fit his already-set image as a bumbler. (Some readers may remember how *Saturday Night Live*'s Chevy Chase popularized that image in hilarious send-ups of Ford falling off stages and tripping over his own feet.) Similarly, Howard Dean's scream confirmed for journalists that he was an untested and volatile figure not ready for the national stage ("Campaign Essentials" 2004). Hillary Clinton's teary-eyed moment fulfilled, in some observers' eyes, her supposed willingness to "do anything" to get elected; for others, it was newsworthy because it added a new and surprising twist to the long-standing story of Clinton's alleged coldness.

Women Candidates and the Media

The research on media and elections reviewed here places into larger context the findings of researchers who have focused on how women politicians are treated by the media. It is important to recognize that much of this research does not focus on female presidential candidates, for the obvious reason that there have been few, but nonetheless it yields important predictions that can be tested against the case of Hillary Clinton's presidential bid.

A good starting place for reviewing the findings of this research is with the simple observation that in many cases, female candidates simply receive less news attention than male candidates. Kim Kahn (1996), for example, found that across a number of races for the Senate, contests that included a female candidate received less coverage than all-male contests—a difference not attributable to the size of the state or the competitiveness of the race.[15] She speculates that journalists typically devote less attention to female candidates because they see female candidacies as less politically viable; her analysis of news coverage shows that female Senate candidates are typically portrayed as less likely to win (1996, 46).[16] Kahn observes that "the scarcity of women senators and governors makes the female candidate's gender especially salient to journalists, thereby encouraging greater stereotyping" (Ibid., 13)—a statement that would seem to be even more true of presidential candidates. One consequence of this stereotype appears to be even more emphasis on horse-race coverage: Since reporters are focused (consciously or not) on doubts about women's ability to win Senate races, their reporting focuses even more on the "who's up, who's down" of the contest (Ibid., 47).

Indeed, Hillary Clinton's predecessors were dogged by the media's emphasis on the "novelty" of their campaigns, as well as questions regarding their viability and subtle denigration of their competency. The media consistently framed Elizabeth Dole, for example, as the "first woman" to be a viable presidential candidate, and this focus on gender arguably made Dole's campaign seem more of a novelty than a serious bid for power (Heldman, Carroll, and Olson 2005). Indeed, Erika Falk's study finds that every woman who has run for the presidency has been dubbed a "first" by the media. "It would not be surprising," she argues, "to find that the persistent framing of women as firsts de-normalizes them in the political field, making the proposition of a woman candidate and president seem more risky and less likely" (Falk 2008, 37). The horse-race coverage that attaches with particular tenacity to female candidates thus also brings a more negative tone (in terms of their chances for winning) to the coverage of women's candidacies. When Elizabeth Dole dropped out of the 2000 presidential race, for example, "reporters immediately considered whether the 'female factor' contributed to the lack of success. . . . like a tooth about to fall out, reporters could not help picking at the point" even while they and their sources denied that sexism played a role (Heith 2003, 127).

An illustrative example of these findings is the media coverage of Senator Margaret Chase Smith, who ran for the Republican nomination in 1964. Smith received "less coverage, less serious coverage, and a minimization of her accomplishments" compared with her main competitor for the nomination, Nelson Rockefeller (Falk and Jamieson 2003, 48). Coverage of her campaign was less substantively focused on issues, and she was more likely to have her official title of "Senator" replaced with "Mrs." than Rockefeller was to have his replaced with "Mr." Furthermore, Smith was "often treated as though she were not running for president and was 'really' interested in the vice presidency" (Ibid., 49).

Women candidates also tend to receive less substantive coverage focusing on policy issues—a corollary to the finding that women are subjected to more horse-race framing. Kahn finds that in Senate races, "almost four paragraphs are published about male candidates' issue positions each day, while fewer than three paragraphs a day are published about the issue priorities of female candidates" (1996, 50–51). In her study of female presidential candidates, Falk finds on average 16 percent of paragraphs focused on substantive policy issues in conjunction with women candidates, versus almost twice as many (27 percent) for male candidates (2008, 119). Similarly, a study of media coverage of Elizabeth Dole's presidential campaign found that while she received more coverage than some of her opponents for the Republican nomination, less coverage was focused on issues and more on Dole's personality traits, and Dole was directly quoted less often and paraphrased more than her (male) opponents (Aday and Devitt 2001). In fact, some scholars have concluded that "the news media much more faithfully represent the messages of male candidates, virtually mirroring the content of their political communications. In contrast, the news media are less accurate in their representation of the messages of women candidates, often distorting the messages of these candidates" (Woodall and Fridkin 2003, 77).

Kahn also finds more emphasis in news coverage of Senate campaigns on "male" issues like foreign policy and the economy than "female" issues like health care and education. In races without a female contender, male issues dominated the coverage by a margin of roughly two to one; in races including a female contender, that margin improved slightly, though male issues still dominated (1996, 52). Since the public tends to associate women with inherent capabilities regarding "care" issues, this focus on "male" issues can further disadvantage women candidates.

Overall, Kahn concludes that gendered patterns in news coverage, plus the incumbency advantage that typically accrues to male office-holders, leads the public "to view female challengers as less electable than their male counterparts" (1996, 72). As her experimental research revealed, "gender differences in news coverage hurt women senate candidates. . . . these press patterns lead people to view male incumbent as stronger leaders, more viable, and better able to deal with defense issues" (1996, 72).

Some research has suggested that these gendered patterns of news coverage are giving way to more evenhanded treatment as women enter the political field in greater numbers. Smith (1997), for example, finds little evidence of the gendering of issues in news coverage of statewide campaigns in 1994 and that the coverage tone was largely neutral for female candidates, but negative for male candidates. Similarly, a study of news coverage of primary election campaigns in 2000 found that more articles focused predominantly on female than male candidates; that female candidates were mentioned significantly more often than males; and that both female and male candidates received more neutral coverage than positive or negative coverage (although both received more negative than positive coverage) (Bystrom, Robertson, and Banwart 2001; see also Bystrom et al. 2004). It may also be that previous groundbreakers like Margaret Chase Smith and Elizabeth Dole experienced more blatantly sexist coverage than their successors will precisely because, for this generation of journalists, those women were the pioneers who helped make reporters more sensitive to charges of sexism (Heith 2003, 127).

Yet a basic challenge for female candidates identified by this literature seems to remain and reinforces the gendered political terrain we analyzed in Chapter 1: to set the issue agenda in a way that capitalizes on stereotypes about women's abilities in "female" issues, yet fits with expectations for the office for which they are running, while also managing impressions of their "femininity." The challenge is multiplied by the news media's tendency (at least in Senate races) to focus on male issues, leaving the female candidate with a tough strategic choice: try to change the news media's typical issue focus, or try to compete on the stereotypically "male" turf of foreign policy, national defense, and the economy. As we shall see, this choice was particularly consequential in Hillary Clinton's campaign for the White House.

Finally, gender stereotypes appear to shape the ways that both male and female candidates' personal traits are portrayed in the news. In general, women candidates have been subject to more discussion of their physical characteristics and their gender than have male candidates. One study found that female candidates received more mentions of their gender, children, and marital status, though not of their physical appearance (Bystrom, Robertson, and Banwart 2001), while others have found more numerous references to female candidates' physical attributes as well (Aday and Devitt 2001; Devitt 2002; Heldman, Carroll, and Olson 2005). This pattern in media coverage has become so well known among women politicians and the scholars who study them that it has been dubbed the "hair, hemlines, and husbands" problem, or, alternatively, the "lipstick watch" (Heith 2003). Personality is also a focus of media coverage of women politicians. As discussed above, media coverage of elections tends to focus heavily on the candidates' characters, but this pattern appears to be heightened for women. Falk's study of women presidential candidates finds that "the extra issue coverage garnered by men is mostly converted to character coverage for the women" (2008, 133). Thus, the media's lack of attention to policy issues can be particularly damaging to women, who get even more coverage of their appearance, emotions, and personalities. In particular, the women and politics research warns female candidates to avoid showing much emotion in public, since doing so will presumably generate media coverage that plays into public stereotypes of female emotionalism (Kahn 1996).

Even as women candidates are treated more superficially in the media—as women historically have been in public life—they are in another sense subjected to masculinized standards. Kahn (1996) finds that Senate candidates—both male and female—are more likely to be described in terms of stereotypically "male" traits such as knowledge, competitiveness, leadership, and strength than in terms of "female" traits such as noncompetitiveness, emotionality, and compassion. News coverage may marginalize women when they fail to adopt masculine political behaviors, yet overemphasize "nonfeminine" behavior when female candidates are combative; as one study contends, women candidates' performance in campaign debates is framed to fit a "masculine narrative of election reporting" (Gidengil and Everitt 2000). One interesting upshot may be that the media's emphasis on aggressiveness and combativeness makes *women* voters in particular like female candidates less (Gidengill and Everitt 2003).

Of course, it seems likely that stereotypically "female" traits like dependence, passivity, and a dislike of competition would be in short supply in the rough and tumble world of politics, so these findings to some degree reflect the reality of politics that journalists observe. What is striking is how "male" characteristics like ambition and toughness create the framework through which politics is understood—and thus the framework within which female candidates must present themselves to reporters and the public. This dynamic was crucial in Hillary Clinton's case: as Clinton positioned herself as the "toughest" presidential candidate, she ran headlong into these gendered double binds.

Yet the general findings of the women and politics literature and the specific case of Hillary Clinton's presidential campaign do not perfectly coincide. Based on the findings of the literature reviewed thus far, and leaving aside for a moment the particular attributes of Hillary Rodham Clinton, we should have expected media coverage that paid less attention to her campaign than to that of her male opponents; that granted her less substantive issue coverage while emphasizing doubts about the viability of her bid for the nomination; that highlighted her personal and gender-related attributes as well as any emotion she showed on the campaign trail; and that framed her more negatively with regard to her chances of winning the nomination. We test these propositions in Chapter 6; for now, we can preview our findings by saying that the expectations of the women and politics literature appear to have been only partially correct. Given Clinton's strong starting point as the presumptive front-runner and the numerous resource advantages she enjoyed over her competitors when the primary season began, coverage of her campaign was extensive, and questions about her "viability" took on forms different than for previous female presidential contenders. Meanwhile, her front-runner status—a status not enjoyed by any other female candidate in US history—rendered her media coverage even more negative in tone. Coverage of Clinton was also clearly dominated by the horse race and the game frame, although that was the case for her competitors as well; the media marginalized substantive discussion not just of Clinton's issue positions but also those of other candidates, including Senators Barack Obama and John McCain. But for Clinton, who studiously emphasized policy over other political appeals, this may have been particularly damaging. Finally, media discussion framed quite negatively her tactical choices during the campaign and her decision to remain in the race even as her mathematical chances of securing the nomination faded, and bore marks of deep-seated presumptions about appropriate female behavior and roles.

Conclusion: The Gendering of Presidential Campaign Coverage

Most voters can only encounter presidential candidates via the mass media. Thus, the media's persistent emphasis on gaffes, negativity, and the horse race, and their downplaying of the substantive attributes of female candidates in particular, may skew voters' understandings of the candidates and the issues at stake in any election while fundamentally disadvantaging female contenders. Moreover, mainstream media coverage is one of the few avenues by which presidential candidates can reach mass audiences aside from television advertising. As Patterson observes, no other democracy has a system in which the press plays such a central role. In a very real sense, "the road to nomination now runs through the newsroom" (1994, 33).

Quite often, the path to nomination—or defeat—is paved with "key moments" from the campaign trail. Hillary Clinton's near-tears in Portsmouth illustrate the highly gendered aspects of some defining campaign moments. As noted above, some reporters initially expected that Clinton's tears, like Ed Muskie's, would undermine her support among voters by making her seem too weak to be president. This gendered gauntlet of gaffes awaits many presidential hopefuls. Perhaps one of the most-remembered (and most-maligned) moments from a recent presidential campaign was captured when, in 1988, television reporters filmed Democratic candidate Michael Dukakis sitting atop a military tank, a helmet perched awkwardly on his head. Knowing that his national security credentials were perceived as weak, Dukakis visited a tank-making facility in Michigan and his campaign orchestrated a photo-op complete with Dukakis driving an M1 Abrams tank around the lot (mimicking, ironically, a widely publicized image of Great Britain's prime minister Margaret Thatcher riding a tank—while wearing a fashionable scarf—that was credited with helping her win reelection). The plan was to produce visuals that would bolster Dukakis's image as a potential commander in chief, but the effect was quite the opposite. Dukakis failed to seem "manly" even when driving a tank—a lesson that 2004 Democratic candidate Senator John Kerry (D-MA) apparently did not learn, allowing himself to be filmed wind-surfing, thus providing footage that played perfectly into Republican attacks against his steadiness and manliness (Fahey 2007).

It was the same Michael Dukakis who suffered another setback that election season when, during a debate against George H. W. Bush, he was asked what he would do if his wife, Kitty, were to be raped and murdered. Would Dukakis—an opponent of capital punishment—seek the death penalty for his wife's assailant? Dukakis answered coolly, "No, I don't, and I think you know that I've opposed the death penalty during all of my life." He then gave a clinical-sounding discussion of his stance. Almost instantly, his poll numbers dropped, and he was assailed in the media not just for being too "soft" on crime, but for lacking nor-

mal manly emotions. In other words, Dukakis was faulted for not showing the vengeful feelings expected of a man whose woman (and thus his
own honor) had been grievously wronged—and by extension, being
unable to adequately rise to the task of protecting the public.

In light of the patterns of media coverage discussed here, Clinton's
teary moment in Portsmouth takes on special significance. There seems
little doubt that the moment will be remembered as a pivotal one. As
predicted by the women and politics research, the media readily
pounced on Clinton's public display of emotion. But the media did not
frame Hillary Clinton's teary eyes overwhelmingly negatively because
reporters came to believe that her tears had actually improved her standing with the public—particularly with women. Whether or not Clinton's
show of emotion actually mobilized New Hampshire women to vote for
her, reporters believed it signaled a successful shift in her campaign tactics: a new willingness to reveal her real self (or to appear to do so) in an
effort to bridge the emotional distance that many voters reported feeling
with her. According to the conventional wisdom that took hold among
reporters (which was pushed to some degree by Clinton's own staff),
that tactic worked with a key voting bloc: "What turned it around [in
New Hampshire]?" one reporter asked. "Most important Hillary Clinton
won over women, who had abandoned her in Iowa. They empathized
when she showed emotion the day before the election" (*NBC Nightly
News,* 2008a). Ironically, it was perhaps just this kind of strategy-
focused, "who's up, who's down" coverage that Clinton criticized in her
Portsmouth remarks.

The media's framing of key campaign moments snaps into sharper
focus when we compare coverage of Clinton's Portsmouth moment with
an analogous event that received very different coverage. On January 9
(the day after the New Hampshire vote), during a campaign appearance
in Michigan, Republican candidate Mitt Romney had an emotional
moment of his own (one of several during his campaign) after a voter
mentioned Romney's father, a former Michigan governor who passed
away in 1995. Unlike Clinton's moment, Romney's was virtually
ignored in the national media; in a search of the same major newspapers, newsmagazines, and network evening news shows in which
Hillary Clinton's teary moment was heavily covered,[17] we found a single sentence in one newspaper article that referenced this event: "Earlier
in the day, after hearing from a voter who recalled his father, Mr.
Romney choked up momentarily, according to a pool reporter who was
present. 'He was a great man, and I miss him dearly,' Mr. Romney said"
(Santora and Nagourney 2008).[18] In contrast to this dearth of coverage,

Clinton's teary moment was referenced in 27 news stories in just three days across these same eight media sources.

There are obvious reasons that the Romney moment was not big news, despite its surface similarities and its occurrence right on the heels of Clinton's moment: Romney was discussing his family grief, not his campaign objectives, and the moment apparently was not captured on video. But another reason, from a reporter's point of view, may be that Romney's emotional moment was not perceived as part of a strategy to win over voters and was not expected to "help" him with any particular voting bloc; Clinton's was, and so her tears (or near-tears) were news. At the same time, from the point of view of feminist scholarship, Romney was less likely to be subject to the stereotype of feminine emotionality (and manipulativeness) than was Clinton.

For many women candidates, any show of emotion on the campaign trail can be the kiss of electoral death because it confirms stereotypes of feminine weakness. In Hillary Clinton's case, the press's meta-narrative held that she was "cold," calculating, and scripted, and so her show of emotion was met with a variety of contradictory reactions. For some, Clinton's near-tears confirmed sexist stereotypes about female emotionality in general; for others who saw her emotions as manufactured to win votes, they confirmed stereotypes of women in general and/or Clinton in particular as manipulative; but for others, her show of emotion defied expectations about Hillary Clinton and were treated as a salutary turn in her campaigning style. Indeed, as one observer intoned, the problem "was not that Senator Hillary Rodham Clinton teared up. It was all the times she did not" (Kantor 2008b).

All US presidential candidates must negotiate the challenges of media routines for covering elections—the focus on "defining moments," the focus on the "game" of politics, and the focus on the "meta-narratives" that reporters bring to their coverage of individual candidates. Male presidential candidates falter when they are portrayed and perceived as inadequately masculine for the job. But female candidates for the White House face particularly complicated challenges.

Arguably, these challenges were especially great for Hillary Clinton. Clinton is in many ways a very different candidate from any woman before her—or any imagined by the scholarly literature. Her unique professional and personal history and well-defined image in the public eye accounts for much of the discrepancy between the predictions of the women and politics literature and the realities of the media coverage she received. We turn next to examining the specific profile of the woman who so far has come closer than any other to attaining the White

House, in order to understand how this one unique case in many ways confounds the predictions of the literature.

Notes

1. Video footage of this event is available at www.youtube.com/watch?v=6qgWH89qWks.

2. According to the *New York Times*, "Some advisers were so concerned that they did not e-mail video of the Monday incident to Clinton supporters, as they usually do when Senator Clinton makes positive news. "We have absolutely no idea how her getting this emotional will play with voters," one adviser said (Healy 2008c). According to biographer Gail Sheehy (2008), after her momentary and uncharacteristic public loss of composure in Portsmouth, Clinton herself "saw only the danger she had feared all her life—to appear female was to court failure—and the driving force of her life since childhood was to win." Chief campaign strategist Mark Penn agreed: "Penn insisted she button up," fearing that "any further exposure of her human feelings would cost them white male voters."

3. The Muskie, Ford, and Reagan "moments" are described in more detail in Patterson (1994).

4. For a video providing a brief overview of some of these key moments going back to the 1952 election, see CQ Politics, "'Make or Break' Moments in Campaign History," http://link.brightcove.com/services/player/bcpid 1374481205?bclid=1377894911&bctid=1488623592.

5. Certain information shortcuts are potentially very valuable as efficient tools for casting reasonably sound votes. Party labels, for example, give less-informed voters a shortcut assessment (if not always a perfect predictor) of the general policy views each candidate is likely to hold. During the nominating phase of a presidential campaign, however, that tool isn't very helpful, since primary voters must choose from a variety of candidates, many of whom are unfamiliar names and all of whom belong to the same party.

6. Studies show that both less-educated and better-educated voters rely on cues about the candidates' personal characteristics when deciding how to vote (Glass 1985; Keeter 1987), with those who rely on television being most likely to focus on candidates' personal qualities (Graber 1976).

7. Not all information shortcuts revolve around candidate gaffes. Some involve substantive policy questions. For example, as the 2008 Democratic primary race entered its final rounds in North Carolina and Indiana, a key debate in the campaign became Hillary Clinton's call for a "gas tax holiday" that would temporarily lower gasoline taxes for the summer. Her opponent for the nomination, Senator Barack Obama, criticized her proposal as a "gimmick," and other critics decried Clinton's "pandering" for votes. Most voters, it is safe to assume, did not fully inform themselves of the details of the gas tax, Senator Clinton's proposal, or the arguments of Obama and others for how the tax "holiday" would ultimately simply raise the price of gas. But the intense media focus on the "gas tax holiday" likely served as a shortcut for some voters as they assessed the candidates' respective stands on questions of economic policy—

and the candidates' "character" (since Obama's criticism was that Clinton's tax holiday proposal revealed a characteristic dishonesty in his opponent).

8. For example, in an interview about his experiences covering the campaign, Dave Davies of the *Philadelphia Inquirer* described reporters at campaign events no longer talking with voters and each other, but "all buried in their laptops," leading to a more "insular" culture of reporting and increasing the importance of "undigested nuggets" like campaign gaffes (Davies 2008).

9. The Center for Media and Public Affairs coded network television news stories for both issue and horse-race content and found that in the 2000 campaign, 71 percent of stories included horse-race coverage, while 40 percent included issue substance. In 2004, the center found a closer balance, with 48 percent of stories including horse-race aspects and 49 percent including issue aspects (Center for Media and Public Affairs 2004).

10. Other studies have found less lopsided patterns, particularly during those phases of the campaign season, such as the summer before the general election, in which the horse race aspects are less pronounced. Aday (2004) for example, found that newspaper coverage during the summer of 2004 was about evenly balanced between issue and horse-race stories—although most issue stories did not appear on the front pages. A different study of that election year found that in the 2004 Democratic primary, 68 percent of news stories focused on the competition among candidates, followed by 18 percent focusing on candidate character, and 14 percent focusing on policy (Harper 2004).

11. Cognitive and political psychology uses the "schema" concept to describe the cognitive structure within the human brain that organizes, filters, and stores incoming information (see Graber 2001). Scholars who study the news have borrowed the concept as a way of explaining certain patterns in the news. In this sense, a "schema" is any organizing principle that seems to structure news organizations' decisions about what is newsworthy (see Patterson 1994).

12. The game frame may be useful to reporters as a simplifying organizing tool, but it also reflects some attitudinal baggage the national press acquired during the Vietnam/Watergate years. During that time, the press corps became (in the positive version of the story) more willing to question the pronouncements of political leaders and (in the less positive version) more openly cynical about politics. "Unmasking" politicians and "decoding" their messages became a more common element of political coverage, and the press became more focused on the strategies and tactics politicians employ to gain power and win political battles. As Thomas Patterson observes, "The rules of reporting changed with Vietnam and Watergate, when the deceptions perpetrated by the Johnson and Nixon administrations convinced reporters that they had let the nation down by taking political leaders at their word. Two presidents had lied; therefore, no politician was to be trusted" (Patterson 1994, 19).

13. Republican nominee Senator John McCain experienced this kind of script-driven coverage when he visited Iraq during his 2008 campaign. Speaking to reporters, McCain asserted, "It's common knowledge . . . that al Qaeda is going back into Iran and receiving training and are coming back into Iraq from Iran that is well-known, and it is unfortunate." After Senator Joseph Lieberman, McCain's companion on the trip, apparently whispered a correction into McCain's ear, McCain leaned back into the microphone and said, "I'm

sorry. I'm sorry the Iranians are training extremists, not al Qaeda" (quoted on Reliable Sources 2008d). Despite the transparency of this effort at spin control, McCain's comment was not treated by the media as a moment of attempted news manipulation, but rather as a "senior moment" that raised questions about whether he was "too old" to be president. In other words, the preexisting script about McCain—a tough, straight-talking but aging war hero—filtered the press's framing of the event and thus signaled to voters its "real" significance.

14. Moreover, prescripted reporting is problematic because it is often dependent upon the candidates' standing in the polls and election returns. Generally speaking, losing candidates can expect their news coverage to become more negative in tone, and for the media to focus even more on negative campaign moments that "prove" the script. As Patterson (1994, 97) observes, "The tendency to say unfavorable things about a faltering candidate is nearly tautological: the candidate is doing poorly, therefore, something is wrong with him." However, this basic correlation has an ironic twist: the presumed "front-runner" during a presidential election is also quite likely to receive negative media coverage—a dynamic that played out dramatically, as we shall see, in Hillary Clinton's campaign for the White House.

15. Kahn (1996) finds less pronounced patterns in media coverage of female gubernatorial candidates across virtually all of her variables. The media terrain does not disadvantage women to the same degree in races for governor as in races for the Senate, and sex stereotypes have less impact. Running for the White House, while it bears similarities to a gubernatorial campaign, is more comparable to running for the Senate because of the issue competencies demanded (particularly in foreign policy and national defense) and the dynamics of running for a national as opposed to a state office.

16. It is well to note that the media are not alone in doubting female candidates' viability. Work by Woodall and Fridkin (2003) reveals that the public questions female viability, and Sanbonmatsu's work indicates that party leaders do as well (2005).

17. To find relevant coverage, we searched three major newspapers (the *New York Times*, *Washington Post*, and *Los Angeles Times*), the three broadcast network evening news shows (ABC, CBS, and NBC), and in *Newsweek* and *U.S. News and World Report*, between January 9 and 16, 2008, for mentions of Romney in conjunction with words or roots of words including "cry," "emotion," "tears," "misty," and "choked up."

18. Romney's multiple emotional moments on the campaign trail did receive some fleeting coverage in the news organizations we surveyed, though nothing like the attention devoted to Clinton's Portsmouth moment. Moving beyond the six main newspapers and television news programs that we analyze throughout this book, none of which covered Romney's January 9 tears, we found two broadcast television segments, one on ABC's *Good Morning America* and one on NBC's *Today* show, that focused on the issue of candidates showing emotion. Romney was mentioned once in each segment while Clinton was the focus of both segments, mentioned by name multiple times; both aired in the immediate aftermath of and focused on the Portsmouth moment, with Romney's shows of emotion less specifically identified. One Romney teary-eyed moment that was covered by the *Boston Globe* received no coverage in

any of the news organizations we surveyed. (Appearing at a military contractor site in New Hampshire on December 17, 2007, Romney described seeing a military casket returning on a plane from Iraq and said, his eyes welling with tears, "I have five boys of my own. . . . I imagined what it would be like to lose a son in a situation like that.")

Interestingly, fleeting comments sprinkled throughout news coverage in the weeks before and after Clinton's Portsmouth moment indicate that Romney had developed a reputation among reporters and pundits for emotionalism on the campaign trail. Appearing on the *Today* show (in a different segment), for example, commentator and Clinton surrogate Paul Begala remarked in passing, "You know, the next big contest is Romney and McCain are going to square off in Michigan. And, you know, Romney's so desperate in Michigan, apparently he's pledged to cry for 24 hours straight," to which the show's host Matt Lauer replied, "A cryathon." Unlike Clinton's Portsmouth moment, which was singled out in the news and treated as a unique gaffe–cum–turning point in her campaign, Romney's emotional moments were not singled out and never became "key moments" in the campaign.

4

Hillary Clinton in Context

Hillary hate is something profound, something that may never be fully unraveled. . . . Is it about her womanhood? Or is it about this woman? Is that a false distinction?

—Libby Copeland, *Washington Post*

A s the year 2007 came to an end and the contest for the Democratic nomination tightened, the two main candidates traded jabs about Senator Hillary Clinton's claims of foreign policy experience gained while she was First Lady. Here's how a *Washington Post* reporter described the exchange:

A day after Sen. Barack Obama dismissed her foreign policy experience as little more than sipping tea with potentates, Clinton fired back by portraying herself as a virtual secretary of state during her husband's administration.

To listen to her tell it, she brought peace to Northern Ireland ("I went to Northern Ireland more than my husband did"), parachuted into the hottest of the world's hotspots ("If it's too dangerous, too small and too poor, send the first lady") and improved U.S. ties with the other countries ("I was part of the diplomatic team that conveyed America's values across the world").

She said she saved Kosovar refugees by persuading Macedonia to reopen its border. And in a direct jab back at Obama, she recalled visiting Bosnia on a plane that made a tight corkscrew landing to avoid potential attacks. "Somebody said there might be sniper fire," she said, adding tartly, "I don't remember anyone offering me tea on the tarmac." (Baker 2007)

For almost three months, the former First Lady would repeat these claims about landing under sniper fire during her Bosnia stopover in

March 1996. Clinton only began to retract her claim, saying that sleep deprivation may have clouded her memory, after a number of reporters and eyewitnesses had undermined her story—most dramatically, a *CBS Evening News* reporter who had traveled with the Clinton entourage to Bosnia. Her report juxtaposing Clinton's claims with press pool video of a sniper-less landing quickly went viral on the Internet, gaining more views than the inflammatory rants of Senator Obama's former pastor, the Rev. Jeremiah Wright (Rich 2008c). Some puzzled over the senator's stalwart repetition of the "Bosnia fairy tale" in the face of mounting evidence that her account was inaccurate and proposed that her drive to "tough it out" in the face of a wave of public criticism revealed a weak understanding of the twenty-first century YouTube media environment (Ibid.). Others, like Clinton biographer Carl Bernstein, reminded the public that Clinton had long had a "difficult relationship with the truth," arguing that the "Bosnian episode is a watershed event, because it indelibly brings to mind so many examples of this tendency" (Bernstein 2008).

The Bosnia vignette illustrates both the difficult pressures that exist for women running for the White House and simultaneously the particular trials of running as Hillary Clinton. Clinton's "Bosnia fairy tale" highlights, among other things, the imperative for the female presidential candidate to burnish her national security credentials. Clinton may have felt pressure to exaggerate her foreign policy experience to establish her "toughness" in the foreign policy arena, especially in a time of war. Additionally, the vestiges of sexist assumptions about a woman's trustworthiness may have shaped the public reaction. As students of Machiavelli learn, "fortune is a woman": fickle, prone to duplicity, and conniving. Yet the incident also highlighted Senator Clinton's own particular personality and political style, as well as her history with the press. As biographer Bernstein noted, Hillary Clinton has a long, documented history of questionable statements, dating back to the secrecy she imposed on her 1993–1994 health-care task force and her role in the Whitewater and Travel Office scandals (2007). Due to her own lapses, as well as her husband's notorious parsing, the public easily read the Bosnia sniper-fire episode as another instance of Clintonian truth-bending.

In this chapter, we consider not simply the gendered expectations that challenge all female contenders for the presidency or the media norms that govern modern campaigns, but the particular constellation of advantages and liabilities that Hillary Rodham Clinton brought to her quest. Here we also consider the intersection of this specific woman's campaign with the received wisdom about how a woman must run for the nation's highest office. We find that, while she faced many of the predicted challenges for a female presidential candidate, Clinton also represents exceptions to the rule book of presidential politics. Ultimately, her campaign for the presidency held great promise because she had overcome barriers that held other women candidates back. It was undone not just by the generic dynamics of gendered politics, such as the competence/femininity bind, but by her particular path to power—specifically, the double bind of independence/dependence surrounding the individual woman named Hillary Clinton.

Leapfrogging over Institutional Barriers

Unlike the women who preceded her, Hillary Clinton entered the presidential election with a resume that resembles a primer for the "first woman president." A multiterm US senator from a state that produces presidential candidates, Clinton entered the race from one of the typical "pipelines" to the presidency. With both name recognition and fundraising strengths, this articulate woman also claimed a moderate Senate voting record that would serve her well in a general election. Moreover, she was experienced with the press. Senator Clinton is, as she often remarks herself, one of the most watched political figures of our time. "I have a lot of baggage and everybody has rummaged through it for years," she reminded the crowd at the April 16, 2008, debate in Philadelphia (*New York Times* 2008). Indeed, the former First Lady has been the subject of more than three dozen biographies (most unauthorized), though most of them are unflattering (Tomasky 2007). But along with that baggage came considerable electoral resources: By the time she launched her presidential campaign in 2007, Hillary Clinton had surmounted important institutional barriers that had stymied her predecessors.

Considering the women who have gone before her reveals important financial and name-recognition advantages for a Clinton presidential bid. While Elizabeth Dole (D-NC) and Carol Mosley Braun (D-IL) were also US senators when they ran in 2000 and 2004, respectively, their length of service at the time they ran for president was shorter. Though she was the wife of a long-time politician, Dole did not have the name recognition Clinton enjoys (but neither did she have the "negatives" of the Clinton name that we discuss further below). In the end, both Dole's and Braun's chances of success were challenged by limited fundraising ability; Dole's chances were also undermined, as indicated in Chapter 2, by a striking lack of public support from her husband, then–Senate majority leader Bob Dole.

Going farther back in time, Clinton was also preceded by congress-women Shirley Chisholm (D-NY), Patsy Mink (D-HI), and Patricia Schroeder (D-CO). As the first African American and first Asian American women to seek the nomination, both Chisholm and Mink made history with their 1972 efforts at the White House, though both would remain better known for their congressional achievements than for their presidential races; moreover, recall that no modern president has been directly elected from the House of Representatives. Some years later, Congresswoman Schroeder briefly sought the Democratic nomination in 1987. She is well remembered during that campaign for her clever rejoinders to those in the press who treated her candidacy as a curiosity. When asked what it felt like to run as a woman, Schroeder would retort dryly, "What choice do I have?" (Lawrence 2007). Schroeder may in fact have been the first woman with a serious shot at the Democratic nomination, as early polls showed her leading other potential contenders on questions of trust, managing the economy, and whom voters would be "proud" to have as their president (Ferraro 1990). Yet in the end, she too was bedeviled by fundraising hurdles. As the press queried her about her quest in June 1987, she declared, "If there is dough, we go. If there isn't, we don't" (Weaver 1987). At a September press conference, Schroeder had her own infamous "teary moment" as she announced the suspension of her campaign, a moment endlessly lampooned by comedians (with her trademark wit, Schroeder would later joke that she could make a fortune selling tissues). In the end, for Clinton's predecessors, the dual challenges of name recognition and money presented insurmountable barriers.

In contrast to these recent trailblazers, Senator Clinton began the presidential election with a stellar dossier. Her name recognition was unmatched by any other Democratic hopeful, and she was, by mid-2007, the preferred candidate of Democratic voters over her rivals by a com-fortable margin (Blumenthal 2007). She raised over $175 million between her 2000 Senate campaign and early 2008 (Green 2008d)—a formidable record for any candidate. And her years in the Senate, during which she carefully cultivated relationships within and across party lines and mastered the norms of the institution, provided valuable connec-tions; during those years she also played a key role, along with Bill Clinton, in Democratic Party institution building, giving her access to the power players and purse strings of the party (Green 2006). Meanwhile, her First Lady title gave her enormous clout with and loyal-ty from many in the party (Green 2006). NBC political analyst Chuck Todd observes that the common wisdom early in the campaign season was that the Democratic contest "would be a primary within the primary between all the Democrats not named Clinton to establish an alternative to Hillary" (Todd and Gawiser 2009, 4).

Political reporter Mark Halperin listed Clinton's advantages going into the 2008 campaign in his 2007 book *The Way to Win*:

> Imagine . . . a senator from New York who dominated the field for her party's nomination in every national public opinion survey taken in the years leading up to the election; who had a strong record as a legislator; an authoritative command of policy issues across the board; unparalleled ties to her party's interest groups, activists, and elected officials; the ability to call on many of the party's leading strategists, in addition to national and key state operatives; vast media experience; the capacity to make news and get on network television without effort; a household name to capture the imagination; and unquestioned star power. (Halperin 2007)

Thus, even in the midst of two wars, which might be considered ill-timing for a female candidate, Clinton began her race the anointed front-runner. What remained to be seen was the extent to which cultural hurdles would dominate the race and whether Clinton's unique set of strengths and weaknesses would allow her to transcend those hurdles—or, alternatively, be tripped by them.

The Framing of Hillary Clinton

As discussed in Chapter 2, US presidential politics are fundamentally shaped by gender stereotypes that juxtapose masculine "strength" with feminine "nurturing," weakness, and emotionalism. It is tempting to attribute Clinton's failed presidential bid exclusively to these deeply rooted gendered attitudes that have hampered women's bid for equality for centuries. For example, it is often noted that from her earliest moments of national recognition as the nation's first First Lady with a postgraduate degree and a professional career of her own, Clinton's public image was troubled, and she struggled to find equilibrium in the public eye. She was quickly criticized during her husband's 1992 campaign for her appearance, and her dowdy headband, evolving hairstyles, and pantsuits have been fodder for the punditry and late-night comedians ever since. In fact, even as she returned to her work in the Senate after ending her nomination quest, the media noticed her haircut. Covering a speech she gave on the Senate floor, MSNBC ran a photo with the caption, "Hillary's New 'Do'—Senator Clinton Moves from Left to Right—Her Part, Not Her Positions" (2008b).

Thus, Ms. Clinton has obviously been subject to the "hair, hemlines, and husbands" theme (and in particular, the "husband" part, as we explore further below), as well as a host of other gendered challenges experienced by many powerful women. But we contend that more must be taken into account when considering the successes and failures of her run for the White House. A more nuanced and accurate view, we believe, highlights the liabilities specific to Hillary Clinton as well and bears in mind the interlocking variables of gender stereotypes, media routines, and the candidate and her context that shaped Clinton's campaign.

In fact, in one sense, gender stereotypes would seem to have mattered less in Hillary Clinton's bid for the presidency because she is famous. Since stereotypes function to fill in missing information, they tend to have less impact the more we have specific information available for evaluating specific people. For example, the literature on race suggests that when African American individuals become well known and are well regarded by the public, they are no longer viewed as "representatives" of their race. Famous, well-liked African Americans such as Bill Cosby and Oprah Winfrey become delinked in the public mind from the larger, more politically complex category of "blacks" (see Entman and Rojecki 2001). From this perspective, understanding Hillary Clinton's political fortunes as the first viable female candidate for the presidency cannot be understood simply in terms of gender stereotypes and the patterns of media coverage they generate for lesser-known women politicians.

Yet gender stereotypes certainly still mattered, not least because stereotypes work in two directions: We use them to fill in missing information about specific individuals belonging to a stereotyped group, but we also use them to compare specific individuals to that group. As some experts in cognition and stereotypes note, "Americans don't hate women, but they do frequently stereotype them as warm and friendly, creating a mismatch with the stereotype we hold of leaders as tough and strong" (Kristoff 2008). According to Joshua Correll, a psychologist at the University of Chicago, "Clinton runs the risk of being seen as particularly cold, particularly uncaring, because she doesn't fit the mold" (quoted in Kristoff 2008). It is in this comparison between her and these "typical" female attributes that Hillary Clinton has often come up short in the public's eyes.

Famous, Yet Unknown

Hillary Rodham Clinton is perhaps one of the best-known female figures in the world. As the wife of an Arkansas governor, and later First

Lady, she has been in the national spotlight for three decades, giving the press and the public (and Clinton herself) ample opportunity to set a frame for her public persona. In many respects, Clinton's fame was a distinct advantage as she entered the presidential race, since name recognition can translate into better fundraising and clearer public recognition of one's policy stances. Yet her unmatched name recognition was also a disadvantage: The very surname and privileged political position that gave her an advantage over previous female contenders as well as her male competitors for the 2008 nomination also evoked particular connotations associated with the name "Clinton," and instantly reminded people of her even more famous husband. Hillary Clinton's best defense against the media's predictable treatment of female candidates that emphasizes their novelty and dissects their viability was her name recognition. Yet with that name came considerable cultural costs.

Moreover, even though she is very famous, Hillary Clinton is not a known entity. More precisely, she is not one entity, but many. Her friend and advocate Susan Estrich argues, "People project on Hillary. You fill her in, usually for the worse. That makes it hard to define what you don't like, and hard for her to overcome it" (Estrich 2005, 69). She has long been perceived by the public and pundits as a kind of human Rorschach test, as scholar Kathleen Hall Jamieson argued in her 1995 book *Beyond the Double Bind*: "Hillary Clinton became a surrogate on whom we projected our attitudes about attributes once thought incompatible, that women either exercised their minds or had children but not both, that women who were smart were unwomanly and sexually unfulfilled, that articulate women were dangerous" (Jamieson 1995, 23). It was also Clinton's own observation: "I'm a Rorschach test," Clinton herself once said (quoted in Morrison 2008, xiii). Twelve years later in 2008, a book titled *Thirty Ways of Looking at Hillary* (each of the thirty essays was authored by a different woman) observed that

> although she is probably the most famous woman in the world right now, Hillary Clinton has a lot of people stumped. It could be that we think we should know her well already, having watched her and her husband for eight years in the White House (and having learned more about their marriage than we had a right to, thanks to Kenneth Starr). Or it could be that, because she is a woman, we have different expectations of her and how cozy we ought to feel with her.
>
> To some Hillary is a sellout who changed her name and her hairstyle when it suited her husband's career; to others she's a hardworking idealist with the political savvy to work effectively within the system. Where one person sees a carpetbagger another sees a deft politician; where one sees a humiliated and long-suffering wife, anoth-

er sees a dignified First Lady. Is she tainted by the scandals of her husband's presidency or has she gained experience and authority from weathering his missteps? Cold or competent, overachiever or pioneer, too radical or too moderate, Clinton continues to overturn the assumptions we make about her. (National Public Radio 2008b)[1]

Even in defeat, Clinton evoked the same contradictory responses. A Sunday *New York Times* piece solicited perspectives from a dozen analysts the day after she conceded the Democratic nomination to Senator Obama. True to form, these analyses offered fundamentally conflicting views on the causes of Clinton's defeat: While Richmond, Virginia, mayor L. Douglas Wilder blamed Clinton's hubris, Congresswoman Heather Wilson (R-NM) cited "a latent and lamentable sexism" ("What Went Wrong?" 2008).

Mixed feelings about Hillary Clinton have been perhaps even more prevalent among women than men, a pattern also seen in reactions to her presidential campaign. Since Hillary Clinton's bid for the presidency was a history-making attempt to put a woman in the White House, her candidacy could not help but be seen in highly symbolic terms. For many US women, Clinton's campaign was inspiring, and her difficulties on the campaign trail symbolized only too well the difficulties that professional women face in a still male-dominated work world. Thus, many women identified with Clinton, seeing their own challenges in hers. One *Wall Street Journal* article captured this dynamic well:

> Katherine Putnam, president of Package Machinery Co., a West Springfield, Mass., equipment manufacturer, recalls that at a lunch she attended recently, a group of male chief executives "started talking about what an awful b—— Hillary was and how they'd never vote for her." She says she kept quiet. "I didn't want to jeopardize my relationship with them," she says. "But their remarks were a clear reminder that although I could sit there eating and drinking with them, and work with them, instinctively their reaction to me isn't positive." (Kaufman and Hymowitz 2008)

Many women's identification with Clinton helped to create a significant gender gap in public attitudes toward her candidacy. As the same article also reported, in a March 2008 poll,

> Democratic women favored Sen. Clinton over Sen. Obama, 52% to 40%. Among Democratic men, the results were reversed: Sen. Obama garnered 52%, versus 36% for Sen. Clinton. In addition, negative views about Sen. Clinton were more prevalent among Democratic men than women. Fifty-one percent of men said they had negative views of

Sen. Clinton, while 32% reported positive views. Among Democratic
women, 44% reported negative views about her, and 42% reported
positive ones. (Kaufman and Hymowitz 2008)

Yet even as Ms. Clinton inspired female identification, she also
aroused negative feelings, including among many women. As Jill
Abramson, managing editor of the *New York Times,* said of Clinton's bid
for the presidency: "With Hillary there's a sort of double factor. There's
[*sic*] women are excited about the prospect of the first woman making a
serious and possibly successful bid for the presidency, but then, there's
sort of a pause, and step two, which is do you like *her*, do you think she
will make the best president?" (National Public Radio 2008a). Indeed,
public opinion polls registered this ambivalence, and Clinton struggled
in the "likeability" department.

For many women (and men) who were ambivalent about or opposed
to Hillary Clinton as president, the objections were in many ways specific to her own particular constellation of attributes. Yet at the same
time, those objections appear, on closer inspection, to be rooted in
deeply gendered attitudes about women, marriage, the presidency, and
power. In the sections that follow, we examine how societywide and
Clinton-specific double binds have structured public reactions to Hillary
Clinton, and how these binds overlap to create a deeply set public image
of her.

Hillary Clinton and the "Feminine" Communicative Style

As Jamieson (1995) contends, Hillary Clinton has long been a canvas
onto which the double binds faced by many powerful women have been
projected. In Clinton's case, the femininity/competence bind has played
out in myriad ways, even around something as mundane as the way she
communicates. An essay by the enigmatic social critic Camille Paglia
published in *Salon* in March of 2008 crystallized this perennial problem
of being Hillary Clinton. Criticizing Clinton's appearances on Saturday
Night Live and other nontraditional venues, Paglia observed, "All that
canned 'softening' of Hillary's image would have been unnecessary had
she had greater personal resources to begin with." Problem number one,
in Paglia's estimation, was Clinton's personality, which many perceive as
imperious. Some interpret her public stiffness as a simple result of her
preference for privacy (Gerth and Van Natta 2007) or a result of her domi-
nating father's influence (Bernstein 2007). Whatever its source, as former
Bush administration official and prominent Republican female politician

Linda Chavez put it, "the problem for Hillary has been, she's had no difficulty showing how tough she is, she has more difficulty showing how human she is" (National Public Radio 2008a).

This lack of "humanness" for which Clinton is often criticized stems in large measure from her communicative style. As rhetoric scholar Karlyn Kohrs Campbell has observed, "Hillary Rodham Clinton's style of public advocacy typically omits virtually all of the discursive markers by which women publically enact their femininity." Clinton's method of persuasion makes very limited use of personal anecdote or self-revelation. "Instead, she plays the roles for which she has been professionally trained, the roles of lawyer, advocate, and expert" (Campbell 1998, 6).

This style rankles, arguably, because gender stereotypes include the expectation that women are more compassionate, empathetic, and emotional than men. Thus, although a large part of the negative reaction to Hillary Clinton is based on the nontraditional way she went about being a First Lady, Campbell argues, "her rhetorical style exacerbates this problem significantly" (Campbell 1998, 14).[2] As Clinton supporter and CNN commentator Paul Begala observed during the 2008 campaign, "Usually, you know, there's about two feet of bullet-proof glass between her heart and that TV camera" (CNN, April 22). She also tended to "emotionally outsource" her speeches by using video presentations to convey her personal biography (Green 2006).

Women are not only thought to be inherently more compassionate and empathetic, they are "supposed" to display compassionate, empathetic behaviors. In her famous book *In a Different Voice*, education professor Carol Gilligan argues that women express themselves through an "ethic of care" infused with concern for complex webs of human relationships, while men more frequently communicate with an "ethic of justice," focused primarily on rules. Though feminist scholars debate the accuracy of Gilligan's analysis,[3] Gilligan's theory seems to accurately describe widely shared cultural gender norms. Women who seem lacking in compassion and empathy are therefore unsettling because they violate the invisible markers that define the category "woman," and, in Jamieson's framework, sacrifice femininity as they demonstrate competence. The public expects empathy and compassion; Clinton has often had trouble conveying those attributes in public. In striving to straddle Jamieson's "femininity/competence" bind, Clinton, it seems, tips too far to the competence side, sacrificing familiar markers of femininity and therefore losing public favor.

This policy-oriented, nonemotive style of speech won her few fans among the reporters who were assigned to cover campaign events and speeches that, to reporters (and apparently to some voters), were "boring." Here's how a reporter with the *New Yorker* described one such event:

> The ninety-minute conversation among Clinton and fourteen politicians and business and labor leaders, and Ohioans with hard-luck stories, had all the drama of a Senate committee hearing. Some no doubt found the discussion riveting, but at one point the former Ohio senator and Mercury astronaut John Glenn, a panelist, was either very deep in thought about college loans, or fast asleep. Scores of audience members were similarly benumbed and fled the event before it was over. But Clinton seemed confident about the electoral power of relentless policy tedium. It was as if the sheer display of iron-pantsed discussion would further underscore her insistent theme: the hollowness of Obama's charisma. (Lizza 2008b)

Interestingly, throughout her political career, Clinton has been able to win over the public at key moments by speaking in more intimate styles and settings. Campbell notes that Clinton's "pushy," "arrogant," and "cold" qualities made her unpopular in Arkansas until she mounted a speaking tour to help her husband pass an education reform bill. "Traveling and speaking throughout the state, she transformed herself into a respected figure. Many people were pleasantly surprised by the passion and humor and intelligence she revealed" (1998, 13). A very similar process occurred during Clinton's bid for the Senate, and again during her presidential campaign: People who had thought of her as cold and impersonal were surprised to find that in small venues she is warm, personable, and humorous (Green 2006). Indeed, as we noted previously, Clinton's teary-eyed moment in Portsmouth was considered noteworthy to many journalists and pundits precisely because it showed a more personal, emotional (and, implicitly, a more "feminine") side of the candidate. In stark contrast to that moment, Clinton's usual mode of self-presentation deemphasizes stereotypically feminine attributes.

The Independence/Dependence Bind

A similarly mundane feature of Clinton's political career illustrates another of her daunting, and more particular, double binds: her name. Hillary Rodham Clinton used alternately her given and married names during her husband's political ascendance. During her own presidential campaign, the former first lady dropped her surname Rodham in her presidential campaign communications, retained it when communicating with her New York constituency, and shortened her name further to simply "Hillary" on yard signs, T-shirts, and bumper stickers. This latter decision was perhaps an attempt to distinguish herself from her husband and to personalize and soften her image. Though perhaps politically necessary, that choice also raised criticism; being called by her first name seemed to some observers to render her little more than "an odd, exasperating, or vaguely frivolous child" (Kramer 2008, 68). At the same time, her last name carried both considerable clout and bountiful baggage, a dilemma that her opponent Senator Barack Obama underscored in their January South Carolina debate; when Obama criticized comments made against him by the former president, Hillary Clinton responded, "I'm here, not my husband," to which Mr. Obama retorted, "I can't tell who I'm running against sometimes" (Healy and Zeleny 2008b).

The controversy over her name illustrates a deeper bind. Clinton has for years struggled against perceptions of her as simultaneously a flagrant feminist yet a typical politician, "bitchy" and strident yet craven. She is seen as both too independent from gendered social norms yet too dependent on others in her acquisition of power.

Discomfort with Clinton's independence was underscored and the frame around her set by two incidents from Bill Clinton's 1992 presidential campaign. When pressed about her husband's affair with nightclub singer Gennifer Flowers during a February 1992 interview on CBS's *60 Minutes*, Clinton intoned that she was "not sitting there, some little woman standing by my man like Tammy Wynette" (Jamieson 1995). A month later, Ms. Clinton responded to critics of her decision to retain her own career and to questions raised about whether she had used her marriage to the Arkansas governor to funnel business to the law firm in which she was a partner. In a comment that became infamous, Clinton tartly retorted that she supposed she "could have stayed home and baked cookies and had teas," but instead had chosen to maintain her professional career while her husband was governor. In both episodes, Clinton appeared to reject traditional social norms surrounding homemaking and marriage. The news stories covering these episodes framed Ms. Clinton as radically independent, disrespectful of more conventional women's choices, and downright ambitious (Parry-Giles 2000). (After the strong reaction to her "tea and cookies" comment, Ms. Clinton engaged First Lady Barbara Bush in a cookie bake-off sponsored by *Family Circle* magazine [Beasley 2005, 213].)

Yet Hillary Clinton did stand by her man on more than one occasion when he was caught in private infidelities and public lies, improving her image among some observers, but for others feeding the opposite image of her as dishonest and craven and, ironically, as a parasite on her husband—a sentiment captured in Tammy Wynette's public response to Clinton's comment: "I believe you have offended . . . every person who has 'made it on their own' with no one to take them to the White House" (Jamieson 1995, 25). Her loyalty to her marriage (whatever its motive) during the 1999 impeachment of Bill Clinton for lying under oath about his sexual relationship with White House intern Monica Lewinsky improved Hillary Clinton's standing in public opinion polls. This perhaps unexpected improvement in her public image may have been a reaction to news coverage that often erased Hillary Clinton's history as a professional woman and portrayed her simply as a wronged wife in emotional distress (Parry-Giles 2000). But her fierce public defense of her husband against what she termed a "vast right-wing conspiracy" added a layer to her image as a dishonest and power-hungry member of a dishonest and power-hungry team. As one author recently wrote, "After Bill Clinton was exposed as both a cheater and a liar, Hillary Clinton became the public's proxy—a walking Rorschach test for our feelings about infidelity. And she started having (even more) difficulty being honest" (Levy 2008, 91). Standing by her man repeatedly in the face of public humiliation left many people asking what was in it for her: Was her marriage really a means to power?

Thus, Hillary Clinton's marriage became the canvas upon which contradictory images were painted: She was at once too stridently feminist to "stay home and bake cookies," yet too dependent upon her husband to achieve political power on her own. This image, long a part of Hillary Clinton lore, reemerged strongly during her presidential bid, with various observers and critics questioning whether Hillary could have "made it" without Bill. Of course, other observers pointed out, no one asks of Bill Clinton "how far his own gifts would have taken him with a different wife." Yet many believe that "it's not that Mrs. Clinton hasn't paid her dues, but rather that she hasn't paid most of them from her own account" (Thurman 2008, 78). As her presidential bid unfolded, this frame of the former First Lady as too-independent/dependent was hard to shake off.

Marriage, Bill, and Other Liabilities of Being Hillary Clinton

The independence/dependence bind was all the more binding for Hillary Clinton because of the nature of the political career she has shared with her husband. Ms. Clinton's central place in many of the most heated political battles of the 1990s meant that every time she invoked her "experience" and "readiness" to lead during the 2008 campaign, she also evoked memories of those battles. These connotations of the Clinton name—along with her consistently high negative ratings among Republican voters—helped cement the widely shared perception of Clinton as "polarizing." As writer Ezra Klein noted in the *Los Angeles Times*,

> It's a bit misleading to say "she" is polarizing. Polarization isn't a character trait; it's the outcome of a process. And that process is American politics. Clinton was a central player in most of the high-profile political controversies between 1992 and 2000. Remember them all? The bruising healthcare reform fight of 1993 and 1994, the endless Whitewater scandal, the weird resuscitation of the '60s-era culture wars, the Lewinsky mess and all the rest. Fifteen years in the hothouse of national politics will leave you "polarizing" as surely as 15 minutes in a tanning bed will leave you bronzed. (Klein 2007)

But Hillary Clinton's problems with the public, and with women and feminists in particular, are also rooted in the sense that she is not really her own woman. Clinton's penchant for policy, which goes back to her days on the editorial board of the Yale Law Review and her internship with Marian Wright Edelman at the Children's Defense Fund, not to mention her years of policy experience thereafter in the White House and the Senate, arguably should have given her policy credibility in her own right. But in another reflection of Clinton's independence/dependence double bind, even as many dislike Clinton for what they see as her imperious personality and her obvious ambition, they simultaneously discount her as a woman to be taken seriously. Paglia's criticism along these lines was sharp: "Her cutesy campaign has set a bad precedent for future women candidates, who should stand on their own as proponents of public policy" (Paglia 2008).

That Hillary Clinton benefited from proximity to those in power and advanced her own interests through dubious channels became a running theme of media commentary in 2008 (even though, if true, it arguably makes her quite like the long parade of male presidents that precedes her), echoing a long-running narrative about the Clintons. Bill Clinton himself had called attention to his wife's considerable policy and advocacy talents during his 1992 campaign, famously confiding in voters that they would get "two for the price of one" if they elected him: "If I get elected president, it will be an unprecedented partnership, far more than Franklin Roosevelt and Eleanor. They were two great people, but on different tracks. If I get elected, we'll do things together like we always have" (quoted in Troy 2000, 591–592). But Bill Clinton's "two-for-one" promise cemented public concern around Hillary Clinton's unconventional access to power as First Lady, as well as her preference for policymaking over the traditional, family-oriented tasks of the First Lady position. The secrecy, and then the failure, of the health-care task force that Bill Clinton appointed his wife to lead in 1993 further cemented the frame of Hillary Clinton as a self-interested professional climber realizing her ambitions through her husband.

The influential MSNBC commentator Chris Matthews returned to this narrative during the 2008 campaign when he claimed, just after Ms. Clinton won the New Hampshire primary, that "the reason she's a U.S. Senator, the reason she's a candidate for President, the reason she may be a front-runner, is her husband messed around. That's how she got to be Senator from New York. We keep forgetting it. She didn't win it on the merits" (quoted in Leibovich 2008a). In Matthews' estimation, it was the Lewinsky scandal and New Yorkers' sympathy for the scorned wife that earned her a seat in the US Senate, not her own talents and accomplishments. Even in humiliation, Senator Clinton was viewed as succeeding through her husband's actions.[4]

Matthews was not alone. Novelist Lionel Shriver made the same claim. Clinton's rise to power, he argued, "is anti-feminist: former First Lady is elected on her husband's coattails" (Shriver 2008, 47). Hillary, he claimed "owes [her Senate election] to the fact that she is Bill Clinton's wife" (Ibid. 51). Clinton's Senate seat therefore was commonly seen as ill-gotten gains. This preconceived notion of her wielding unearned power powerfully shaped the narrative of the former First Lady's presidential candidacy.

The "Gossamer Shackles" of the First Lady Role

Much of this public discourse on Clinton and her ambition is informed by our cultural expectations of a First *Lady*—a position with historically few responsibilities other than the ceremonial and decorous (Beasley 2005; O'Connor, Nye, and Assendelft 1996). In assuming the role in 1993, Clinton was stepping into a preconceived office that resembles the True Woman role. Indeed, despite the fact that it has carried far more informal power than many realize, the First Lady role is commonly viewed as "feminine window dressing" that does not and should not convey formal political power (Watson 2000). (Commenting on press coverage of presidents' wives over the years, journalism professor Caryl Rivers notes wryly, "The best sort of first lady, one would assume after reading the press, would be like Mr. Rochester's first wife in *Jane*

Eyre—locked in the attic and neither seen nor heard, except for an occasional muffled shriek" [in Beasley 2005, ix].)

As a highly educated and independent working woman, and later as a lead policymaker in the Clinton administration, Ms. Clinton stretched the limits of the First Lady role. Her early approval ratings were quite positive—significantly more positive than her husband's—and the public responded approvingly to her appointment to head the health-care task force (Beasley 2005, 219). But that appointment "violate[d] the traditional separation of the masculine sphere and the feminine domestic sphere that ha[d] previously defined the role of First Lady" (Burrell 1997, 18). Indeed, in her role as head of the task force, Hillary Clinton "could easily appear 'too strong' in relation to a husband many thought was 'too weak,'" symbolizing the social advancement of career women that evoked distrust and resentment among gender traditionalists (Skocpol 1997, 152–153, quoted in Winter 2008, 124–125). As the Whitewater affair and other negative news about the Clinton administration came to dominate the front pages, her key role in the White House inspired increasing criticism that she had exceeded her proper scope of influence, and her press coverage and approval ratings became markedly more negative (Beasley 2005; Guy 1995). (Moreover, as Winter [2008, 131] demonstrates, negative feelings toward Hillary Clinton became associated with negative reaction to health-care reform.) In response, Elizabeth Kolbert argues, "when Clinton has been attacked for being too ambitious, her response has been an elaborate show of femininity" more in keeping with the First Lady trope (2008, 14). Following the defeat of the Clinton health plan for example, Hillary Clinton retreated to that ceremonial role while publishing her book *It Takes a Village* to refocus her image squarely on children's interests.

Thus, the First Lady role offered Clinton a path to power, but her unconventional approach to the role met what one biographer refers to as the "gossamer shackles" of that office (Troy 2006). In fact, none of the US women and politics literature predicts that the first US woman president would ascend from the East Wing to the West Wing (even with an intervening seat in the Senate), which is perhaps why Clinton's determination to occupy a West Wing office was so unsettling to some. She was literally attempting to move from a ceremonial location to the hub of political and policymaking power.[5]

Similarly, even as it offered her an unprecedented opportunity to wield power, Hillary Clinton's marriage has also been a hindrance. Some have argued that being a wife at all is a political liability for ambitious women. When surveying the members of Congress, one finds more married men than married women. Even on the unelected side of public service, the patterns remains. Some of the most powerful women in presidential cabinets are single: Janet Reno, Condoleezza Rice, and Madeleine Albright all fit this mold. While having a wife shows a softer, caring side of the male candidate, and thus rounds out his image, the female candidate's husband is a puzzlement. In presidential candidates, having a husband inspires distinct challenges—whomever he might be. One could argue that "the standards by which wives are judged differ radically from the standard by which Americans typically judge their president. . . . [the female candidate] has to project strength and power. As a wife, however, she dare not do anything that might emasculate her husband" (Pogrebin 2008, 104–105).

Of course, Bill Clinton is not just any husband. Being related to this particular husband both improved and hurt Hillary Clinton's odds of succeeding at becoming president herself. Bill Clinton was a popular president, with above-average approval ratings during his two terms— even in the midst of the Lewinsky impeachment scandal (Zaller 1998). His popularity, in theory, was an essential ingredient of Hillary Clinton's own presidential bid. As Bill Clinton's vice president, Al Gore, learned in his own 2000 presidential campaign, it is critical for a candidate of the same party to symbolically affiliate with a popular president; Gore's decision to try to distance himself from Bill Clinton during the 2000 campaign may well have cost him his shot at the presidency (Johnston, Hagen, and Jamieson 2004). And given Bill Clinton's legendary skill on the campaign trail, many had predicted he would be a formidable advocate for his wife, particularly given her lack of personal charisma in large venues.

This apparent advantage proved to be a two-edged sword, however, as the "two-for-one" narrative returned and President Clinton's own baggage weighed heavily on his wife's campaign. The publication of the unauthorized biography *Her Way* in 2007 proffered a theory that the Clintons had crafted a "twenty-year project" to elect Bill president, a plan they then extended to Hillary. The historian to whom the book attributes information about this theory denounced it as "preposterous" and issued a stinging disavowal (Tomasky 2007), but the "project" theory was nevertheless plausible to many because it played to the independent/dependent narrative about Hillary Clinton. Given Bill Clinton's extramarital scandals and his impeachment, as well as his commanding personality, the notion of him as now the "two for" gained critical scrutiny. Would he bring further scandal to the White House? Could he step back from a policy role, and "let" his wife govern? Or would this in fact be a third term for Bill Clinton, an extension of what Carl Bernstein calls the Clintons' "co-presidency" (Bernstein 2007)?

There are important and historically unprecedented questions raised by the possibility of a president being followed in office by his wife— even if she were to win election in her own right. Since the Clintons portrayed themselves unabashedly as a political partnership, critics were within their rights to wonder if this kind of presidency would be acceptable and constitutional. Yet these questions also have an unavoidably gendered cast. Just as the script for president has been written in masculinist terms, the script for his life partner has been feminized. Resistance to Hillary Clinton's bid for the presidency thus reflected, to some perhaps immeasurable degree, discomfort with the concept of a first gentleman—discomfort reflected in popular culture portrayals. In the first television show to feature a female president, *Commander in Chief*, for example, the president's husband was given a pink office and treated to a social secretary; feeling irrelevant and perhaps cuckolded, the first gentleman sought employment in the masculine terrain of Major League Baseball. In that fictional narrative, only through being hired as baseball commissioner could the president's husband salvage his masculinity. In real life, while former president Clinton joked that his Scottish friends would dub him "first laddie," the blogosphere offered up feminized versions of Bill Clinton in the role: one common image for sale on T-shirts and bumper stickers depicted Bill Clinton sporting a Monica Lewinsky–styled hairdo with an oversized pink bow, inquiring, "Do you really want Bill as your First Lady?"

These demasculinized images of the former president serve to underscore the novelty (inappropriateness?) of a woman president by reminding voters that she does not have a proper wife to serve in the First Lady role. Such images also recall an effective strategy of undermining presidential candidates by calling into question their sexuality and proper gender attributes. Similarly, contemplating a "first gentleman" destabilizes that delicate balance the female candidate must strike between femininity and competence.[6]

The questions that swirled around the Clintons' "two-for-one" partnership were also unavoidably gendered because they implied that Hillary would not be able to "control" Bill (ironic, since Hillary Clinton had long been portrayed in popular culture as a demasculating dominatrix). Why would the nation doubt Hillary's ability to command the office of the presidency? The answer, for feminist writer Letty Cottin Pogrebin, "presupposes that Hillary is able to strike a pitch-perfect note on the femininity scale." As a wife and former First Lady, she needed to be "believably *wife-ish* while studiously avoiding any behavior that might be construed as *wifely*" as she pursued the White House (Pogrebin 2008, 112). Pogrebin offers this acerbic conclusion: "If a husband is a liability for a candidate and wifehood is a normalizer for a woman, the ideal status, obviously, is for a woman [candidate] to be a widow" (Ibid., 113).

Hillary Clinton's partnership with the former president raised another concern often echoed in media coverage of her presidential campaign: political dynasty. While in other countries women have been elevated to executive positions by virtue of their familial ties, the very notion of family dynasty strikes a discordant note in the United States (with the possible notable exception of the Kennedys). By 2008, either a Clinton or a Bush had occupied the White House for twenty years, and a Hillary Clinton presidency would extend the alternating family administrations for at least another four years. While Clinton attempted to mute these concerns by highlighting her husband's policy successes and the relative economic prosperity during his administration, she could not avoid the central argument that too few families seem to govern at 1600 Pennsylvania Avenue.

Moreover, raising her husband's policy achievements as she campaigned for the presidency prompted further questions about her own role in support of his less popular policies. Particularly damaging was her position on Bill Clinton's North American Free Trade Agreement (NAFTA). As the primary election process extended into spring contests in industrial states like Ohio and Pennsylvania, Hillary Clinton struggled to distance herself from NAFTA and its effect on blue-collar industry; while Sally Bedell Smith wrote in her Clinton biography, *For Love of Politics*, that Hillary Clinton had disapproved of NAFTA, the public had a difficult time distinguishing the former First Lady's views from those of her husband (2007). Hence, yet another liability in having been First Lady: One's job in that role is not to undermine publicly your husband's policy stances, even when one disagrees. That silence as First Lady hampered Hillary Clinton the presidential candidate.

Finally, there were campaign-specific liabilities of Clinton's marriage—specifically, in Bill Clinton's role as her campaign surrogate. To a considerable extent, media coverage of Hillary Clinton's presidential bid was inextricably linked to media coverage of her husband, the former president. While the campaign may have hoped Bill's legendary capacity to connect with audiences would rub off onto Hillary,[7] his magnanimity waned on the campaign trail. Moreover, the national press corps had not forgotten the "soap opera" of the Bill Clinton presidency, as it was often referred to, and there seems little doubt that the media approached him, as they did his wife, with a well-established script. Reporters wondered whether Bill would bring "another scandal" to his wife's presidential campaign; "Will Bill behave?" became a key topic of speculation (Mueller 2008, 199). This may help to explain why the former president's clumsy and, to some, offensive remarks on the 2008 presidential campaign trail instantly became major news stories that persisted long after his wife had suspended her campaign.[8]

Long perceived to be a friend of the African American community, Bill Clinton made several remarks that quickly tainted his reputation as the so-called "first black president" when he dismissed popular perceptions of Barack Obama as "fairy tales," and then compared Obama's victory over Hillary Clinton in South Carolina to Jesse Jackson's primary victories there in the 1980s: "Jesse Jackson won South Carolina in '84 and '88. Jackson ran a good campaign. And Obama ran a good campaign here," the former president observed, a comparison viewed by some as inflammatory and marginalizing, since Jackson had won limited support outside the black community while Obama had been winning white voters in large numbers. Several African American leaders publicly denounced the former president for this remark and others, with some contending that he had created a permanent rift with the black community (see for example Leibovich 2008b).[9] This episode and the public rebukes contributed to Hillary Clinton's dismal levels of African American support in subsequent primary contests; meanwhile, fundraising stalled in response to the uproar (Sheehy 2008). In more ways than one, Bill Clinton had become a liability on the campaign trail.

The Problem of Political Ambition

The charges against the Clintons of race-baiting in the 2008 campaign resonated in large part because they fit a larger narrative about the Clintons, as did negative coverage of her "Bosnia fairy tale" described earlier. As one prominent Washington journalist said, that moment "so completely fits into the narrative of the Clintons, which is that they will say anything or do anything or exaggerate in order to kind of get the edge in a political battle. So . . . even if this was an accident, it fits too neatly with . . . the larger story about them" (Reliable Sources 2008d).

Indeed, it seems that at the heart of Clinton's problems with the public and the media lies this perception of her (and her husband's) overweening ambition, which many apparently believe has led her to marry for power, to remain in a marriage that smacks of an "arrangement," and to use the First Lady office inappropriately to gain power.[10] And her Senate position—a virtual requirement for her viability as a presidential contender—affirms for some the view that "New York was just a vehicle for Clinton's ambition" (Kolbert 2008, 10).[11]

As Joseph Schlesinger once observed, "Ambition lies at the heart of politics" (1966, 1). Indeed, "by virtue of being candidates, individuals make a declaration of their ambition for political power and authority" (Palmer and Simon 2008, 55). Yet, US citizens have a deep and abiding suspicion of politics and political ambition stemming back to the founders (Lipset 1990; Wills 1999). So it is not surprising that anyone as clearly ambitious as Hillary Clinton would evoke some negative reaction from the public. Yet the intensity of the reaction suggests that the perception of Clinton's power as unearned and her ambition as overweening is gendered. Katha Pollitt argues that in the public mind, "she's a powerful liberal woman. An *older* powerful liberal woman. An older powerful liberal woman whose power is illegitimate because it is bound up somehow with sex—how else could a woman get power over men, its rightful possessors?" (in Morrison 2008, 17).

According to deep-seated US cultural norms, ambition to professional political advancement by women is unseemly—even unwomanly. We see this social prohibition enforced against Hillary Clinton by the many commentators who focused on what they saw as her *inappropriate* political ambition. As one author summed it up, "What is hardest to take about [Clinton] and what accounts for her success are basically the same thing: she is willing to do whatever it takes. *Women should wish for a more principled candidate*. They should wish for one who's more honest" (Kolbert 2008, 15, emphasis added). Hillary Clinton's ambition—that willingness to do "whatever it takes" to achieve her goals—is fundamentally antithetical to the notions of True Womanhood, leading *New York Times* opinion writer Judith Warner to conclude at the end of the 2008 Democratic primary season, "Clearly, in an age when the dangers and indignities of Driving While Black are well-acknowledged, and properly condemned, Striving While Female—if it goes too far and looks too real—is still held to be a crime" (Warner 2008b).

Ambition is particularly problematic for women when it is framed as "selfish." Indeed, Diane Kincaid notes the long-held stereotype of congressional women as merely "reluctant placeholders" for deceased husbands (1978, 96). Some female candidates for lower offices inoculate themselves against perceptions of selfishness by couching their ambition in the context of service to others. Oregon's only woman governor, Barbara Roberts (D-OR), famously entered politics because she was motivated to solve the education challenges faced by her autistic son and other disabled children; various female candidates' descriptions of themselves as "just moms" play to this social expectation as well. These messages, while often genuine, also serve to protect women candidates against charges of personal ambition by justifying their bids for power as motivated entirely by service to others.

This problem was arguably intensified for Hillary Clinton because of her own characteristic lack of self-revelation. As noted above, Clinton has long opted not to embrace the rhetoric of self-revelatory storytelling expected of female candidates. Without these personal narratives, the audience is left wondering why the candidate is seeking office, and the media and voters may easily insert the personal ambition moniker, a potentially dangerous inference for a "first" female contender who might then be understood as seeking power for power's sake. Indeed, some pundits' main criticism of Clinton's presidential campaign was that she offered "nothing else other than 'I'm in it to win it'" to explain why she was running for president (Todd and Gawiser 2009, 10).[12]

Again, the New Hampshire "teary moment" stands out, for in that moment, candidate Clinton came the closest to providing a compelling story line for her ambition: "I have so many opportunities from this country. I just don't want to see us fall backwards." But even in this instance, she told a general story of the needs of "the country," while couching that story line in terms of opportunities the country has provided to *her*.

At the same time, it is important to acknowledge that despite ongoing negative public framing, Clinton's ambition and toughness were not seen by everyone as negatives. An October 2007 Pew Center poll revealed that,

> In fact, some of the traits most often associated with Hillary Clinton—that she is "ambitious," "tough," and "outspoken"—are widely seen as positive traits, not negative traits. Fully 93% of voters say they think Clinton is ambitious, and 72% of these voters say her ambition is something they like about her. Similarly, 78% say Clinton is tough, and 81% view her toughness positively. The one trait that has a slightly more negative connotation for Clinton is being outspoken. Fully 84% say this applies to Clinton, and while 68% say they like this about her, 26% say they dislike this trait. (Pew Research Center 2007b)

It is critical to note, however, that there is a "Clinton factor" in these responses:

the terms "ambitious" and "outspoken" carry a slightly more negative connotation when people are thinking about Clinton than when they are thinking about female politicians in general. Overall, 21% of those who see Clinton as ambitious dislike this about her, compared with 16% who dislike this in female political leaders more generally. (Ibid.)

All of this is not to suggest that Hillary Clinton is not an ambitious person, as indeed anyone who seeks high political office must be. As one of her closest chroniclers observed simply, "Hillary Clinton is viewed through the lens of her larger ambition—and ambition is definitely there" (Green 2006). It is rather to point out why her ambition lies at the center of the negative public perceptions that posed such a challenge to her campaign.

Ambition, Missteps, and the Hillary Script

As we discussed in Chapter 3, a key pattern in media coverage of presidential campaigns has been the press's tendency to write prescribed stories about the various candidates' personal qualities. This tendency makes it difficult to know whether candidates' blunders (or triumphs) really do reveal something essential about their character, or whether the media emphasize the moments that seem to reveal the candidate's "true" character as defined by their preset script. Without resolving that chicken-and-the-egg question, we can simply observe that many of the key moments from the 2008 campaign trail fit quite neatly with the press's preestablished narrative about Hillary Clinton, and that Clinton's campaign did not significantly alter that preset narrative.

Indeed, it must be said that some of Clinton's campaign trail missteps played right into that narrative, all too easily confirming the suspicions of the press and many in the public that she is essentially manipulative and willing to do anything to get elected. Exhibit A might be her statement to *USA Today*, after she won resoundingly among rural voters in the Ohio, Indiana, West Virginia, and Kentucky primaries, that her campaign was resonating (and Obama's was not) with "hard-working Americans, white Americans"—a statement roundly criticized as not so subtle race-baiting.[13]

Clinton's campaign featured a mini-panoply of communicative missteps such as these that reinforced the ambition script. Interestingly, several of the most inflammatory of these moments involved Clinton's own reading of US political history (and the historical roles into which she implicitly cast herself). Take for example her comment implicitly comparing herself to former president Lyndon Johnson and Barack Obama to Martin Luther King Jr.: "Dr. King's dream began to be realized," Clinton said, "when President Lyndon Johnson passed the Civil Rights Act of 1964. It took a president to get it done" (Valbrun 2008). The comment drew immediate fire. PBS reporter Gwen Ifill told a National Public Radio audience that many black Americans reacted to Clinton's comment as she initially did: "Wait a second—are you dissing Martin Luther King?" (National Public Radio 2008a). Journalist Marjorie Valbrun asked, "What was Clinton thinking? King's name is sacrosanct in most black households. . . . Clinton managed to insult a beloved black leader in her eager attempt to insult a rising black leader" (Valbrun 2008). From a different perspective, though, Clinton's comment could be taken as a defensible illustration of the importance of governing experience in bringing about social change. Historian Robert Mann observed, "for all he did and for the many millions he inspired and persuaded, King's power was limited. He had the influence to start a movement, but little or no power to finish it. To quote Clinton, 'it took a president'" (Mann 2008). Whatever her real intent, and while biographers of the Clintons document the couple's long-time support of civil rights, these clumsy comments made while she was trying to wrest the nomination from the nation's first viable African American contender sounded flat-footed at best, and led some to charge her with "playing the race card."[14]

A particularly devastating moment occurred when Clinton compared the 2008 nominating race to the 1968 contest. In answer to a question about why she continued to campaign with so little chance of winning the nomination, Clinton reminded the editorial board of the Sioux Falls *Argus Leader* in late May of 2008 that historically, nominating contests have lasted well into June, and she gave two examples: her husband, who didn't "wrap up the nomination" until the California primary in June of 1992, and June of 1968, in which "we all remember Bobby Kennedy was assassinated" (Hamby 2008).[15] But the subtext seemed to many observers inescapable: Clinton was comparing Barack Obama, the first black man likely to win the presidency, with the assassinated Robert Kennedy. Given persistent fears in the black community for Senator Obama's safety,[16] the comment seemed at best highly insensitive. The Obama campaign quickly issued a statement saying that Clinton's comments "have no place in this campaign"; other reactions were more heated.[17] Without downplaying the significance of these missteps (or deliberate manipulations, depending upon one's perspective), we can also note that preestablished notions of Clinton as selfishly power hungry provided a convenient way to make sense of her unfortunate remarks.

The Back Story: The Clintons and the Press

As is true of all national political figures in contemporary politics, the public's image of Hillary Clinton has been focused—or distorted—through the mass media. The accumulated negative images of Clinton described here have, to a significant degree, grown out of how the press has covered her, and how she has attempted to manage her press coverage over the many years she has been in the public eye. The press's negative reaction to Clinton's campaign missteps did not arise sui generis on the 2008 campaign trail but had roots in long-running battles between her and the national press corps stemming back to her years as First Lady.

To some degree, a contentious relationship with the press is a feature of virtually every contemporary White House. As one long-time Washington reporter has noted,

> If [presidents] have seemed paranoid at times, it may be because they had real tormenters in the basement of the West Wing, ready to pounce on their hypocrisies. How presidents handle the ordeal of press coverage can be revealing of character. Some pretend to shrug it off better than others. The Clintons have been theatrical in their resentments and aggressive about pushing back. But in the realm of press relations, the most important difference between Hillary Clinton and Barack Obama or John McCain is that she has lived for eight years in the White House and they have not. (Thomas 2008b)

Hillary Clinton's path-breaking approach to her First Lady role made her a challenging subject for a news media accustomed to covering traditional First Ladies. Moreover, as one history of First Ladies and the press observes, "Positive portrayals of first ladies seem to stem from symbiotic relationships between them and the news media, cemented by personal contacts" (Beasley 2005, 23). Hillary Clinton eschewed such relationships with the press corps, pursuing a mode of news management very different from that of her most similar predecessor, Eleanor Roosevelt. First Lady Clinton held only one press conference during her husband's eight years in office, and avoided rather than cultivated influential newspaper reporters, preferring instead to reach out to the public via television programs and the White House website. "Not comfortable with reporters," Maurine Beasley observes, Clinton "tried to ignore the Washington press corps, even when she was in the midst of pushing her complicated health care reform proposal, which desperately needed public understanding and backing" (2005, 215). Clinton once confided to veteran reporter Helen Thomas that her aloofness with the press had been a mistake (Ibid., 217), though her press management style, for the most part, did not subsequently change.

Hillary Clinton's contentious relationship with the national press crystallized in the various scandals that plagued her husband's presidency, Whitewater in particular. According to analyst Michael Tomasky (2007), her "grave error" as First Lady "was to attempt to stonewall the press and the prosecutors, creating suspicion of serious wrongdoing where at worst some corner-cutting of the sort that passes unremarked nearly every day in Washington had occurred" (see also Kurtz 1998; Thomas 2008b). That approach to handling the media stemmed in part from her experiences in the early years of her career in public life, particularly when she served as counsel on the Watergate hearings (Mueller 2008). Her attempts to carefully control interactions with the press and her sometimes aggressive pushback to negative media coverage engendered long-lasting distrust among many reporters. As one biography of the Clintons' relationship with the press has observed, her "years on [Bill Clinton's] presidential campaign trail and in the White House were spent in a cold war with reporters over access" (Ibid., 56).

Though Hillary Clinton became more experienced and comfortable handling the media during her two Senate campaigns (Ibid.), she vacillated in 2008, at times experimenting with a more open style, but often reverting to her customary distance. As the *Washington Post*'s Howard Kurtz observed when we asked him about this, "her insistence on keeping reporters at arm's length in the early months of the campaign, until she began losing" contributed significantly to the negative coverage she received (Kurtz 2008a)—an observation echoed by many other reporters. Clinton's "arm's length" approach only cemented the press's view of her as scripted, cold, and arrogantly certain of victory—and flew in the face of every campaign reporter's most basic desire: access to the candidate.

More important than whether reporters personally like a candidate is whether they can get close enough to them to gain a glimpse of the candidate's real personality and gain some fresh news material.[18] CNN commentator Gloria Borger claimed, "It's not about 'like' with reporters, it's about access," but that Clinton only "reached out" to journalists when she was "in trouble" (Reliable Sources 2008a). Veteran political analyst Charlie Cook, who traveled briefly with the Clinton campaign press corps, observed that given how separate reporters were kept from the candidate, he would have had a better chance of seeing Clinton on television than catching a glimpse of her in person (Cook 2008b).

Indeed, the all-important background variable of accessibility helps explain why the press did not frame Clinton's "teary moment" in New Hampshire as a flat-out gaffe. Because Clinton's press tactics changed in the run-up to New Hampshire and she had begun interacting more directly with the traveling press corps assigned to cover her, reporters were getting up close and personal with the candidate in unscripted settings she did not usually allow. As one reporter described it,

> Senator Hillary Rodham Clinton has become the open and accessible candidate—sharing beers with reporters, taking endless questions from voters at campaign events and showing rare glimpses of emotion. Senator Barack Obama meantime, has been cautious, guarded and strenuously on message—Clinton-like, in other words. (Leibovich 2008c)

Noting, almost as if surprised, that Clinton "was funny, candid and apparently comfortable" talking personally with reporters, this one continued, "She has become more accessible and personable as she has become less of a sure bet" (Ibid.).[19]

Yet this new accessibility did not last; as the race for the nomination tightened, the campaign circled the wagons. Indeed, the Clinton team was infamous among reporters for its tight message control. According to one reporter, "Her team is frighteningly disciplined; no one talks out of turn or without prior approval, and even when they do, aides repeat the same anecdotes almost robotically" (quoted in Mueller 2008, 64). Members of Clinton's campaign staff were also infamous for their rudeness and attempts to intimidate reporters. Kurtz, for example, described to us "her staff's very aggressive attitude toward the media," including how "they treated reporters personally, being especially aggressive when they didn't like stories" (Kurtz 2008a). Anecdotes circulated of respected reporters receiving blistering e-mails from Clinton staff for coverage the campaign didn't like, and the staff made a habit of going straight to reporters' bosses with their complaints (Thomas 2008b). Journalist Josh Green (whose 2007 story on the Clinton campaign for *GQ* magazine was killed, reportedly by flack from Bill Clinton) argues that the Clinton campaign managed news coverage more "aggressively" than other campaigns. According to Green, "they often times treat the press the way a dog treats a fire hydrant" (quoted in Abrams 2008). MSNBC's Chris Matthews referred to the Clinton staff as "kneecappers," and ranted that "her press relations are lousy. . . . If all you do is intimidate and punish and claim you'll get even relentlessly . . . human reaction to intimidation is screw you. . . . and that has been their whole policy. We're going to win this thing. Get out of the way" (quoted in Stein 2008).[20]

To be fair, a good deal of the tension between the press and the Clinton campaign also stemmed from the campaign's frustration with the media's scripts for covering the campaign.[21] Clinton herself was reportedly infuriated with what she saw as the press's effort to settle old scores from her White House days and force her from the race (Green 2008b).[22] And indeed, as we will show in later chapters, Clinton's coverage was markedly more negative than that of her main competitors. *Washington Post* reporter Anne Kornblut, who watched the Clinton campaign from her front-row seat on the campaign trail, told us, "I get it. After all she had been through [as First Lady] I can see why the media was treated with suspicion." But, Kornblut says, "It was baffling why she didn't make a bigger effort to try and sway us. Every campaign makes an effort to co-opt reporters," but the Clinton campaign, she says, made "no effort to reason with us" and did not seem to see the press "as a potentially helpful force" (Kornblut 2009).

Whoever was most to blame, the result was a press corps in 2008 that seemed eager to write Hillary Clinton's political obituary. As Evan Thomas of *Newsweek* said on the *Charlie Rose Show* in February, reporters would "for sure rather cover a contest between Barack Obama and John McCain than between McCain and Hillary Clinton" (Rose 2008). In a segment devoted to the question of media bias against Clinton, MSNBC's Dan Abrams interviewed political analyst Lawrence O'Donnell, who described reporters going "en masse" to her postprimary New Hampshire appearance expecting to see the "end" of the Clintons—and, according to O'Donnell, the mood among reporters was "gleeful" (Abrams 2008). O'Donnell added that he knows and likes Hillary Clinton, but that most members of the press "never get to see that person."

"Likeable Enough"

Thus, in more ways than one, many of the challenges that faced Clinton's presidential campaign might have been mitigated through the candidate's likeability. Particularly in a primary contest in which there was very little ideological and policy difference between the candidates on most issues, personality and identity arguably were heightened in the choices made by voters. Hillary Clinton's low likeability ratings have been widely reported, and during the 2008 campaign, her "negative" ratings were consistently higher than those of her competitors. (At the same time, Clinton topped the nation's list of most admired women in 2007, beating out even Oprah Winfrey [Jones 2007], a fact that was not as widely remarked upon.) In February 2008, a Pew Center poll of Democrats and Democratic-leaning independents found 38 percent described Clinton as "prepared to lead the country," but 42 percent also described her as "someone who is hard to like" (Pew Center 2008c). In May 2008, even as 53 percent of Democratic respondents reported that she would be a "strong and decisive leader" (to Obama's 37 percent), 45 percent offered an "unfavorable" opinion of Clinton (to Obama's 37 percent) (*USA Today* 2008).

The "likeability" data shown in Figure 4.1, and the intrigue in Clinton's ratings in this area, highlight the double bind she faced as a presidential candidate. For while the femininity/competence bind forces women to waver between tough competence and soft familiarity, oftentimes those same women are then punished for waffling. As in the case of Hillary, who has been criticized for both pandering and no-holds-barred ambition, women who are striving to stay perched atop the thin

**Figure 4.1 Unfavorability Scores for
Senators Obama and Clinton over Time**

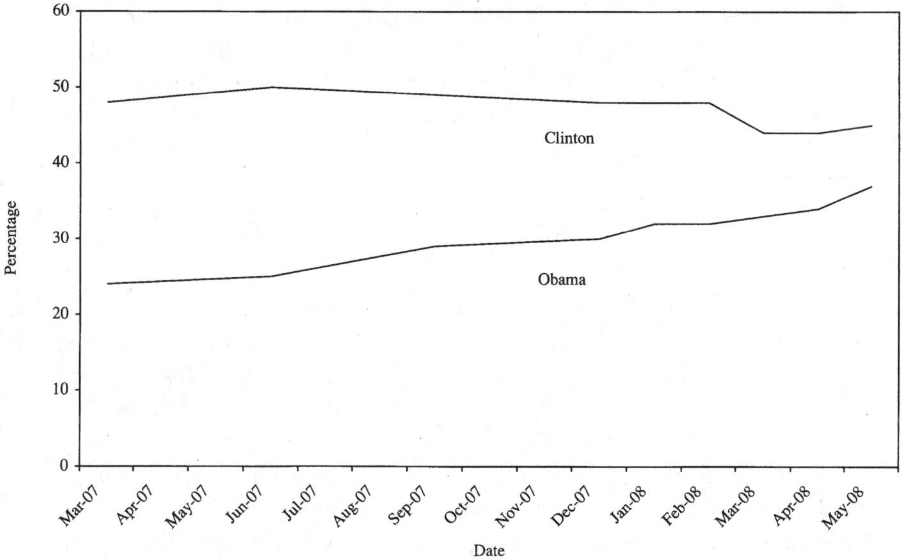

Source: USA Today/Gallup Poll, May 4, 2008.

tightrope of the double bind may easily be charged with self-serving ambition as they seek just the right balance.

As Figure 4.1 demonstrates, Clinton's likeability challenge would persist throughout the campaign. It appears that she attempted to address this concern in a variety of ways, from her early Web-based "conversations" with her supporters to her coy response to a question posed during a January Democratic debate regarding what the debate moderator called her "personality deficit": "Well, that hurts my feelings." Her response, delivered with a wry smile, brought appreciative applause from the studio audience, but the personality question would not so easily be put to rest; Senator Obama's retort that "You're likeable enough, Hillary" quickly reminded the public of doubts about her personality. As her campaign wore on, Clinton continued to battle her personality problem. During an April 17 Pennsylvania campaign appearance, when she was asked by a male supporter what arguments he could use to persuade undecided voters as he canvassed, she replied, "Knock on the door and say, 'She's really nice.' Or you can say, 'She's not as bad as you think'" (Shapiro 2008b).

Negative perceptions of Clinton's personal traits are so widely shared that mocking and derisive messages about her presidential campaign could be easily conveyed on an unspoken undercurrent. For example, one of the most popular videos on the file-sharing site YouTube throughout Clinton's campaign was an early Obama supporter's "advertisement" that characterized her, in a parody of Apple computer's famous "1984" ad, as "the face of oppression" (Cohen 2008a). The piece portrays Clinton in a "Big Brother" posture, intoning passionless messages via a huge video screen to an audience of lifeless prisoners. The ad struck a chord, appearing in the top ten viewed videos for the entire primary season.[23]

Conclusion

While unsurpassed name recognition, unprecedented fundraising ability, and the right resume appeared to position Hillary Clinton for electoral success in 2008, these advantages came tethered to preset public perceptions of her that proved difficult if not impossible to change. To some she is the bright young woman giving Wellesley College's first student graduation speech, or a mold-breaking First Lady giving global voice to the cause of children and women; but to many others (or, perhaps, to many at the same time), she is an imperious interloper: the quintessential Rorschach test. As Clinton herself once observed, "Everything I do carries political risk because nobody gets the scrutiny that I get. . . . It's not like I have any margin for error whatsoever. I don't. Everybody else does, and I don't. And that's fine. That's just who I am, and that's what I live with" (Green 2006).

Thus, although Clinton's resume and political connections allowed her to leap over the institutional and structural hurdles to the presidency, her candidacy stumbled against cultural constraints. In addition to the competence/femininity bind faced by so many women seeking power, the independent/dependent foil assigned to her many years ago proved a difficult frame to negotiate, let alone shake off. These difficulties were reinforced by Clinton's communicative and press management style. Ultimately, a prediction made before the 2008 campaign appears vindicated: Hillary Clinton was "a candidate that perhaps has too many labels to live down and too much political baggage" to win the nomination, let alone the presidency (Han 2007, 10).

It is important to remember that Clinton's campaign also stumbled against more benign and less gendered barriers. Though she leaped over institutional barriers that tripped her female predecessors, she would find that some "rules of the game" would prove decisive in this historic year (Ohlemacher 2008). So, careful to check all the boxes a female candidate must check along her route to the White House, she appeared cavalier in some tactical choices that would prove decisive: her choice to run essentially a general election campaign during the primary season by speaking to the ideological center rather than the more liberal Democratic base; her campaign's decision to work toward a Super Tuesday target for winning the nomination rather than preparing for a longer, broader fight; and her campaign's reliance on old-style fundraising and communications against an opponent exploiting new technologies to their fullest (Cottle 2008; Kuhn 2008; Sheehy 2008; Smith 2008). All proved missteps in hindsight. (For readers wanting to understand more about the nominating process rules and Clinton's strategic response, see the Appendix to the book.)

If there are lessons to be found in the particular case of Hillary Clinton for women and presidential politics, one must surely be the importance of good press relations. Unfortunately for Clinton, her characteristic discomfort with self-disclosure, sealed into place by her scorching experiences with the press as First Lady, played into media scripts that would haunt and perhaps deeply undermine her presidential campaign. Another crucial lesson may be the difficulty of ascending to the Oval Office via the East Wing. A former First Lady seeking the Oval

Office faces a unique challenge because her authority is viewed by definition as derivative of her husband's. A bid for the presidency runs contrary to the narrative of First Lady: Though that role affords unmatched name recognition, it is so thoroughly cast in the True Woman mold that it would seem to undermine any grasp at formal power as both dependent and illegitimate. Perhaps the literature has not considered a female president rising through the First Lady role precisely because the path seems untenable.

Many friends and well-wishers argue that Hillary Clinton would be where she is today without her husband. As a young attorney, she staffed the House Judiciary Committee while it investigated the impeachment of President Richard Nixon. As the first female partner at Rose law firm, she was once named one of the 100 most influential lawyers in the country (an honor that two recent biographers claim was undeserved, which underscores this frame of unearned power [see Tomasky 2007]). But in the public's eye, Hillary Clinton's achievements are largely her husband's. As the editor of *The New Statesman* observed in an article titled "Hating Hillary,"

> Hillary Clinton, a successful senator for New York who was re-elected for a second term by a wide margin in 2006—and who has been a political activist since she campaigned against the Vietnam War and served as a lawyer on the congressional staff seeking to impeach President Nixon—has been treated throughout the 2008 campaign as a mere appendage of her husband, never as a heavyweight politician whose career trajectory (as an accomplished lawyer and professional advocate for equality among children, for example) is markedly more impressive than those of the typical middle-aged male senator. (Stephen 2008)

There is no other potential female contender for the White House that has walked the path of Hillary Clinton, set against the backdrop of public distrust not just of female ambition, but distrust of "the Clintons" in particular. When combined with Bill Clinton's various blunderings on the campaign trail, the public was easily reminded of the independent/dependent trope set for Hillary Clinton since the early 1990s, and Clinton's name recognition became more a hurdle than a help.

Political scientist and women and politics expert Kathy Dolan sums up what is one of the critical findings of this chapter: "For all the postmortems we do on 2008, I don't think we'll ever be able to separate out what is gender stereotypes from what is Hillary Clinton" (quoted in Toner 2008). We must also agree with Pogrebin, who concludes that for female candidates, "wifehood comes with potholes" (Pogrebin 2008, 115). The variety of reactions she evokes are directly related to Hillary Clinton's role as an ambitious, complicated woman first entering the White House as the equal political partner of her president-husband, and then attempting to reenter as president herself. This is a professional and personal profile Hillary Clinton shares with no other woman in US history.

Notes

1. For a provocative analysis of even more heated reactions to Clinton among "Hillary Haters," see Horowitz (2008).

2. Clinton's speaking style not only violates gendered expectations of how women should speak, it violates expectations of how all politicians speak in the television era. Kathleen Hall Jamieson writes that TV has changed the repertoire of acceptable rhetorical styles of politicians; now a "feminine" style of self-disclosure, using personal anecdote and emotional self-disclosure, is more acceptable—indeed, virtually demanded by the medium (Jamieson 1998).

3. Essayist Katha Pollitt says of Gilligan's theory, "Speaking in a different voice is, after all, a big step up from silence" (1994, 54), while law professor Catherine MacKinnon is more pointed in her view of Gilligan's "different voice" theory. A woman speaks differently than a man, she once famously chided Gilligan, because "his foot is on her throat" (Conversation 1984).

4. Gender and politics scholar Georgia Duerst-Lahti, among others, had hoped Clinton's Senate experience would allow the public to see her as her own person, with her own accomplishments: "Having served successfully as a senator, she gains credibility in her own right. No longer must she rely upon derivative power as first lady . . ." (2006, 39). We come to a different conclusion; either because Clinton herself did not elaborate on her Senate achievements, or because the public could not see those achievements as truly hers, Clinton's record is still viewed as derivative by many.

5. Hillary Clinton actually had already made inroads into the West Wing as "the first president's wife to set up an office alongside her husband's advisers in the West Wing of the White House as well as to have her own office for social affairs in the East Wing" (Beasley 2005, 202).

6. As explored further in later chapters, attacks questioning Hillary Clinton's sexual orientation abounded in 2008.

7. Others were skeptical about the former president's ability to woo the press on behalf of his wife. According to one of the skeptics, "I don't think he knows the press that well. His press relations ended badly," particularly over the president's last-minute pardons of rich and infamous supporters who had run afoul of the law. "It's been 10 years since he had good [press] relations. . . . Bill's lessons on how to work the press are not current" (quoted in Mueller 2008, 113).

8. Indeed, two full months after Hillary Clinton bowed out of the presidential race, the controversy over her husband's remarks as her surrogate was still winning air time and ink in the national media (see for example Phillips 2008b).

9. Bill Clinton adamantly denied that he had played the race card, claiming, "I've never made a racist comment and I never attacked [Obama] personally" (Phillips 2008b). Mr. Clinton also blamed the Obama camp and journalistic gullibility for the debacle: "They are feeding you this because they know this is what you want to cover," he said. "What you care about is this. And the Obama people know that. So they just spin you up on this and you happily go along" (Seelye 2008a). But many reporters seemed to agree with ABC's Jake Tapper, who sarcastically observed that the former president's comment was in response to a question in which "Jackson had not been mentioned. Boy, I can't understand why anyone would think the Clintons are running a race-baiting campaign to paint Obama as 'the black candidate'" (Tapper 2008a).

10. It is important to recall here that the "ambition" narrative was one of the underlying challenges facing Hillary Clinton in 2008, while her opponent Barack Obama's own apparent ambition was rarely questioned. In December 2007, the Clinton team pushed a story that Senator Obama's kindergarten teacher remembered his boyhood essay titled "I Want to Become President," presumably in order to undermine the Obama team's argument that Clinton was overly ambitious by showing that Obama had sought the presidency, in a sense, since childhood (and perhaps to remind voters of their own argument that Obama was too young and inexperienced for the job). The tactic flopped, however, as bloggers and pundits poked fun at the unlikely "kindergate."

11. Ironically, none other than Robert Kennedy had "made the same mad, carpetbagging dash to New York to pick up that very same Senate seat in a state he was not really from, clearly with an eye to the 1968 presidential election" (Moore 2008, 30).

12. In fairness, Todd and Gawiser (2009) also criticize Republican candidate John McCain for failing to give a formal "why I'm running" speech, as Barack Obama did. Interestingly, Hillary Clinton did tell a personal story to explain her ambition in several of her campaign speeches. She presented perhaps the most fully elaborated version to a friendly audience at her alma mater, Wellesley College, on November 1, 2007, where she told her audience about going to work right out of law school for the Children's Defense Fund ("I didn't want to go to work for a law firm, I didn't want to clerk for a judge . . ."), where her work involved going door to door to investigate why some children weren't going to school. According to her narrative, she discovered that the missing were disabled children who weren't accommodated in public schools. Clinton concluded the story by explaining that she was motivated to public service by the plight of these children. The full text of this and other Clinton speeches can be found at www.presidency.ucsb.edu/ws/index.php?pid=77072.

13. Clinton later apologized for her remark; when "told that a top black supporter, Rep. Charles Rangel, D-N.Y., had called the remark 'the dumbest thing you could have possibly said,' Clinton said, 'Well, he's probably right'" (Associated Press 2008a; MSNBC 2008a).

14. Indeed, having lost the black vote, including the black female vote, to Obama after South Carolina, Clinton repositioned herself as the candidate best able to win rural white voters. Pennsylvania governor Ed Rendell, one of Hillary Clinton's most powerful advocates in that state, said bluntly, "I think there are some whites who are probably not ready to vote for an African-

American candidate." "This toxic issue," wrote one columnist, "is at the core of the Clinton camp's relentless effort to persuade super delegates that Senator Obama 'can't win' the White House" (Herbert 2008).

15. The evidence suggests that Clinton made her comment in an attempt to argue that her continued campaign, despite the odds against her, was not a historical anomaly. Indeed, Clinton followed her assassination comment with the observation that "people have been trying to push me out of this ever since Iowa" and said that position "historically . . . makes no sense" (Hamby 2008). The editors of the *Argus Leader* issued a statement later that day explaining that Clinton's comments had been an attempt to explain the campaign timeline, and some reporters traveling with the Clinton campaign posted an in-depth description of the circumstances of her comment—and her quick apology—that seemed to suggest that Clinton had been surprised by how her comments were interpreted (Seelye 2008d).

16. See for example Seelye (2008a).

17. Putting the negative reaction bluntly, one blogger commented, "You just said that it was too early to drop out in May because Bobby Kennedy was assassinated in June. FUCK YOU, HILLARY CLINTON" (www.americablog.com/ 2008/05/breaking-hillary-reportedly-invoked.html).

18. Of course, being accessible to reporters carries risks, but it can pay off significantly for the candidate. According to the *New Yorker*'s Ryan Lizza, Senator John McCain's practice during the 2008 primary of perpetually holding court with reporters—providing them ongoing inside access to the candidate while he traveled—"disarm[ed]" them. "The incentive to ask 'gotcha' questions that feed the latest news cycle is greatly reduced, and the hours of exposure to McCain breed a relationship that inclines journalists to be more careful about describing the context of his statements." Therefore, "his back-of-the-bus rambles rarely produce gaffes" (2008a).

19. As if to confirm this analysis, later in January Senator Clinton played one of several friendly jokes on the press when she took the steward's microphone on her "Hil-Force 1" campaign plane to announce to the traveling press corps, "We know you have choices when you fly, and so we are grateful that you chose to fly with the most experienced candidate" (www.youtube.com/ watch?v=_umButQ-diU).

20. By far the most infamous of the Clinton campaign staffers was senior strategist Mark Penn, who was deplored by many journalists for his highly scripted and attack-oriented approach to politics, and for having, as *Newsweek*'s Jonathon Alter described it, the "'EQ' (emotional intelligence) [sic] of an eggplant" (Alter 2008). It was also a staff riven by unclear lines of authority, longstanding personal feuds, and deep divisions over strategy. The campaign's internal conflicts, which increasingly leaked out to the press, helped fuel coverage questioning Clinton's judgment and managerial skills and portraying her campaign as on the ropes. Reporter Dave Davies, for example, described the "spin room" at campaign venues as a "churning sub-campaign, in which the campaign operatives are spreading venom and vitriol, which insiders and reporters see and hear, which is really at odds with what's going on in the campaign that voters see. . . . The insiders see this nasty, divisive campaign that's sort of sub rosa" (Davies 2008).

21. One *Washington Post* reporter provided a window on that frustration while describing a breakfast briefing the Clinton campaign team held with senior political reporters. Pressed continually on whether their positive spin on their candidate's chances for winning Ohio and Texas (which she did ultimately win) were realistic, senior adviser Harold Ickes exploded, "For the love of God, we can't say there's not much chance here." When a reporter suggested that campaign spokesman Phil Singer was being antagonistic, Singer responded, "Sixteen months into this . . . I'm just angry" (Milbank 2008c). For his part, Singer, like some others working for Clinton, was known for his explosive temper and long tirades against coworkers and reporters (Green 2008b).

22. At the same time, internal squabbling within the campaign team about how aggressively to attack Barack Obama exacerbated tensions between the press corps and the Clinton campaign. As Green (2008b) writes, based on analysis of internal campaign memos:

> About the only thing the campaign's warring factions did agree on was that the press ought to be criticizing Obama more severely. The more the Clinton team became paralyzed by conflict, the more it was forced to rely on the press to write negative stories that would weaken Obama—to, in effect, perform the very function it was unable to do for itself. This led the campaign to aggressively pressure reporters throughout 2007 and launch the outright attacks against the press that backfired once the primaries began.

23. We measured the popularity of this and other videos about Clinton on YouTube by cataloging the ten most popular videos retrieved with the search term "Hillary Clinton" on the Monday of each week during the campaign, beginning in November of 2007 and continuing through June of 2008. Another popular motif in pop culture drew comparisons between Obama's "Mac" image versus Hillary's as a "PC," portraying Clinton as the slogging, unglamorous electoral option. Blog chatter would continue to find similar analogies; at *Vanity Fair*, Senator Clinton's candidacy was equated with "warmed-over meatloaf, comfort food for those too old or fearful to Dream" (Wolcott 2008). Each of these analogies served to emphasize Hillary's age, lack of charisma, and strained relationship with the public.

5

Clinton's Gender Strategy

Well, we could have had a different kind of campaign where she ran as a woman from the first day. But for her it was the question of who would be the best president.
—Neera Tanden, policy director for the Clinton campaign, personal interview, May 12, 2008

I am also running to break through the highest and hardest glass ceiling.   —Senator Clinton in New Hampshire, January 2008

Senator Hillary Rodham Clinton's run for the 2008 Democratic presidential nomination offers a historic test case for the women and politics literature. This chapter examines expectations from that literature about how the first woman to run a viable campaign for the presidency would and should present herself to the voters. In particular, we assess the expectation (and the counsel) of that literature that the female "first" will present herself in terms of her experience, credentials, and policy positions, and that she will (and should) emphasize the "sameness" of her qualifications for office, staking her bid in terms of equality rather than difference. We find that Hillary Clinton followed this prediction (and advice) to a significant degree. But we also find feminine gendered messages interwoven into her gender-neutral claims of policy competence in often subtle and occasionally straightforward ways. Finally, we find a decided turn in the latter months of her campaign toward a heavily masculinized message strategy. All of these tactics arguably may have helped her with various groups of voters, even while they arguably hurt her with others and contributed to negative narratives about Clinton prevalent in the media. Overall, we find that in the case of Hillary Clinton, the predictions of the literature do not fully capture the complexities of how Clinton ran, and the counsel of the literature proved a problematic prescription for how to win.

This chapter presents data analyzing the gendered elements of Hillary Clinton's messaging strategies. Several sources of data we bring together—including press coverage, political blog postings, Clinton's own campaign appearances, advertisements, and websites, as well as postcampaign interviews with her staff that appeared in the national press and our own interviews with members of the campaign—all make clear that Clinton chose not to run primarily "as a woman." Indeed, the dominant messages throughout most of her campaign largely avoided explicitly gendered appeals. Yet the campaign did evoke gender at critical moments. In particular, as we show below, the Clinton team attempted in the months leading up to the Iowa and New Hampshire contests to layer a message of femininity and feminine solidarity on the foundation of "toughness" the candidate had laid, in an explicit attempt to mobilize women voters. Then, in the early months of 2008 as the nomination began to slip from her grasp, Clinton's messaging featured not so subtle efforts to "outmale" her opponents. In both cases, these efforts to some degree appear to have worked, but also entailed significant costs to Clinton's campaign.

We also find that Clinton's early decision to emphasize her experience in order to overcome the usual presumption that women are not as qualified as men for high office began to work against her once the media settled on an "experience versus change" narrative for understanding the Clinton versus Obama contest. Thus, in the specific electoral context of 2008, Clinton's "experience" claim formed a double bind in which she found it difficult to simultaneously frame herself as a change agent.

Arriving at a Gender Strategy

As the first woman to run in all her party's primaries, Hillary Clinton faced critical strategic decisions with respect to messaging. Senator Clinton brought to the campaign a specific package of advantages and challenges unique to her, and as she faced the gendered hurdles inherent in seeking the presidency, the job of the Clinton campaign strategists was to align their particular candidate's strengths with cultural expectations, and to try to break free of the particular burdens Clinton carries. How do you run a woman—and this particular woman—to be president of the United States?

As her policy director, Neera Tanden bore a good deal of the burden in dealing with the double binds presented to her candidate: Understanding well the masculinized presidency and her boss's skills and downfalls, Tanden's job was to create messaging through Clinton's policy positions. Critical among Tanden's obligations, one might think, was the need to position her candidate to walk the fine lines imposed by double binds. Yet when pressed in a personal interview, Tanden consistently argued that the strategic team had never considered Senator Clinton a "female candidate," and that their job was simply to allow Ms. Clinton's policy expertise to shine. While admitting frustration with the media's oversimplification of her candidate, and with the media's portrayal of Clinton as cold and calculating, Tanden would not acknowledge any effort within the campaign to address deliberately the gender issue.

Admittedly, Tanden's response may simply reflect campaign strategy; we visited her while the primary process was ongoing and she may well have been trying to affect the public framing of the campaign through the interview. Whether strategic or sincere, in hindsight, Tanden's statement supports our analysis in this chapter: that Senator Clinton preferred to position herself on the equality-based twin platforms of political experience and policy expertise, rather than to embrace her difference and hold up her gender as a unique and important quality in the campaign. As we show below, however, gender *was* a consideration in her campaign team's strategizing.

Gender Power and Presidential Campaigns

Gender power is an intrinsic aspect of political campaigns. Certainly, in earlier eras, gendered expectations were more readily apparent: In the late 1970s, when Congresswoman Pat Schroeder (D-CO) was asked how she could be both a mother and a Congresswoman, she responded bluntly, "God gave me a brain and a uterus and I intend to use them both" (*Time* 1978). But gender exists in every campaign, not just when women are prominent (or even present). Male presidential candidates and presidents employ muscular versions of masculinity to emphasize their authority. In an earlier day, the nation witnessed Teddy Roosevelt the outdoorsman, striding across the plains, rifle in hand. More recently, George W. Bush donned his flak jacket astride a fighter jet to demonstrate military prowess and international dominance. Even when women are absent from the stage, gender dynamics are at play.

We also can recall the instances where gender strategy has backfired for male candidates, because "the feminine is deployed to denigrate the man and his masculinity" (Duerst-Lahti 2007, 91), as in the ruinous images of Michael Dukakis atop an army tank in 1988 or John Kerry gliding on his snowboard in 2004. Some efforts at gender strategy have been clear attempts to overcome an image of weakness: Franklin D. Roosevelt, bound to a wheelchair, was generally photographed upright, while John F. Kennedy allowed himself to be photographed playing family football games, in order to draw attention away from his physical ailments.

These examples are simple reminders that past presidents and presidential hopefuls alike attempt to manage gender to their benefit. In the case of the presidency, the benefit generally goes to the candidate who is perceived as most independent, sure, and tough—all considered masculine traits, which, when no woman is vying for the office, masks the fact that gender is present at all. As Georgia Duerst-Lahti concludes, presidential elections are in the end about "[m]anly men, doing manly things, in manly ways" (2007, 87). For women candidates, the dilemma becomes how to prove one's (manly) competence for the job while retaining reassuring markers of femininity. In the 2008 presidential nominating elections, Hillary Clinton's very presence reminded the nation of gender, though often the media was prone to ascribe any revelation of gender to the only woman onstage—as if the context was gender-neutral until she showed up.

Against the ubiquity of gender, Clinton faced tough strategic decisions. As one *Newsweek* columnist observed,

> As a woman, Clinton feels constrained to portray herself as tough, competitive, willing to take on the bad guys. She has to be more male than men, in the same way that women are reluctant to leave the office early to pick up their children at day care because they fear they will not be thought of as serious about their careers, while men are applauded for doing so. (Linsky 2008)

Perhaps because "presidential elections have been very much about picking the right or best *man* for the job" (Duerst-Lahti 2007, 87, emphasis added), Clinton did not overtly feminize her candidacy; she kept the pantsuit and ran as the toughest guy on the dais.

Strategy Conflicts in the Clinton Camp

Postmortem analyses in the national media have revealed that the dominant voices within Clinton's campaign team clashed over the competence/femininity bind. Key advisers made a concerted effort to avoid falling into the "softness" side of the double bind, while other staff members apparently disagreed with this strategy:

> For more than a year the Clinton campaign has grappled with how it should portray Sen. Clinton, the first viable female presidential candidate. Chief strategist Mark Penn has advocated for presenting Sen. Clinton as a tough commander-in-chief by emphasizing her "strength and experience" and her deep knowledge of issues.
>
> But chief ad maker Mandy Grunwald and others worried that the campaign was overlooking the fact that many voters disliked Sen. Clinton. They argued that the campaign's message should humanize her and present her as a more personable, likeable candidate. (Chozick and Timiraos 2008)

Some others on the Clinton team apparently agreed with Grunwald. "'Everybody already knows Hillary is plenty tough,' [Harold] Ickes argued. 'If they know she's a tough operator, who could kick aside anyone who gets in her way, and they still don't like her, she needs to show the very human side of herself'" (Sheehy 2008).

The Penn-Grunwald divide represents one part of the bind that Hillary Clinton faced: If she took the Grunwald tack, she could be accused of failing to possess the credentials necessary for the "toughest job in the world." If she explicitly presented herself as a "woman" candidate, she could be accused of "playing the gender card," thus evoking gender in quite negative ways and reinforcing the public image of her as conniving and undeserving. (And indeed, on several occasions when Clinton did raise the gender issue, she was roundly accused of exactly that, as we discuss later in the chapter.)

Gail Sheehy, *Vanity Fair* writer and author of a sympathetic biography of Hillary Clinton (*Hillary's Choice*), noted in August 2008 that the senator "as always, had surrounded herself with brilliant, egocentric, hypercompetitive men," with Mark Penn at the helm (2008). In Sheehy's estimation, "Hillary's chief strategist proved to be an old-fashioned sexist. Penn did not appreciate the strength of her character as a woman. He and Bill Clinton insisted that she not run as a woman. They ran her as tougher than any man" (Ibid.).

Yet Penn's own thinking about gender strategizing proved complicated, for even as he tried to position his candidate as tougher than any other, he also believed that Hillary's bid for the presidency would powerfully mobilize women voters (Green 2008c). Reflecting this mixed strategy, during October of 2007, the campaign launched an effort to reach out to older, married women in particular by staging a weeklong Women Changing America theme, complete with local events across the country, to "highlight the decisive role women can play in this election, discuss issues important to women, and celebrate the ways that women are changing America everyday." On her website, the candidate enthused, "America is ready for change—and I believe women will lead that change. . . . It's up to us to do our part to take back the White House and change this country, and that's exactly what we're going to do. I say this nation can shatter the highest glass ceiling—because that's what Americans have been doing for over 200 years."[1] A subsequent news story headlined "Clinton Shows Femininity to Court Key Constituency" captured the strategy: "Everywhere she goes, Hillary Clinton asks voters to help her make history as the first woman president. Yet Clinton is increasingly portraying herself more as motherly and traditional than as trailblazing and feminist, sometimes playing up the difference between men and women" (Bombardieri 2007).

The Clinton campaign's initial gender strategizing was thus premised on a complex mix of toughness and feminine appeal, with toughness in the lead and feminine solidarity playing a supporting role. According to internal campaign documents obtained by Green (2008c), Penn's December 2006 "Launch Strategy" memo argued that "most voters in essence see the president as the 'father' of the country. . . . They do not want someone who will be first mama. . . . But there is a yearning for a kind of tough single parent. . . . They are open to the first father being a woman." Penn's "Overall Strategy for Winning" included themes of breaking gender barriers, being the "most competent and qualified in an unfair, male dominated world," and "the infusion of a woman and a mother's sensibilities into a world of war and neglect" (Green 2008c).

During these crucial months, the campaign made no secret of its gamble that a significant number of Democratic (and even Republican) women would vote for the first woman candidate to come along in their lifetimes. Penn predicted to a large group of reporters in mid-October that the influx of female voters in support of Clinton could tip the electoral map decisively in her favor (Balz 2007a). This was not an idle claim. Women were a potentially decisive voting bloc that had helped deliver control of the US Senate to Democrats in 2006, and who comprised 54 percent of the 2006 electorate (Center for American Women and Politics 2004, 2006), and 54 percent of Democratic primary voters in both Iowa and New Hampshire (Toner 2007). Moreover, as Democratic strategist Joe Trippi told us in a personal conversation, the 2006 election results proved the country was clamoring for change, and Clinton's team could have won women's support while also claiming the theme of change by saying, for example, "Every woman in the room knows what I'm talking about when I say that a vote for me is a vote for change, not the status quo. We need to educate children. We need to end war—not just this war, but all war. We didn't start this fire but we're sure the hell going to put it out" (Trippi 2008).

Instead of staking her campaign on explicitly feminized appeals, the Clinton team switched gears. By early February it became increasingly clear what a serious challenge Clinton faced in Obama, persuading the campaign to pursue a more aggressive attack-oriented strategy and a more overtly masculine message. Penn's strategy memo of March 5, 2008, shows him arguing forcefully against too much effort to feminize the candidate by those in the campaign team who wanted to "soften her and get warm and personal." Although "we did need a second track of [showing] that Hillary was also connected to our culture and to everyday life," Penn contended, "the idea that . . . this can be won on all smiles, empathy, and emotions is simply wrong," particularly since "white men became the pivotal post-Edwards vote" after Senator John Edwards exited the race (Green 2008c). Ultimately, Penn's preferred toughness strategy won the day, and it was the masculinized fighter narrative that Clinton embraced and amplified as the campaign extended into the spring of 2008.

Issue Positioning and Gender Strategy

Hillary Clinton's policy positions represented an added messaging challenge, shaped by generic voter expectations that female candidates are more adept with domestic policy than foreign policy, and by Clinton's own particular political history and the context she faced in 2008. Clinton's initial strategy, aimed at women voters in Iowa and New Hampshire in particular, emphasized domestic "care" issues. But sticking exclusively to "female" issues is not an option in most presidential contests, particularly in the post-9/11 era with the United States engaged in two wars. Therefore much of Clinton's strategizing, particularly as the fight intensified, involved priming the "male" presidential issue of national security.

Clinton had positioned herself as strong on defense when in 2002, as a member of the Senate Armed Services Committee, she voted to authorize the war in Iraq and gave a stern speech on the Senate floor justifying her vote.[2] As public opinion turned against the war, Clinton's 2002 vote came under closer scrutiny, particularly from the liberal wing of the

Democratic Party. Her main competitor and new Senate colleague Barack Obama criticized her openly for this vote, instructing voters that he had opposed the war consistently from the beginning.[3] Perhaps in an attempt to avoid the "flip-flopper" designation used to devastating effect against Democrat John Kerry in the 2004 election, Clinton refused to apologize for her vote (as her opponent John Edwards did). Indeed, Clinton told the crowd at the Los Angeles Democratic debate on January 31, "I've said many times that if I knew then what I know now, I would never have given President Bush the authority," but that at the time there had been a "credible case" for the war resolution (Milligan 2008). According to one account, "Her private refrain, say insiders, is the same as her public one: 'I've done nothing wrong, so I have nothing to apologize for'" (Ambinder 2007). At a deeper level, Clinton's decision reflected gendered political dynamics. Deborah Tannen, Harvard linguistics professor, explained that "for her to apologize would be far more face threatening than for a man to, because [Obama] started with the assumption [by the public] that he is stronger" because he is a man (2008).

Clinton continued to take a hard line on foreign policy throughout the primary season, and her positioning as tough on foreign policy registered with some voters. She took every available opportunity to play up her toughness contrasted with Obama's, calling him "naïve" and telling the ABC News program *Good Morning America* that under her presidency the United States would "totally obliterate" Iran if it launched nuclear weapons at Israel. While this tough talk may have seemed imprudent to some, especially given that the Democratic primary voter tends to be more liberal and antiwar than the general electorate, Clinton's fervent language assuaged concerns that a female president would be "soft" on foreign policy; though it seems to have been aimed squarely at the general electorate, it worked with many Democratic primary voters as well. A March 2008 *Wall Street Journal* poll showed 48 percent of Democratic voters ranking her as the best candidate to deal with international crises, and 44 percent saw her better than her rivals at dealing with foreign leaders (Hart/McInturff 2008). (For his part, Obama argued that Clinton's Iraq vote might count as "experience," but it also indicated poor judgment. At the California debate in January 2008, Obama proclaimed, "It is important to be *right* on Day One," to thunderous applause.)

Clinton's credentials as a woman's rights advocate created yet another policy positioning dilemma: Her long history in advancing rights for women and children[4] would fit well with public stereotypes about women's areas of expertise, but also would fit easily into the established narrative of her as a strident feminist—and could sit uneasily with a campaign grounded on her equal qualifications rather than her feminine "difference." The Clinton campaign apparently attempted to manage this challenge by suppressing this aspect of her professional résumé. Failing to invoke these areas of notable personal and professional accomplishments in order to avoid being branded a feminist or to appear an expert only on issues of women's and children's welfare left Clinton on shaky ground to establish her own independent arenas of expertise. It also left her relying more heavily on her other experiences as First Lady unrelated to women's issues.

In the domestic policy arena, Clinton's health policy credentials were well known, and survey respondents affirmed her competence in that arena. For example, the *Wall Street Journal* poll taken in early March found that 50 percent of Democratic voters believed Clinton would be the "better" candidate on the issue of health care (versus 23 percent who thought this of Barack Obama) (Hart/McInturff 2008).[5] Still, emphasizing her health policy credentials presented a two-edged sword: relying on health policy as the best index of her experience recalled her "dependence" on Bill Clinton for that opportunity to gain experience.

Finally, Clinton faced a delicate challenge in forming her electoral stance on abortion. While Democratic primary voters generally support a woman's reproductive rights, general political opinion on the subject is complex and moderate—a reality any presidential contender must navigate (Rose 2007). As a woman, voters might assign to Clinton a more liberal position than is accepted in the general electorate, and her own previous record as a staunch supporter of abortion rights might in this context be a liability—a liability Clinton began addressing in 2005 as she moderated her message on the issue.[6] By acknowledging the complexity of abortion, Clinton may have derailed it as a major campaign issue, though some in the liberal wing of her party then questioned her loyalty to this Democratic issue.[7]

Ultimately, Clinton's moderate issue positioning in the years leading up to her presidential bid seemed to make good sense for a woman contemplating a run for the White House. But these moves simultaneously codified the existing image of her as a calculating politician willing to shift policy positions for political gain (an image captured succinctly by the always-acerbic Maureen Dowd: "There is nowhere she won't go, so long as it gets her where she wants to be. That's the beauty of Hillary" [2007]). And while these decisions could have bolstered her odds in a general election, they hurt her with some liberal Democratic primary voters—the very voters she needed to win first. Thus, Clinton's issue positioning, which dovetailed with her gender strategy, was fraught with drawbacks.

The campaign's internal struggle over gender strategy, and the constrained terrain she faced on her issue positions, constitutes the crucial context for understanding many of the Clinton campaign's messages. Clinton's "experience" theme, which sought to establish her competence, fit comfortably with her equality-based appeal, and also came to serve the masculinized vision of the candidate that emerged ever more strongly over the course of the campaign. This theme rested her claim to power squarely upon the notion that her résumé and personal qualities were the same as the men's, and avoided bringing special or unique features of the candidate's gender into the foreground. Yet feminine gendering also played a key role in Clinton's messaging, particularly in late 2007.

The Femininity Interregnum

Close attention to the trajectory of the campaign reveals two key time periods with distinctively different gender messages.[8] In the earlier stage of the campaign, particularly October 2007 through January 2008, the Grunwald strategy of softening the candidate through nods to feminine-gendered messages punctuated an otherwise equality-based narrative. During this time period, Clinton evoked feminine gender in a variety of ways, some subtle and some more overt.

Clinton's very first television ad, aired in August of 2007 in Iowa, illustrates the general thrust of her gender messaging during the months leading up to the first primary contests. "Invisibles"[9] offers on its surface a straightforward gender-neutral appeal, highlighting key issues of concern to Democratic voters and demonstrating Clinton's ability to command respect from audiences. Yet the rhetorical theme, the choice and framing of issues, and some of the visual cues subtly highlight gender considerations. The ad intersperses footage of Clinton traveling and meeting with rural Americans (presumably Iowans) with footage from a campaign speech. The first line from the ad makes its message clear: "As I travel around America, I hear from so many people who feel like they're just invisible to their government." A male narrator interjects: "Hillary Clinton has spent her life standing up for people others don't see." The audio track and the visuals return to Clinton's speech, in which she discusses a family without health care and a single mom without affordable child care—both examples that fit with gendered policy arenas and send subtle cues of feminine empathy. She then mentions that troops who have served in Iraq and Afghanistan are also "invisible" to the current administration. Thus, the issues mentioned in the ad are primarily domestic, with the exception of the war in Iraq, which is treated obliquely, with an emphasis on caring for soldiers (not on prosecuting the war). The ad concludes with shots of Clinton driving home her argument—these people "aren't invisible to me, and they won't be invisible to the next president of the United States"—mixed with warm reaction shots from the audience. One visual moment from the ad stands out: As Clinton is shown talking with various groups, striking an authoritative yet personable posture, she is also shown talking with an elderly woman; as the woman confides something to Clinton, Clinton reaches out and holds the woman's shoulder and pulls her slightly closer with a look of deep concern and understanding, in a movement that distinctively conveys womanly empathy. The overall message is clear: This (female) candidate sees, hears, empathizes with, and "stands up" for others.

Gender cues would become less subtle as the Iowa and New Hampshire contests approached. For example, in New Hampshire, the campaign ran radio ads that again featured domestic "care" issues and, this time, real-world women as campaign surrogates: Barbara Marzelli, whose ten-year-old son had had four open-heart surgeries made financially possible by the Children's Health Insurance Program (CHIP), a program of insurance for children in low- and middle-income families that Senator Clinton supported; and Ann Marie Morse, whose daughter Michelle was diagnosed with colon cancer at age twenty, prompting her mother to health-care activism. The Web versions of these ads, lengthier than most TV ads, offer a window into the campaign's gender and issue strategy.

The ad with Marzelli focuses on her first-person description of her child's health problems and the importance of the CHIP program for covering his medical expenses.[10] The emotional highlight of this ad is the moment when Marzelli describes meeting Senator Clinton (the camera cuts to footage of them speaking at a campaign event): "I remember walking up to her and saying, 'I would feel a lot more safe if you were to become president than I have in many, many years.'" In the parting message of the ad, Marzelli says of Clinton, "She's got the courage, she's got the heart, she's got the experience—she's got everything that we need, and I know that she'll stand up for everybody. That's how I feel about her." The second ad features Morse's description of how her daughter was denied health-care coverage when colon cancer forced her to drop out of college, and Morse's continuing efforts to enact

"Michelle's Law" to prevent insurance companies from dropping coverage in similar circumstances.[11] The emotional highlight in this ad is footage from a public event in which Morse, seated next to Clinton, explains that her daughter died at the age of twenty-two. Morse barely maintains her composure, and Hillary Clinton reaches over, resting her hand on Morse's arm and appearing moved as she talks about the need to pass a federal version of the law. The last line in this ad features Morse saying of Clinton, "As a mom, she's passionate about what she's doing. . . . My motto is never mess with a mom who's passionate about a cause." Nodding affirmatively and smiling, Morse says, "She's also passionate about this cause." The keywords in both ads are emotional: "passionate," "heart," "feel," "care."

In mid-December, the Clinton campaign aired a new television ad in Iowa: "Dorothy."[12] The ad begins with a black-and-white photo marked, "Dorothy and Hillary 1948," featuring a toddler Clinton in a bonnet, apparently taking her first baby steps. Dorothy Rodham's description of her daughter forms the audio track of the ad: "What I would like people to know about Hillary is what a good person she is. She never was envious of anybody. She was helpful. And she's continued that with her adult life, with helping other women." At this moment, the words "Hillary's mom lives with her" appear at the foot of the screen in a font that looks hand-written. Next, the camera cuts to footage of Clinton appearing onstage with her mother and her daughter (the footage had been shot a week earlier at a campaign event in Iowa); interestingly, at the moment the camera cuts to this new scene, Clinton is engaged in an uncharacteristic and quintessentially feminine gesture, delicately sweeping hair behind her ear as she speaks. "She has empathy for other people's unfortunate circumstances," Rodham's voice continues, while the camera cuts to footage of her and her daughter talking and smiling together. "I've always admired that because it isn't always true of people. I think she ought to be elected even if she weren't my daughter."

The "Dorothy" ad is particularly noteworthy because it featured Clinton doing what previous research (Bystrom et al. 2004) suggests women candidates generally avoid: Surrounding herself with her own family (though notably, in this particular effort, not her husband). The campaign made no secret that Dorothy (both the ad and the person) was being deployed to mobilize female voters, particularly older women who, in the words of one reporter, "might feel an emotional bond with Mrs. Clinton—seeing her like a daughter or seeing something of themselves in her" (Healy 2007b). Probably not coincidentally, both Chelsea Clinton and Dorothy Rodham were brought to Iowa on the heels of

Oprah Winfrey's high-profile Iowa event on behalf of Barack Obama—part of the Obama team's own explicit effort to win over women voters (Toner 2007).

Clinton's Christmas season ad, released just prior to the Iowa and New Hampshire contests, is closer to the classic female candidate "videostyle" found by Dianne Bystrom et al. (2004). While holiday season ads for her opponent Barack Obama featured him in a homey holiday sweater flanked by his beautiful wife and children,[13] Clinton's ad, "Presents,"[14] finds her alone by the Christmas tree, thus affirming her independence and competence as an individual. Tying ribbons as she puts the finishing touches on her holiday gifts, the camera zooms in on the gift tags: "universal health care," "alternative energy," and the like are placed with care by the candidate, dressed in business attire, without Bill, Chelsea, or her mother in sight. In this ad, again, the focus is largely on domestic issues; the only gift tag hinting at the vexing area of foreign policy offers a reassuring message: "Bring Troops Home." The ad concludes by driving home the public's associations between women, domestic "care" issues, and Hillary Clinton herself: "Where did I put universal pre-K?" the candidate asks herself, lighting up with a smile as she finds the final package.[15]

The feminine messaging evident in these ads was not limited to Clinton's advertising. Notably, it was in the fall of 2007, during the more feminized months of her campaign, that Senator Clinton made an appearance on *The View,* a daytime TV show with an overwhelmingly female audience. On that show, she joked about how long it took her to get ready for campaigning each day compared to her male colleagues and shared a rare story about Chelsea as a baby (Bombardieri 2007). Not coincidentally, on the campaign trail that week, Clinton quipped, "I've noticed that the last couple of weeks I've been getting a lot of attention from the men in this race. And at first, you know, I didn't know what to make of it. And then a good friend of mine said, 'You know, when you get to be our age, having that much attention from all these men . . .'" (she allowed the punch line to go unspoken, to loud laughter from the audience) (Bombardieri 2007). Clinton repeated the joke on several occasions that month, including on Keith Olbermann's *Countdown* on MSNBC (*Countdown with Keith Olbermann* 2007). This air of feminine accessibility extended into the New Hampshire contest, where, fresh from her unexpected Iowa defeat, the senator "opened herself up to as many unscreened questions as the audience could throw out" (Sheehy 2008)—the context for the widely discussed "teary moment" in Portsmouth. On January 15, 2008, toward the end of the femininity interregnum, Clinton appeared on *The Tyra Banks Show*, sharing stories with the audience about dating Bill, the pain of the Lewinsky scandal, and other personal anecdotes.

The Clinton team's strategy to reach out simultaneously to women voters and to address her likeability challenge was portrayed by some reporters with barely disguised disdain. For example, the *Washington Post* reported in December of 2007 that

> her aides are trying a last-minute fix for a potentially fatal flaw: Voters like her brains and her experience, but they don't necessarily like, well, her. And so the campaign rolled out (what else?) a new slogan— "The Hillary I Know"—and a new Web site with 38 videotaped testimonials from the senator's friends and constituents. (Milbank 2007)

Many of these testimonials were from women; more importantly, all of them portrayed Clinton in traditionally feminine terms as warm, supportive, a good friend. Notably, these testimonials were a departure, in terms of their gender cues, from the overall content of Clinton's campaign website, which since early in her campaign had featured women-focused items only sparingly.[16]

Zooming in on these particular messages illuminates the gender cues built into the campaign's strategy leading up to Iowa and New Hampshire. Yet we should not lose sight of the fact that Clinton's overall gender strategy was complex. For a general, national audience, particularly in her network news appearances and debate performances, Clinton more often than not avoided calling attention to her gender and instead focused on demonstrating her policy expertise and toughness (though occasionally with subtly gendered flourishes). Nor should we leave the impression that Clinton only employed feminine gender cues during late 2007. Indeed, the style that would characterize the "femininity interregnum" of late 2007 was on display in the January 2007 videocasts by which Clinton launched her campaign, in which, wearing soft pastels, Clinton invited the nation to "start a conversation": "So let's talk. Let's chat. Let's start a dialogue about your ideas and mine" (Clinton 2007). By providing a sense of virtual intimacy and inviting participants to "start a dialogue," she seemingly sought to avoid the imperious manner often attributed to her. In fact, these videocasts were perhaps the closest Clinton came, stylistically speaking, to "running as a woman." (Notably, some have argued that this way of launching her campaign ultimately undermined it, providing voters with no clear sense of why Clinton was seeking the presidency [Todd and Gawiser 2009]).

Nor did messages of feminine solidarity entirely disappear after

January 2008. In fact, perhaps the most significant example of overtly feminine messaging came in the form of well-known female political surrogates deployed throughout her campaign. Though she rarely appeared onstage with them, Clinton relied on major feminist figures to make this aspect of her case, including Geraldine Ferraro (1984 vice presidential candidate), Kim Gandy (president of NOW), Ellen Malcolm (president of Emily's List), Gloria Steinem (founder of NOW), Maya Angelou (poet laureate), and even former Texas governor Ann Richards (who died in 2006). The campaign's use of Richards leading up to the Texas primary/caucus in early March represented perhaps the most direct appeal to women that Clinton made during her candidacy, and featured one of its most explicit "girl power" messages. In the two-minute ad, made with permission from Richards' daughter, a female announcer tells viewers, "So many women around Texas and America are saying, 'Wish Ann was here, for us and for Hillary.'" Showing a photo of Richards and Clinton together, the ad ends by intoning, "Today, Ann would be asking all of us to make a statement. She would be traveling to every small town and big city in Texas, urging us all to take a stand, be counted, to make a difference, to make history. . . . This one's for Texas. This one's for our country. This one's for Ann."[17]

October Surprise: The Gender Card

One episode from the femininity interregnum illustrates well the risks lying in wait for a female presidential candidate who brings attention to her gender. At the Democratic candidate debate at Drexel University on October 30, 2007, Hillary Clinton delivered her most unimpressive debate performance since announcing her candidacy: her policy statements on immigration and the Iraq war were uncharacteristically garbled, and her six male opponents and the two male moderators did not miss the opportunity to draw attention to the front-runner's missteps. (Indeed, this was the same week that both John Edwards and Barack Obama had announced they were going on the attack against Clinton, the front-runner.) The following day, the Clinton team released a video on YouTube called "The Politics of Pile On."[18] The 30-second spot compiled over 20 instances, in lightning fast succession, in which her Democratic opponents had criticized her and her positions during the debate; it ended with Clinton's comment at the debate that "I seem to be the topic of great conversation and consternation, and that's for a reason." Though the ad did not spell out this reason, it seemed to insinuate that her (male) counterparts had ganged up on her.[19]

The following day, campaign manager Patti Solis Doyle sent supporters an e-mail reinforcing the pile-on theme by calling the debate a "six against one," explaining it as a typical attack on the front-runner by opponents trying to boost their own flagging poll numbers. But Clinton seemed to offer a more transparently gendered interpretation of the "pile on" during a visit to her alma mater, Wellesley College, that same day. During her speech she reflected on her years at Wellesley, observing that, "In so many ways this all-women's college prepared me to compete in the all-boys' club of presidential politics" (Thrush 2007). Coupled with the release of the "Politics of Pile On" video, the senator's remarks fueled the emergence of the "gender card" as a campaign issue.

The debate imbroglio was curiously reminiscent of Clinton's 2000 New York Senate race debate against Congressman Rick Lazio, in which Lazio appeared overtly aggressive when he strode across the debate platform to challenge Ms. Clinton to sign an anti–soft money pledge. In that case, the public reaction ran in support of Clinton. Lazio's performance "trigger[ed] a reaction because it seemed an inappropriate physical attack by a man on a woman" (Duerst-Lahti 2007, 88), and many who viewed the debate concluded that Lazio was unlikeable (Nagourney and Connelly 2000). The "Pile On" ad may have been intended to elicit a similar response from sympathetic viewers; however, the public's reaction proved more varied in the presidential context.

In subsequent days, Clinton made efforts to distance herself from blatant charges of sexism, telling audiences, "People are not attacking me because I'm a woman. They're attacking me because I am ahead." "I'm not trying to play the gender card," she claimed, "I'm trying to play the winning card." But even then, Clinton added a gendered flourish: "If you can't stand the heat, get out of the kitchen. . . . Well, I'm really comfortable in the kitchen, and I'm going to stay in there and absorb the heat" (Nagourney and Healy 2007). Overall, the Clinton messaging subtly referenced female challenges in running for the presidency through the nonverbal cues of the "Pile On" video and Clinton's comments, while not overtly claiming bias or asking for special treatment.

Some were unconvinced. On November 2, when Senator Barack Obama was asked in a *Today Show* interview about the gender card flap, he interpreted the events differently. "One of the things that she has suggested why she should be elected is because she's been playing in this rough-and-tumble stage," Obama responded, "so it doesn't make sense for her after having run that way for eight months, the first time that people start challenging her point of view, that suddenly, she backs off and says, don't pick on me" (Balz 2007b).

Clinton's use, or nonuse, of the gender card emerged as a key theme of election coverage in a week in which she received significant amounts of negative media coverage. The Project for Excellence in Journalism (2007c) found heavy coverage of the presidential campaign on radio and cable TV talk shows that week, "and the conversation was virtually all Clinton all the time. The former First Lady was a significant subject in about 75% of the talk segments" the project cataloged that week, "many of them . . . not flattering or friendly." Indeed, the report found, "the triggering event for last week's outpouring of Hillary hammering" was the Drexel debate and the pile-on controversy. Our own search shows that within major mainstream media outlets, while the term "gender card" had emerged only sporadically before the Drexel debate, it suddenly made a strong appearance in the week after the debate.[20]

Close reading of mainstream news coverage of this incident in leading newspapers and the evening broadcast news, along with reaction in the blogosphere, suggests that the reaction to this episode fell into two competing frames: that Clinton was right to play the gender card, or, more frequently, that she played the card, but shouldn't have. Virtually absent from the coverage was the notion that Clinton did not play the gender card at all, or that Senator Obama or media pundits had played the card.[21] Much of the commentary also implicitly suggested that until the "Pile On" video and Clinton's Wellesley comments, gender was absent from the presidential electoral stage. There were a few notable exceptions, like the opinion piece penned by feminist Susan Faludi: "Keep in mind: The gender card is *always* played. It's even played in presidential campaigns in which the candidates are all men, and (given our political culture and our history) it usually involves a morality tale in which men are the rescuers and women the victims in need of rescuing" (Faludi 2007, italics in original). But in most accounts in the mainstream media and the blogosphere, the question came down to whether it was fair or right for Ms. Clinton to raise gender—and what the consequences would be for her candidacy.

She did and she should. This response was evident in the blogosphere and among some elite feminists in the mainstream press, but it was a minority position in the diverse news sources we monitored. Closely linked to discussions about women and the political landscape, this perspective argued that Clinton should wield feminine difference to her (positive) advantage. Eleanor Smeal, president of the Feminist Majority Foundation, likened "the debate scene to the congressional grilling of Anita Hill when she challenged Clarence Thomas' Supreme Court nomination in 1991" (quoted in Smith and Kuhn 2007). "Turnabout is fair play. . . . When you're the one and only, those stereotypes are coming at you all the time. If she has one time when she can make them work for her, why not?" declared Marie Wilson, the president of the White House Project, a nonpartisan organization that seeks to elect a woman president (Ibid.).

Perhaps the finest point put on this topic was by Geraldine Ferraro. Ferraro hypothesized that a black man would not suffer the same treatment a white woman had: "John Edwards, specifically, as well as the press, would never attack Barack Obama for two hours the way they attacked her [at the debate]. . . . It's O.K. in this country to be sexist. . . . It's certainly not O.K. to be racist. I think if Barack Obama had been attacked for two hours—well, I don't think Barack Obama would have been attacked for two hours" (Nagourney and Healy 2007).[22]

She did; it was wrong. Not all feminists stood by Smeal, Wilson, and Ferraro. Notably, some high-profile feminists interpreted the alleged gender card episode as evidence of Clinton wanting special treatment; these women argued that Clinton's ploy was demeaning to women by suggesting victimization or inferiority. Contending that the debate "pile on" was in fact a fair reaction to Clinton's poor performance, Kate Michelman, president of NARAL Pro-Choice America (and a campaign adviser to Clinton's opponent, Senator John Edwards), said in a written statement, "Any serious candidate for president should make their views clear and let the American people know where they stand on issues. . . . Have we come a long way? Well, far enough to know better than to use our gender as a shield when the questions get too hot" (quoted in Smith and Kuhn 2007). Feminist writer Naomi Wolf argued the pile-on narrative was good strategy, but lousy feminism, accusing the Clinton team of "yielding to gender stereotypes" by suggesting that Clinton had been bullied by powerful men.

Beyond feminist circles, critics argued that the "gender card" was lousy strategy and typical Clinton manipulation. In fact, the dominant perspective in reaction to the pile-on episode, from both the political left and right, seemed to be that Clinton was disingenuously playing the victim. One blogger for the conservative *National Review* complained, "She's supposed to be the tough one in this field; why is her campaign acting like there's something wrong when everybody's focused on her? Why is she whining about a 'pile-on'?" (The Campaign Spot 2007). A liberal blogger took umbrage at the "pile on" metaphor, arguing that "the Clinton campaign is trying to push women's buttons, getting them to rally around Clinton out of a sense of shared victimhood" and accusing them of a more insidious effort to rally the support of male voters through subtle, emotional appeals to their chivalry: "no doubt there are a lot of men whose sympathies can be pricked with the image of a bunch of guys 'piling on' one woman" (Sanders 2007). Conservative talk-radio host Rush Limbaugh also characterized the pile-on narrative as a scheming victim-status ploy: "How stupid . . . one day she wants to be thought of like a man, as a member of the boys' club. Then other times, she's just this victim. . . . She's blowing this big time . . . Mrs. Clinton playing the gender card" (Sargent 2007). Echoing his remarks was *New York Times* columnist Maureen Dowd, who, like Limbaugh, frequently made analogies between Clinton's path to the Senate and her presidential aspirations: "If she could become a senator by playing the victim after Monica, surely she can become president by playing the victim now" (Dowd 2007).

Beyond the opinionated realm of the blogosphere and the editorial pages, the chief concern for many reporters seemed to be whether Clinton's presumed use of the gender card would indeed attract female voters. For example, Dan Balz, writing for the *Washington Post* online, concluded the strategy would work for Clinton because "no one should underestimate the underlying power of a message that aims to appeal to the aspirations—and the sense of exclusion—of the majority of the population. No wonder Clinton and her advisers have decided to play the gender card at every opportunity" (2007b).

Notably, there was little discussion about the consequences for the male candidates that were said to have picked on Clinton during the debate—or afterward. Rather, her opponents were credited with simply avoiding any question of gender politics. The implicit understanding of this discourse seemed to be that until gender was specifically named, gender dynamics were not at play—and that only a woman can play that particular card from the electoral politics deck. Indeed, according to popular reaction to this event, the "card" was not "played" by the men who framed Clinton's messaging as a gender-card ploy.

Given its timing, the "Pile On" video and Clinton's comments may have been an aspect of the Penn strategy for bringing women voters to the campaign. However, for all the attention the October debate moment got, it didn't seem to affect Clinton's public standing for better or worse. Gallup polls conducted the week of October 12–14, and again November 2–4, found that Clinton's commanding lead had remained unmoved by the Philadelphia debate and the ensuing chatter over the "gender card" (Newport 2007). However, the debate kerfuffle may have added to the "information bits" that can accumulate over time to shape voters' evaluations of the candidates (Jamieson 1993), and it certainly provoked a national discussion—though a rather tortured one—of gender, perhaps for the first time, in the 2008 campaign.

The Testosterone Blitzkrieg

If a voter who had closely followed the Clinton campaign in Iowa and New Hampshire had fallen asleep, reawakening just in time for the primaries in Texas and Ohio, she would notice distinctly different messages coming from the campaign. In the short time between December 2007 and mid-February 2008, everything had changed. Barack Obama had won the Iowa caucuses, and though Clinton had won New Hampshire, she had lost twelve of the twenty-two contests on February 5 and suffered a string of losses in subsequent primaries. By the end of February, the Texas and Ohio contests loomed as "do or die" hurdles for a campaign that had been rocked by a series of negative stories about squandered campaign funds and bitter in-fighting. Between February 2 and February 24, polls registered a 22 percent drop in the number of Democratic primary voters predicting Hillary Clinton would win the nomination—down to 23 percent, versus 68 percent predicting victory for Senator Obama (*New York Times*/CBS poll 2008a). In response, the campaign shifted to an aggressive strategy of attack against Obama, employing potent masculine rhetoric that overshadowed the (feminine) gender-conscious messaging of the campaign's early months.

This shift in messaging was evident in Clinton ads targeted at voters in key post–Super Tuesday contests. Interestingly, the two ads that were most revealing of the gendered communication devices at play during the latter months of the primary season were also among the most controversial of her campaign. The first was the so-called "3:00 a.m." ad released in late February, prior to the Texas and Ohio primaries.[23]

In this ad, a gravelly male voice establishes Clinton's credibility in the arena of national security:

> It's 3 a.m. and your children are safe and asleep. But there's a phone in the White House and it's ringing.
>
> Something's happening in the world. Your vote will decide who answers that call, whether it's someone who already knows the world's leaders, knows the military—someone tested and ready to lead in a dangerous world.
>
> It's 3 a.m. and your children are safe and asleep. Who do you want answering the phone? (Alexovich 2008b)

Some of the ad's nonverbal cues feature a classic feminine "videostyle" (Bystrom et al. 2004), showing a sleeping child (not Clinton's grown daughter) dreaming in her bed with an anxious mother (not Hillary Clinton) checking in on her. But the ad also strongly emphasizes the tough competence theme. Only at the end of the ad does Clinton herself appear: bespectacled, calmly at work in her business suit—presumably at her desk in the White House, keeping watch while a nation unaware of the lurking danger sleeps. Clinton, the ultimate protector and unflappable figure of experience, appears alone.

The second notable—and highly controversial—ad was "Kitchen," released before the Pennsylvania primary in April. The text of that ad, recorded by a male announcer, was a tongue-in-cheek turn on a gendered aphorism. But the visuals provided the macho message: amid historic images of US crises, from the stock market crash of 1929 to Hurricane Katrina, reeling gas pump prices, and most significantly, the image of Osama bin Laden, we hear:

> It's the toughest job in the world. You need to be ready for anything—especially now, with two wars, oil prices skyrocketing and an economy in crisis.
>
> Harry Truman said it best: "If you can't stand the heat, get out of the kitchen."
>
> Who do you think has what it takes?[24]

These advertisements offered tough visual images reminding the nation that a president's unique role in US government is foreign policy—a challenge not for the faint of heart. There is no hint in these ads that a Hillary Clinton presidency would create a "kinder and gentler nation," a campaign message once delivered by George H. W. Bush, and no mention of the domestic policy arena highlighted in Clinton's earlier ads. "This is the choice we face: One of us is ready to be commander in chief in a dangerous world," Clinton began telling campaign audiences (Healy and Zeleny 2008c), repeating on the campaign trail the admonition earlier deployed to call attention to Clinton as the only woman on the presidential stage—"if you can't stand the heat, get out of the kitchen"—but that now seemed to carry a more complicated connotation.

The campaign also dispatched a series of tough-talk surrogates to regender the campaign along traditionally male lines. Actor Jack Nicholson proved the quintessentially macho surrogate. Appearing in his own Internet ad purchased for Clinton in March[25]—an ad viewed 1.2 million times by the end of that month—Nicholson offered a montage of his many famous movie lines to lend his hypermasculine identity to the candidate. The mash-up featured footage from Nicholson's various film roles, in a series of manly poses and costumes, while questions like "Don't we need a president who is ready to go on day one?" appeared between movie clips. A gender twist at the advertisement's end featured Nicholson's quip, in his role as a hardened Army colonel from the film *A Few Good Men*, that "there's nothing on this earth sexier, believe me gentlemen, than a woman you have to salute in the morning." Though we cannot know whether Clinton herself approved of that (or any) line in the ad, Nicholson's effort appeared to lend Clinton masculine gravitas and toughness on the one hand, while acknowledging and crediting not just her sex, but her sexuality.[26]

In Ohio and Texas, the tough-talk messaging arguably played well (Clinton won in both states), and the strategy was carried into Pennsylvania, Indiana, and North Carolina. Indeed, Clinton's Indiana campaign appearances were widely noted (and, by some, derided) for featuring the candidate in a series of manly postures, including drinking shots with union workers in a local bar. Cementing the masculine strategy, three tough-as-nails surrogates delivered a manly message on behalf of their candidate in a single week in April. Pennsylvania governor Ed Rendell used the "Rocky" theme song at Clinton campaign events leading up to his state's April 22 primary. One week later, in offering his endorsement to Hillary Clinton, North Carolina governor Mike Easley echoed the winning Pennsylvania theme by brashly stating, "This lady right here makes Rocky Balboa look like a pansy. . . . There's nothing I love more than a strong powerful woman" (Suarez 2008). The next day, in Indiana, United Steelworkers Local 6787 president Paul Gibson introduced Clinton as the kind of leader with the requisite "testicular fortitude" to make difficult decisions. "I do think I have fortitude," Clinton said to laughter and applause. "Women can have it, as well as men" (Pearson 2008). Some weeks after the April trilogy of tough-guy surrogates (and after Clinton won Pennsylvania), strategist James Carville put a fourth, and finer, point on the message when he told Eleanor Clift of *Newsweek*, "If she gave him [Obama] one of her cojones, they'd both have two" (Clift 2008).

The Power and Peril of Historical "Firsts"

We have seen how Hillary Clinton's campaign attempted to layer two distinctly different gender messages over the competence-and-experience theme that formed the campaign's bedrock message, moving from a more feminine to a more masculine posture. It is striking, however, that one message that might have been used more overtly in service of the feminized strategy did not come through clearly: the fact of Hillary Clinton's history-making potential as the first woman within striking distance of the White House.

In running for the Senate seat from New York in 2000, Clinton's opponent, New York mayor Rudy Giuliani frequently referred to Ms. Clinton as the "First Lady" in what seemed an effort to undermine her independent achievements. In response, Clinton ran a biographical ad titled "First," reminding viewers that "her first cause was children, fighting abuse, and chairing the Children's Defense Fund," and that she had an impressive legal career before becoming First Lady.[27] Bystrom maintains that "the strategy behind 'First' was to attempt to educate New York voters about Rodham Clinton's pre–White House life and her thirty years of work on child and family issues. . . . The ad uses word-play, redefining Rodham Clinton not as a first lady, but as a woman with many other 'firsts'" (Bystrom et al. 2004, 196). Obviously, during her run for the Senate, Ms. Clinton was fresh from the First Lady role, and she apparently decided she had to remake her image to establish her credentials for the office she sought in 2000.

In seeking the presidency, Clinton could have chosen once more to remind voters that she was more than a former First Lady: that she was in many ways a trailblazing "first," not least as the first woman to stand a good chance of winning the presidency. Many scholars and campaign consultants would be wary of this approach, however, particularly in a presidential election, because of the gendered way in which voters might hear the "first" label (Falk 2008). Perhaps not surprisingly, Clinton avoided overtly embracing the mantle of historic "first" in 2008, opting to invoke the concept indirectly rather than foregrounding it in her message strategy. While the Clinton team's strategy for the femininity interregnum included this notion of Clinton making history, chief strategist Penn apparently backed away from this strategy once Senator Obama advanced in the contest, fearing that Obama had upstaged Clinton's ability to claim the "first" narrative (Ambinder 2007). One consequence was that any benefit Clinton might have gained by reminding voters of her trailblazing career was lost.

Indeed, as best as we can tell, there was no 2008 equivalent of Clinton's 2000 "First" ad, and none of the key ads analyzed here reminded voters of her "first" status. Neither did the campaign's website, for the most part. While the website was deployed in service of the "Women Changing America" week described earlier, on *none* of the days we logged on, across the six months between mid-December and mid-June, did the "headline" section of Clinton's website highlight Clinton's role in advancing women and children's issues. Significantly, the "spotlight" items, which were updated more frequently than the "headlines" segment of the site, covered more than 60 individual topics across these six months, but only 6 topics were women and/or children specific, representing a mere 13 percent of the cataloged spotlight items.[28] Meanwhile, the website downplayed Clinton's personal biography. Only 6 of the days we cataloged across 26 weeks featured video of Hillary Clinton growing up or other aspects of her life. Overall, just as in her public speaking style, Clinton's "webstyle" (Bystrom et al. 2004) revealed little of herself and featured few references to women-centered policies or issues.

Another indication of how little Hillary Clinton invoked her "first" status is how rarely the media discussed the historical significance of her campaign. Of course, media coverage in 2008 was full of references to the "historic" nature of a campaign that featured a close contest between a woman and an African American. What was often lacking in coverage of Clinton, however, was any discussion that went beyond such fleeting references. To explore this phenomenon, we compared how the media portrayed the historic nature of these two candidacies, zeroing in on Hillary Clinton's New Hampshire primary victory—the first-ever victory for a female candidate in a major party primary—and Barack Obama's historic win in Iowa, both at the time these victories occurred and later, in the aftermath of Clinton's withdrawal from the race, when Obama claimed the nomination.[29]

A close reading of the coverage suggests that greater weight was given to the potential historical implications of an Obama nomination than a Clinton nomination. Out of 49 passages in 31 news and editorial items that referenced these history-making aspects of the 2008 campaign, 25 (50 percent) described Obama's candidacy as historic, while 7 passages (14 percent) described Clinton's candidacy in these terms; the remainder simultaneously described both candidacies as historic, usually pooling Clinton and Obama together in references to a historic campaign season overall.[30] The qualitative differences in coverage of these two victories is captured subtly in one passage from our sample, from a *Washington Post* story appearing the day after Obama clinched the Democratic nomination: "Obama's victory was notable not simply for its historic importance but also because it marked a rejection, albeit by the narrowest of margins, of a candidate who represented the most powerful family in Democratic politics" (Balz and Kornblut 2008). In this brief summation, Obama's win is "historic," while Clinton's very candidacy is framed in relation to her husband. Moreover, as we saw in Chapter 3, Clinton's New Hampshire victory was often attributed to female voters who connected emotionally with her "teary moment" in Portsmouth; Clinton's own political talents and the ground organizing by her campaign were rarely acknowledged as a source of her success. One critical commentary captured in our sample highlighted succinctly the difference in coverage between Obama's Iowa win and Clinton's in New Hampshire (and stands out for its very different framing of history):

> Senator Hillary Rodham Clinton's upset victory in the New Hampshire primary last week was every bit as impressive as Sen. Barack Obama's Iowa caucus breakout five days before—if anything, more impressive, since his win was predicted and hers unforeseen. But the reactions to the two events couldn't have been more different. Obama's Jan. 3 triumph let loose a giddiness bordering on exhilaration among voters and, especially, media commentators, who hailed his triumph as "historic," even though he was not in fact the first African American to win a major presidential nominating contest. (Jesse Jackson won 13 primaries and caucuses in 1988.) By contrast, when Clinton overcame long odds to become the first woman in U.S. history to win a majorparty primary, no leading news outlet trumpeted this landmark feat. Many failed to mention it at all. (Greenberg 2008b)

Interestingly, coverage accompanying Clinton's withdrawal from the race was more respectful of her campaign in hindsight, such as in this passage from the *Washington Post*: "Sen. Hillary Rodham Clinton, the most successful female presidential candidate in U.S. history, officially ended her campaign yesterday with a forceful promise to help elect Sen. Barack Obama—and the declaration that, even though she had failed to 'shatter that highest, hardest glass ceiling,' a gender barrier had been crossed" (Kornblut 2008).

Thus, the media seemed to acknowledge most fully the historic contours of the Clinton candidacy after she conceded to Senator Obama. This historical blind spot is not merely the result of media nearsightedness, however. It reflects, at least in part, the Clinton campaign's relegation of this theme to the background of its own message. One small but telling indication of this silence is the fact that many references to the historic nature of Obama's campaign drew directly or indirectly from Obama's speech on the night of his Iowa victory, which the candidate described as "a defining moment in history," subtly calling attention to a storyline the press seemed poised to write. Clinton appears not to have prompted similar coverage in New Hampshire. Her victory speech that evening made no references to "history"; the single moment in the speech in which it seemed she might evoke a gender victory—"This campaign will transform America"—was quickly followed with a rather pat promise to "take on the challenges" facing the country. The closing line of the speech evoked not a history-making victory for women, but the masculinized Clinton that would emerge more strongly in the weeks to come: "This country is worth fighting for!"[31] It appears, then, that the press paid little attention to the historic quality of Clinton's candidacy in part because of the compelling historic importance of her competitor's achievement, and in part because Clinton herself avoided claiming that mantle, leaving us to wonder whether Clinton's decision to avoid the "first" narrative might have undermined the impact of her accomplishment.

Experience: Ready on Day One

Instead of embracing the "first" narrative, Hillary Clinton told the nation that she was the only candidate who would be "Ready on Day One," implying that her experience in Washington as First Lady and senator translated into preparedness for the presidency, and suggesting by implication that any competitor with less experience would take some time to learn on the job—a dangerous liability during wartime. Given the historic gender stereotypes that have plagued public women, this frame seemed well-advised. According to Bill Clinton's former strategy guru, Dick Morris, "(a) it bolstered Hillary's résumé and inoculated her against charges that she was just running on Bill's record; (b) it reassured people about her qualifications for the general election and assuaged anxieties about a female president; (c) but, most of all, it laid down the predicate for an attack, down the road, on Obama's own lack of experience" (Morris 2008). But while this approach had many advantages, it also contained serious risks that were exacerbated by Senator Obama's campaign messaging, and by the way Clinton articulated her message.

Given Obama's relative youthfulness, his more recent emergence on the national political stage, and the old wisdom that Americans at war are conservative about their presidential selections, Hillary Clinton's effort to emphasize her own experience and thereby simultaneously draw attention to Obama's inexperience made sense. Unfortunately for her, as *New York Times* writer Matt Bai observed, Obama "gladly accepted the contrast. Ever since then, 'experience versus change' has been the principal choice that both candidates have been asking Democratic voters to make" (Bai 2008a).

Clinton tried to avoid that dichotomy, as Kathleen Hall Jamieson observed, by casting herself as the candidate with "the experience to bring change" (Jamieson 2008). At a California stop in September 2007, for example, Clinton argued that "'change' is just a word without the strength and experience to make it happen. . . . And I know some people think you have to choose between change and experience. Well, with me you don't have to choose" (Nicholas 2007). But her effort to escape the dichotomy failed. Writing on Super Tuesday, Bai observed,

> Mrs. Clinton has tried, more recently, to establish her own bona fides as a change agent, but her assigned role in that pivotal equation was decided long ago. And this is why she has had to go so strongly on the offensive against Mr. Obama, in a way that has repelled a lot of those who once sympathized with her—because the only course of action available to her after Iowa was to persuade voters that Mr. Obama is, in fact, too flawed to bring about the kind of change he has come to represent. The negative trajectory of her campaign was set those many months ago when she chose to define herself against the change in Washington that many Democrats were craving. (2008a)

In the end, Clinton's emphasis on "experience," while on its face so necessary for a woman running for president, provided Obama an important advantage. As Bai observed, "Mr. Obama's aides . . . were happy to let Mrs. Clinton anoint herself the candidate of Washington experience if it meant their guy could run against the status quo." Bai also argued that, "in doing so, they ceded ground to Mrs. Clinton they need not have ceded, validating this notion that she had far more experience than Mr. Obama, even though she had been in the Senate only four years longer and had actually served less time in elective office. They enabled her to seamlessly transform her tenure as First Lady into presidential preparedness" (Ibid.).

While from Bai's vantage point it may have looked seamless, in hindsight it appears that the translation of First Lady experience into presidential preparedness was fraught with problems—first among them, Clinton's failure to portray compellingly the specifics of her "experience" to voters. With few references to her Senate record on either her website or in her advertisements, the "experience" narrative recalled for many the perception that Hillary Clinton had gotten power through her husband; for others, experience in the Senate boiled down to Clinton's Iraq war vote in 2002, highly unpopular among liberal Democratic primary voters. We are left to wonder what the public response would have been had she filled in details of experience from her law practice, her advocacy for women and children, and her larger

Senate record. Moreover, the Clinton team's gamble that Obama's "inexperience" would undermine his candidacy did not pay off. University of Iowa sociologist Michael Lovaglia (2008) concludes, "In terms of the election, it was right for Clinton to emphasize her credentials and experience. That helped her." But "what she and her campaign didn't expect was that Obama's lack of experience would not be a deficit. Obama has very little experience, but it didn't seem to matter. Lack of experience for a woman, however, would likely eliminate her from contention."

Moreover, when confronted with a youthful male competitor, the experience message contained yet another landmine: age. Hillary Clinton, running for the presidency at sixty years old, was quickly identified as Obama's senior. Leaning on the experience message allowed the message of experience = age to gain traction. The visuals of a lanky, hip Senator Obama underscored the point as he traveled from one enthusiastic, massive college crowd to the next—without ever having to mention his opponent's age. While for many, experience equals competence, for others, older age in a woman is problematic.

Rush Limbaugh gave strident voice to the ageism emerging in the campaign when he responded to an unflattering photo of Senator Clinton being featured on the Drudge Report website, where it ran with the tagline "The Toll of a Campaign." Limbaugh asked his audience bluntly, "Will this country want to actually watch a woman get older before their eyes on a daily basis?" (Traister 2007). One week later, the *Washington Post* extended the story's life to a wider audience by running the photo on the front page of its political news section. Under the banner "Sooner or Later, Candidates Will Surely Look Lost," the story described the image as a typical "hangdog" photo that emerges in many campaigns, showing the politician tired and lackluster (Kennicott 2007).[32] Rebecca Traister, writing for Salon.com, argued that the worn-looking photo of Senator Clinton carried a more distinctly gendered pall: none of us, she says, "are above thinking about how Clinton looks and sounds and what she wears. We are like babies first encountering a new object: a potential president who has breasts and hips and who was once pregnant and whose female skin has changed as it aged" (2007). Traister's remarks are exceptional, a counterframe for a photo that, particularly in the blogosphere, came to represent Clinton as the old, establishment candidate against Obama's youthful, fresh face. Criticism of the use of the Clinton "hangdog" photo was mainly isolated to feminist blogs.

Given either a different competitor, or a different set of liabilities, the experience theme may have been a successful message for candidate

Clinton—indeed, the scholarly argument that women should first and foremost assert their credentials for the job would perhaps have held true. Remembering that women enter political careers generally later than their male competitors, however, suggests yet another double bind for female presidential contenders. On the one hand, most women enter politics on average later than their male counterparts (Thomas 1994; Herrick 2004), and because they must take the time to establish their credibility and suitable experience, women can be expected to run for the presidency later than men. But to the extent that mature women face cultural discrimination in the United States, arguing the "experience" message may inadvertently become code for advanced age, as it surely did in Hillary Clinton's case.

Conclusion

"After 17 months of running for president as a man, and four days of internalizing the loss of a dream, Hillary Clinton conceded on June 7, in the finest speech of her career" (Sheehy 2008). In that speech, Clinton elaborated the gender-specific meanings of her candidacy that she had often left unarticulated during the campaign, particularly with her ringing statement that, "Although we weren't able to shatter that highest, hardest glass ceiling this time, thanks to you, it's got about 18 million cracks in it" (Milbank 2008). Bringing together the material presented here, we see that in her 2008 campaign, Hillary Clinton ran first and foremost on an "equality" platform that emphasized her experience and thus tried to avoid the pitfalls of running "as a woman." The campaign's use of feminine gender cues in order to mobilize women in the pre–New Hampshire period—a strategy that carried risks well illustrated by the October "gender card" flap—gave way by March to a regendered, masculinized strategy of toughness and "testicular fortitude."

Ultimately, while toughness is a leading unstated credential for the presidency and Clinton was thus obliged to demonstrate it, in her particular case it seems to have backfired to some extent because preexisting narratives about Clinton already framed her as overly ambitious. Though to some degree the campaign attempted early on to create a message conveying both "masculine" strength and "feminine" caring, the balance tipped in March to a much tougher fighter image infused with hypermasculine imagery, leaving us to wonder whether a campaign more grounded in a distinctly feminine voice might actually have succeeded.

What impact did Clinton's gender strategy have on her electoral chances? A concrete answer may be difficult to come by. Scholars agree that ideology and party are generally more powerful voting cues than candidate sex. But during a primary process, party is not a distinguishing cue, arguably making sex (and other attributes of the particular candidates) a more important voter consideration; this was probably particularly true in 2008, since Senators Obama and Clinton had relatively similar voting patterns in the Senate (Argetsinger and Roberts 2008, 124; Nather 2008) and rather similar policy proposals.[33] As indicated by the literature reviewed in Chapter 2, gender preferences rarely seem to run in women candidates' favor when US citizens contemplate the presidency, though in some electoral contexts, women candidates benefit by being women (particularly among women voters) (Dolan 1998; Smith and Fox 2001).

A thorough review of voting results is beyond the scope of this chapter; suffice it to say that Clinton drew strong but not unilateral support among white Democratic women—indeed, she won less than 50 percent of white women in only a handful of states. (We leave aside for now the important story of Clinton's fall from grace with African American women.)

Whatever its precise impact on her vote totals, the complicated task of a woman presidential candidate seeking the support of both women and men voters was further complicated, we believe, by Clinton's gender strategy. As the coverage of the gender card episode reveals, public and media reactions to Clinton's messages were mixed. But so, too, were the Clinton team's messages, which alternated not just between feminine and masculine appeals, but between hinting at gender bias and patently sticking to her message of fighting to win on equal terms. Nevertheless, it bears noting that in many of the states treated to the Clinton campaign's testosterone blitzkrieg, Clinton won (though these were also, for the most part, states where she already had stronger voter support).

Whatever its impact upon the vote, the campaign's complex gender messaging contributed to media characterizations of Clinton as "hysterical" and suffering from "multiple personality disorder." In late February, the media watchdog website Media Matters captured a series of comments from old and new media outlets that scrutinized Clinton's emotional state (Media Matters 2008e). Their list included columnist Maureen Dowd's declaration that Clinton "has turned into Sybil. We've had Experienced Hillary, Soft Hillary, Hard Hillary, Misty Hillary, Sarcastic Hillary, Joined-at-the-Hip-to-Bill Hillary, Her-Own-Person-Who-Just-Happens-to-Be-Married-to-a-Former-President Hillary, It's-My-Turn Hillary, Cuddly Hillary, Let's-Get-Down-in-the-Dirt-and-Fight-Like-Dogs Hillary."

Dowd's counterpart at the *Chicago Tribune*, Jill Zuckerman, argued that Clinton's messaging "comes across as a little schizophrenic" (Ibid.). Going further, the *Atlantic Monthly* described a candidate prone to "a paralyzing schizophrenia—one day a shots-'n'-beers brawler, the next a Hallmark Channel mom" (Green 2008b).[34] In the blogs, CNBC host Lawrence Kudlow offered his armchair analysis of the senator's emotional health in a post titled "Hillary's Mental Roller Coaster": "Is it just me, or has anyone else noticed Hillary's erratic, roller-coaster, mood swings these past few weeks? She's all over the map. Irritable and angry. Manic. Pessimistic and sad. One minute she's shedding tears, the next minute she's shouting and attacking, then she's sarcastically ripping on Obama, and on and on it goes." Kudlow concluded, "Now I'm no psychiatrist, far from it, but I think a simple answer is that Senator Clinton could be depressed. . . . Maybe Hillary's taking meds, but they're just not working for her?" (Media Matters 2008e). On February 26, Jack Cafferty of CNN's *Situation Room* concluded that Clinton's antics were "resembling someone with multiple personality disorder" (Ibid.).

Clearly these characterizations were brought to the campaign by media commentators themselves. But to some degree, the Clinton campaign's complicated and incongruent gender messaging contributed all too readily to characterizations rooted in age-old stereotypes of women as inconsistent, overly emotional, and ultimately, untrustworthy. In the end, as one postmortem analysis observed, candidate Clinton had seemed "uncertain how to reconcile her sex with her political persona" (Kantor 2008c).

Notes

1. News release at www.hillaryclinton.com/news/release/view/?id=3716 (accessed October 20, 2007; site now discontinued).
2. "It is clear," Clinton argued, "that if left unchecked, Saddam Hussein will continue to increase his capacity to wage biological and chemical warfare, and will keep trying to develop nuclear weapons. Should he succeed in that endeavor, he could alter the political and security landscape of the Middle East, which as we know all too well affects American security" (Clinton 2002). It may be that as a senator from New York, Clinton could not have cast any vote other than one in support of the Iraq war, given the strong feelings in the state about the September 11 terrorist attacks. Feelings about the war were particularly strong among the Jewish constituency, which at that time saw the vote to authorize the war as "protecting Israel" (Cook 2008b).
3. Some might point out that in 2002, when he publicly opposed the war, Obama was a state senator from a reliably liberal Chicago district unlikely to

punish him for taking such a stance and was not in possession of the intelligence reports provided to Senator Clinton as a member of the Senate Armed Services Committee (to our knowledge, this is not an argument Clinton made in her own defense). Moreover, there is evidence now suggesting that the intelligence reports Clinton read were manipulated by the administration to build the case for war. Like many of her Senate colleagues, Clinton apparently never availed herself of the full, classified report that provided some reason to doubt the administration's claims about the Iraqi threat.

   4. Shortly after giving the first-ever graduation speech offered by a student at Wellesley College, Clinton earned her stripes as a children's rights advocate through her work in this area while still at Yale Law School. Nearly three decades later, her famous speech at the 1995 Beijing Conference on women's rights called upon the world's nations to consider the most vexing of women's issues (domestic violence, literacy, hunger, genital mutilation, slavery, etc.), earning Clinton a reputation for unwavering commitment to women's rights as human rights: "As long as discrimination and inequities remain so commonplace around the world—as long as girls and women are valued less, fed last, overworked, underpaid, not schooled and subjected to violence in and out of their homes—the potential of the human family to create a peaceful, prosperous world will not be realized" (Clinton 1995).

   5. By late March, however, a *New York Times*/CBS poll found that Obama had pulled even: equal percentages (61 percent) of the general public were "confident" in both Clinton and Obama to "make the right decisions about health care" (*New York Times*/CBS, March 2008b).

   6. Senator Clinton attempted to strike a balanced tone on this issue by cosponsoring the Prevention First Act of 2005, which distanced the senator from abortion politics by refocusing the reproductive policy discussion on expanding contraception access. She also moderated her abortion rhetoric in a 2005 speech to the Family Planning Advocates of New York State on the anniversary of *Roe v. Wade* by focusing on the centrality of birth control to limiting unintended pregnancy and therefore abortion. While most of the speech was traditional prochoice rhetoric, one line captured headlines: "We can all recognize that abortion in many ways represents a sad, even tragic choice to many, many women" (Clinton 2005).

   7. Despite Obama's record of voting "present" (rather than affirmatively voting in favor of abortion rights) on abortion bills while in the Illinois state senate, Clinton ultimately lost the endorsement of NARAL Pro-Choice America to Senator Obama in May 2008, perhaps in part because of these tactical choices.

   8. This analysis of the Clinton team's message strategies is based upon a small and purposive sample of her campaign advertisements. Our sampling criteria were three. First, we looked for advertisements run by the campaign leading up to the most crucial contests, such as Iowa and New Hampshire in early January and Texas and Ohio in early March. Second, we focused on ads that received media attention in the news outlets and blogs we monitored throughout the campaign. Finally, we sought to illustrate the range of gender strategies employed by the campaign. Our findings must therefore be treated as suggestive rather than conclusive.

   9. Clinton television ad, August 2007, http://marcambinder.theatlantic .com/archives/2007/08/hillary_clintons_first_ad.php.

10. Clinton ad, Decmeber 13, 2007, www.youtube.com/watch?v= jbUurCogvS4&feature=PlayList&p=F4DAC3EA3738244F&playnext=1&index=1.

11. Clinton ad, December 13, 2007, www.youtube.com/watch?v=FBPdKT-fyq8.

12. Clinton ad, December 13, 2007, http://thecaucus.blogs.nytimes.com/2007/12/13/clinton-ad-dorothy-speaks.

13. Democratic contender Senator John Edwards's Christmas ad, titled "Season," did not feature his family. With a lighted Christmas tree in the background, Edwards appeared alone, speaking directly into the camera about the need to care for the poor and the homeless (http://hotair.com/archives/2007/12/19/video-john-edwards-awful-christmas-ad).

14. Clinton ad, December 20, 2007, www.youtube.com/watch?v=yz BvQ9EeF3k.

15. For conservatives, the ad drove home the association between Hillary Clinton and liberalism. As one blogger complained: "All of the gifts are funded in one way or another with your money. And she's portraying herself as a thoughtful gift-giver by taking your money and giving it back to you in the form of expensive government programs, some or all of which you might not actually want or need. If that doesn't typify liberal thinking, I don't know what does" (http://hotair.com/archives/2007/12/19/video-hillarys-unintentionally-revealing-christmas-ad).

16. For example, during our monitoring of Clinton's campaign website, logging into the site at least once per week over twenty-six weeks, we found only two other videos (beyond the testimonials discussed here) within the "Video" and "HillTV" sections of the site that were labeled as featuring women specifically.

17. Clinton ad, February 27, 2008, http://guerillawomentn.blogspot.com/2008/02/hillary-ad-tribute-to-ann-richards.html.

18. Clinton video, October 31, 2007, www.youtube.com/watch?v= F3Nq6jd579E.

19. In fact, in her comments from which that punch line was drawn, Clinton had been talking about the previous week's Republican debate; the reason she had been attacked by the Republican candidates in that venue, she had said, was "because I have stood against George Bush and his failed policies" (October 30 Democratic Debate Transcript 2007).

20. Searching our mainstream news outlets for the terms "gender card" and "Clinton" yielded only 1 story containing both terms in October prior to the Drexel debate, compared with 17 stories in the seven days between October 31 and November 7. Between January and September 2007, the terms "gender card" and "Clinton" had appeared in a total of only 3 stories in these outlets.

21. One might wonder what "playing the gender card" means, regardless of who might have played it. In none of the coverage we analyzed did anyone formally define this electoral term of art, but in most instances the term was used to suggest that Clinton raised gender deliberately to gain advantage, and that in doing so, she assumed a victim status that was unbecoming of her efforts to become president. Rarely did anyone use the term to argue that the senator was making legitimate claims of bias in the election process, or that she was noting real barriers to women seeking executive office. It bears mentioning that despite the similarity in terms, it is likely that public discourse around "the gen-

der card" differs substantially from "the race card" because of differences in the nature of public attitudes and political formations regarding gender versus race (see Mendelberg 2001, 239–246; Winter 2008).

22. We return in Chapter 8 to Ferraro's other controversial comments on race versus gender.

23. Clinton ad, February 29, 2008, www.youtube.com/watch?v= N-VFA7L2RcE.

24. Clinton ad, April 21, 2008, www.youtube.com/watch?v= Mt6W3rVTLhw.

25. Jack Nicholson ad, March 1, www.youtube.com/watch?v=-h2GF51s-ss.

26. This effort to evoke positive sexual connotations was exceedingly rare in the discourse around Hillary Clinton in 2008. It may be that references to Clinton's sexuality were few due to her age; as we discuss further in Chapter 8, early indications reveal far more such references to vice presidential candidate Sarah Palin's sexual attractiveness.

27. Clinton ad, May 4, 2000, http://archives.cnn.com/2000/ ALLPOLITICS/stories/05/03/hillary.ad/index.html.

28. The Clinton campaign website featured four sections. The "headline" area, which remained relatively unchanged throughout the duration of the primary, featured links to allow visitors to make contributions and sign up for campaign news. Below the headline area were the "spotlight," video, and blog areas of the site. "Spotlight" items were short "news" items about a wide range of topics. Our specific finding is that women- and children-specific topics were quite limited: The issue of equal pay was featured on 4 days we sampled (out of 26 days, one per week from mid-December though mid-June), as were breast cancer and women's history month. A celebrating women theme was featured on 8 of our sampled days, and Texas women specifically on 5 days. Children's issues appeared in the spotlight on 1 day.

29. Specifically, we focused on the period from January 4–13, 2008 (immediately following the Iowa and New Hampshire contests) and from June 1–10, 2008 (straddling Clinton's withdrawal from the race). Our search terms were "(Clinton OR Obama) AND histor! AND (win OR victor!) AND (gender OR rac!) AND (Iowa OR New Hampshire) AND (woman OR black)," occurring in tandem with either "Iowa" or "New Hampshire." Across the six media outlets, we found 31 news stories that contained relevant discussion; across these 31 articles, 49 relevant quotes were cataloged and analyzed.

30. These articles also tended to argue that either nomination would mean victory primarily for a particular demographic group, undermining the wider implications of either an Obama or Clinton nomination, and implicitly pitted the two groups against one another, such as in this passage: "Either Senator Barack Obama will be the first African-American or Senator Hillary Rodham Clinton will be the first woman to win the presidential nomination of a major American political party. One of them will take the stage at Denver's Pepsi Center, specked with confetti and soaked in history as a culminating figure of one of the great ideological movements of the last century—civil rights or women's rights" (Leibovich 2008d).

31. Clinton's speech can be viewed at www.youtube.com/watch?v= kRJWmAS7z2I.

32. Interestingly, in that story, journalist Philip Kennicott gave the photo a masculine-gendered nuance: "The hangdog image conveys a single, tight visual message: fatigue, sadness, *impotence*" (emphasis ours).

33. In fact, the liberal Americans for Democratic Action gave Senators Clinton and Obama the identical "liberal quotient" for their voting records in 2007 (Americans for Democratic Action 2008). The liberal quotient rating is the percentage of liberal votes the senator cast out of a possible twenty votes on key issues. Both senators scored a 75 in 2007, lower than the average for Democratic senators in that year.

34. The reference was to Clinton's hour-long special on the Hallmark channel, known for its heavily female audience and family-friendly fare. Paid for by the Clinton campaign and aired on February 4, the night before Super Tuesday, the unusual event featured Clinton being questioned by a live audience in New York along with remote questioners from campaign debates in twenty-two states (Stelter 2008b).

6

Quantity vs. Quality
of Media Coverage

Let's face it. In the grand scheme of things, Clinton is The Get. . . .
She's the number-one seed. The road to the White House goes
through her.   —*Huffington Post*, December 2007

Am I feeling bitter? You bet. Not because Hillary Clinton seems more
likely than not to lose—I can live with that pretty easily—but because
of how she's likely to lose. Because the press doesn't like her.
Because any time a woman raises her voice half a decibel she
instantly becomes shrill.
     —Kevin Drum, *Washington Monthly*, January 2008

I n February of 2008, with the crucial Ohio and Texas primaries less
than two weeks away, the cast of *Saturday Night Live* (*SNL*) performed a skit lampooning media coverage of the election. Fresh off a
months-long television writers' strike, the skit injected some biting commentary on the media into mainstream discourse and became an instant
campaign season sensation.

As the skit began, an *SNL* player impersonating CNN reporter
Campbell Brown introduced her fellow mock journalists by saying,
"Like nearly everyone in the news media, the three of us are totally in
the tank for Senator Obama"; she then introduced the (impersonated)
Senator Obama as "soon, knock on wood, the first black president of the
United States." The first question directed to the faux Obama: "Senator
Obama, are you comfortable? Is there anything we can get for you?" To
the guffaws of the studio audience, the "journalist" prefaced his next
question by explaining, "I just really, really, really, really, really want
you to be the next president. . . . I was afraid you might be mad at me
because, you know, all the shilling for you in my campaign coverage has

been so obvious." The mock Obama responded, "As I travel around this country, I'm hearing the same sentiment from every journalist I meet." Reporters, he said, "are tired of being told, 'You journalists have to stay neutral. You can't openly take sides in a political campaign.' And they're saying, 'Yes We Can.'"[1]

The *SNL* skit echoed a repeated complaint of the Clinton campaign that the press had covered Obama far less critically than Senator Clinton, and after it aired, the campaign chided reporters by invoking the skit repeatedly. In fact, Clinton referenced it in her (real) televised debate with Obama in Cleveland just a few days later, saying, "Well, can I just point out that in the last several debates, I seem to get the first question all the time. I don't mind, you know, I'll be happy to field them. But I do find it curious. If anybody saw Saturday Night Live, maybe we should ask Barack if he's comfortable and needs another pillow" ("The Democratic Debate in Cleveland" 2008).

The *SNL* skit also captured a perception of media bias among many Clinton supporters. At a Clinton rally the day after the Cleveland debate, one reporter observed, "When someone stood to castigate the news media for being unfair to her, the audience cheered, with some even turning to cast a collective evil eye on the reporters in the high school gymnasium" (Steinberg 2008). Another observed a similar scene in Ohio, where a Clinton supporter

> turned toward the back of the gym where a penned-off area held perhaps 30 reporters and a half-dozen local and network cameras. "You guys have been so unfair to this lady," he declared. "I can't believe you." With that, the crowd of more than 1,200 people roared with approval, many of them rising from their seats to hoot at the media and cheer the questioner. Many turned their cameras on the reporters. (Seelye 2008b)

Newsweek reported in early March that "in these last beleaguered weeks, women started showing up in waves at Clinton headquarters—women who [said] they had never volunteered in a campaign before." According to one grassroots organizer, who would go on to found a group called Clinton Supporters Count Too aimed at mobilizing women in swing states to vote against Senator Obama, "There was just an outpouring about the way she was being treated by the media. . . . It was something we hadn't seen in a long time. We all felt, as women, we had made a lot of progress, and we saw this as an attack of misogyny that was trying to beat her down" (Brown 2008).

The *SNL* skit also captured the sentiments of NOW president Kim

Gandy. Roughly two weeks before the skit aired, Gandy had castigated media coverage in an online column titled "Ignorance and Venom: The Media's Deeply Ingrained Sexism": "At this moment it feels like [Clinton] is a stand-in for every woman who has ever tried to get ahead and be taken seriously by the powers that be" (Gandy 2008). Gandy later observed, after Clinton's campaign had ended, "There was an enormous amount of sexism. She was called a bitch, a witch, shrill, cackle, cleavage—all words that come to mind—and, what was it, thick ankles? There were comments made about her that would never ever be made about a male candidate." Gandy continued, "I expected a little bit. I expected some. But I didn't expect this level of venom directed at her from people in the mainstream media. I expect it from the fringe Fox News types, sure. But from NPR, from CNN, from NBC and MSNBC, no, I didn't" (quoted in Jill Rosen 2008).

Many (though certainly not all) in the general public also shared the perception of unfair treatment of Senator Clinton. A Pew Center poll taken in early February found that "Majorities of Democrats and Democratic-leaning independents say news organizations have been fair in the way they have treated both Barack Obama (71% fair) and Hillary Clinton (53% fair). However, nearly a third (31%) say the press has been too tough on Clinton; just 8% believe the press has been too tough on Obama" (Pew Center 2008e). A *New York Times*/CBS poll taken in late February found "nearly half of those respondents who described themselves as voters in Democratic primaries or caucuses said the news media had been 'harder' on Mrs. Clinton than other candidates. (Only about 1 in 10 suggested the news media had been harder on Mr. Obama.)" (*New York Times*/CBS poll 2008a).[2]

A few in the media agreed that Clinton was being treated differently (though, as discussed in Chapter 3, few were willing to attribute that different treatment to sexism). Veteran journalist Jeff Jarvis claimed that SNL's "shaming" of the media captured one of the biggest uncovered stories of the election: the media's "strange tip-toeing around Barack Obama in this campaign." Jarvis argued that the "empty vessel" of Obama's rhetoric had not been challenged or investigated by the press (Reliable Sources 2008b). Veteran political analyst Charlie Cook of the *Cook Political Report* echoed this sentiment: *Saturday Night Live,* he said, "should win an award" for exposing the "fabulous, fawning" coverage bestowed on Senator Obama (Cook 2008a). *New York Times* columnist Frank Rich, a tough public critic of Hillary Clinton, captured the sense of outrage among many of her supporters: "Clinton fans [believe] their highly substantive candidate was unfairly undone by a lightweight showboat who got a free ride from an often misogynist press and from naïve young people who lap up messianic language as if it were Jim Jones's Kool-Aid" (Rich 2008a).

As it happened, the *SNL* skit was closely followed by the release of a weekly study of media coverage by the Project for Excellence in Journalism (PEJ). That report found that in the previous week, Senator Obama had gotten a greater share of media attention, much of it negative. "Clinton's charges of a pro-Obama tilt reverberated in the media echo chamber last week," the report noted, while "Obama's life and record came under a heightened degree of scrutiny." The PEJ report seemed to confirm that reporters, chastened by the *SNL* skit and the Clinton campaign's repeated complaints, had suddenly turned a more critical lens on Senator Obama. Reflecting this moment of media self-examination, ABC's Diane Sawyer asked, "Have all of us in the media used boxing gloves on Clinton and kid gloves on Obama?" (Project for Excellence in Journalism 2008c).

Roughly two months later, as her chances for winning the nomination faded but her supporters continued to turn out in large numbers, Senator Clinton directly raised the issue of media sexism. "The manifestation of some of the sexism that has gone on in this campaign is somehow more respectable, or at least more accepted, and . . . there should be equal rejection of the sexism and the racism when it raises its ugly head," she told the *Washington Post*. "It does seem as though the press at least is not as bothered by the incredible vitriol that has been engendered by the comments by people who are nothing but misogynists" (L. Romano 2008).

By the time Senator Clinton suspended her presidential campaign in early June, criticism of media sexism had grown into a firestorm among Clinton supporters and feminist groups. Various women's groups and bloggers called for a boycott of CNN and MSNBC, thought to be among the worst offenders, and NOW erected a virtual "Media Hall of Shame" to highlight examples of what it deemed sexist media treatment of Clinton (National Organization for Women 2008). In a fascinating turn of events, a campaign that had begun by rejecting the strategy of running "as a woman" ended amid complaints that sexism had brought down Hillary Clinton.

Assessing Media Bias in the 2008 Primary

Our aim in this chapter and the next is to assess those claims. While it will be beyond our scope to prove or disprove the degree to which media coverage affected the vote, we will show evidence that addresses claims of media bias.

The question of whether the media were unfair to Hillary Clinton has an empirical and a normative side. The normative question is whether the media adhered to abstract standards of objectivity and responsibility when covering this historic election—a question about which thinking people may disagree. But empirically, as we will discuss in the next section, the case seems clear that the tone of media coverage of Clinton was more negative than the tone of Obama coverage, particularly during the critical early stages of the campaign, and continued to be tilted against Clinton in a variety of ways as the campaign wore on—patterns we document with primary and secondary data.

The question of media sexism, however, proves more complicated. Some of the patterns of gendered media coverage predicted by the women in politics literature were evident in mainstream news coverage of Clinton's campaign, although many were not. We will also argue in these two chapters that gender bias does not offer a full explanation for the ways the media portrayed Clinton's campaign. Much of her coverage reflected routines for covering elections that the national media have long relied on: "horse-race" and "game-framed" coverage; scripted coverage of the candidates' "character"; and heavy attention to what the media deemed to be "defining moments" on the campaign trail. These ostensibly gender-neutral routines became intertwined with gender stereotypes at key moments in the campaign; more broadly, these media routines lead directly to the negative tone of much of Clinton's coverage. Clinton's troubled relationship with the national press corps also proved decisive. Her campaign's press management style contributed directly to the negative coverage she received, as did some reporters' preexisting views of Senator Clinton herself.

Ultimately, though outright sexism was not absent from mainstream news, it was not as widespread as many of the media critics seemed to believe. A crucial distinction appears, however, between "traditional" news outlets and the "new" media—the world of cable news and the political "blogosphere" in particular. Traditional news outlets did not *systematically* cover Hillary Clinton's campaign in clearly sexist ways; in those venues, gendering and sexism took more subtle (though perhaps no less pernicious) forms. Indeed, mainstream media sources often (though not always) filtered out blatantly sexist and sometimes ugly, even violent, portrayals of Senator Clinton that were prevalent in cable news and especially the Internet—portrayals that we describe further in the final section of this chapter.

Gendering, Sexism, and Media Bias Across Media Outlets

Before we discuss the evidence for our case, it is important to recall that "media bias" can be a difficult thing to define and demonstrate. Bias can take various forms (some more problematic than others), and what appears "biased" to one observer can seem accurate and objective to another. "Bias" is also a difficult term to use precisely, because it can describe the *amount* of coverage a candidate or issue receives, the *content* and *tone* of that coverage, or the presumed *motives* driving that content. The empirical studies we document below indicate, for example, no discernible bias against Senator Clinton in terms of the amount of coverage she received, yet they do show a more negative tone within her coverage. That tonal "bias" is empirically verifiable, but the news media's motives in covering Clinton in these ways are something about which we can only offer educated guesses, based in scholarly research and the words of reporters and editors themselves. In this analysis, we will talk more in terms of amount, content, and tone of media coverage rather than in terms of "bias."

It is also important to note that "negative" coverage is distinguishable from "sexist" coverage. *Negative* coverage includes content or tone that criticizes the candidate or paints her character, her policy positions, or her campaign tactics in an unflattering light (see, for example, Farnsworth and Lichter 2007, 118). *Sexist* coverage devalues female politicians (and voters) vis-à-vis male politicians (see Falk 2008, 155). Defined in this way, sexist coverage is also negative coverage (at least in the ways it has usually been operationalized and studied by researchers) because it evokes problematic gender stereotypes and diminishes the female candidate's stature.

It must be noted, however, that even outright sexist coverage might not be an unalloyed disadvantage for a female candidate if it evokes a rally effect among supportive voters. Indeed, it is difficult to discuss the topic of Hillary Clinton's presidential campaign without considering whether, at least to some degree, perceptions of media sexism actually may have helped Clinton with some voters—as the anecdotes at the beginning of this chapter suggest (see also Seelye and Bosman 2008). It is also worth considering that sexist media coverage might also include coverage that "goes easy" on a female candidate in the presumption that, as a woman, she cannot withstand or should not be subjected to tough questioning and scrutiny.[3] All sexist coverage, in other words, is not necessarily negative in the sense that it undermines the female candidate's chances of election. Likewise, all negative coverage of female candidates is not necessarily sexist, as when female candidates are treated negatively in the same terms as male candidates.

Determining whether those terms are equal often brings us to the more subtle process of *gendering* in which stereotypes about male and female attributes shape the content and tone of media coverage (Falk 2008, 155–156; Gidengil and Everitt 2003). Gendering can be difficult to analyze rigorously because it often involves a perceived or implicit subtext to the words that are actually spoken or written (to use the formal language of content analysis, gendered negativity is more often "latent" than "manifest" in the media text). To a significant degree, the most pernicious gendered negativity is found in these more subtle aspects of media coverage. Again, as with sexist coverage, gendered coverage might in some circumstances be helpful rather than hurtful to female candidates, as when the media ascribe stereotypically feminine attributes to a candidate that would actually be valued by voters in that particular office (see Kahn 1996)—though a question then remains whether that kind of campaign coverage then becomes an albatross around the neck of the elected female official once she begins to govern. More typically, however—particularly in US presidential politics—gender stereotypes and gendered media coverage are not helpful to women seeking power.

Bearing these definitions in mind, we should not necessarily expect to find large amounts of overt, egregious sexism in mainstream media coverage, especially in newspapers' news pages and on broadcast TV news programs. (In this new era of "24/7" cable news programs, where the lines between "news" and "opinion" have become increasingly blurred, it has perhaps become easier than ever for average citizens to lose track of these distinctions, as we discuss further below.) Among other reasons, editors trained in the norms of objectivity and "good taste" probably screen out much (though not all) of the crudest forms of sexism that might otherwise make their way into mainstream news.[4] This may explain why Pippa Norris, in her study of media coverage of female leaders worldwide, found only a handful of examples: "If one looks very hard," she contends, "one can very occasionally come across clear examples of gratuitous remarks about personal appearance or simple sexism" (Norris 1997, 159).

At the same time, there are reasons to expect at least some overt sexism will get through the mainstream media's editorial filter. The fact that female leaders are less rare in many other countries than in the United States may contribute to (and reflect) a more overtly sexist media environment in the US media; at the same time, the uniquely media-driven presidential elections we have here in the United States (Iyengar and McGrady 2006; Patterson 1994) make any media sexism arguably more consequential than in strong party political systems that do not require individual, "entrepreneurial" candidates to appeal to voters directly via the mass media. Erica Falk's (2008) study of newspaper coverage of historical and contemporary female contenders for the presidency discovered crude sexism on more than one occasion (though she also notes that "some of the most explicitly sexist comments found in the papers were direct quotes from citizens," not reporters [Ibid., 34]).

But Falk's most persuasive and troubling evidence lies in the more subtle and more consistent patterns she found, such as the press's persistent habit across many decades of treating each new female contender as a historically unprecedented "first." Though such coverage is not overtly sexist and may even seem on the surface congratulatory, Kathleen Hall Jamieson (1995) reminds us that this way of thinking about women politicians contributes to the erasure of women's history and the pigeonholing of women as nonleaders. Along similar lines, Elisabeth Gidengil and Joanna Everitt (2003) found clear patterns of gendered coverage of female candidates in Canadian elections, in that the press highlighted and exaggerated perceptions of aggressive and combative rhetoric (which violates stereotypical expectations of female decorum) to a greater degree than similar behavior by male candidates. As these examples illustrate, media coverage that is not prima facie or de facto "sexist" may nonetheless have gendered impacts. Gidengil and Everitt (2003) use the term "gendered mediation" to describe the way that gender norms can be inscribed in media coverage, often in subtle ways.

Gender Bias on Cable News

It is also important to note that "the media" is comprised of a wide variety of outlets, and that individual media outlets sometimes treat candidates in markedly different ways. The PEJ and Shorenstein Center report found, for example, that "network morning news is notable for the degree to which it offered an exceptionally positive personal impression of Hillary Clinton. Fully 84% of the assertions studied in those programs projected positive master narratives of the former First Lady, some 20 percentage points more positive than about Obama" (Project for Excellence in Journalism 2008a; see also Hoyt 2008b).

The most frequent target of charges of anti-Clinton, sexist bias was cable news and other venues where news and opinion mix more freely. As media expert Jamieson noted, "Largely, the problem was on cable and in the blogosphere and on the Internet, and that's a relatively small

audience. . . . But while it was limited, it was limited to influential people" (quoted in Seelye and Bosman 2008). The audiences for the more
opinionated cable news outlets are much smaller than for broadcast
news (Farnsworth and Lichter 2007, 24–25). Among the cable networks,
MSNBC came in for the most frequent criticism, in particular against
one of its biggest personalities, Chris Matthews, anchor of *Hardball* and
a frequent commentator on other MSNBC shows. *Hardball* typically
draws fewer than 1 million viewers per night; in early 2008, the 7 p.m.
show was viewed by an average of 660,000 people per night (Leibovich
2008a), as compared with an average nightly audience in 2007 of over 6
million each for the two leading network evening news programs,
ABC's *World News Tonight* and NBC's *Nightly News* (Project for
Excellence in Journalism 2007b). Given the nature of its programming,
however, *Hardball* and other cable news shows tend to draw more politically knowledgeable viewers, which also means people who are more
likely to vote—one measure of the greater influence such shows might
have compared with broadcast television news (Pew Research Center
2007a). MSNBC's audience skews liberal in its self-identification
(Project for Excellence in Journalism 2007b), which also means it was
more likely to be watched by Democratic primary voters.

The liberal watchdog website Media Matters decried Matthews'
"history of degrading comments about women, in which he focuses on
the physical appearances of his female guests and of other women discussed on his program" (quoted in Leibovich 2008a). More specifically,
critics pointed to Matthews' clear anti-Clinton comments, some of
which were not-so-subtly sexist, like his claim just after Clinton won the
New Hampshire primary that "the reason she may be a front-runner, is
her husband messed around" (see Chapter 4). (Matthews later apologized on air for this comment after women's groups organized a letter-
writing protest, though he also told the *New York Times* that "I was
tonally inaccurate but factually true" [Leibovich 2008a].) As one
lengthy profile of Matthews, published in the *New York Times
Magazine*, observed, "it's hard to watch Matthews and conclude that he
has been anything less than enthralled by Obama and, at the very least,
is sick of Clinton" (Ibid.).

Other MSNBC commentators did not hide their disdain for Clinton
either. In addition to correspondent David Shuster's comment that the
Clinton campaign had "pimped out" daughter Chelsea Clinton in their
efforts to persuade superdelegates, MSNBC's top-rated commentator
Keith Olbermann (whose show *Countdown* draws around one and a half
million viewers per night) drew ire for his hard-hitting tirades following
several of Hillary Clinton's most notable campaign missteps (such as

her reminder that the assassination of Robert F. Kennedy had occurred before the 1968 Democratic nomination had been settled), and for his less substantive, more questionable comments. Most notably, in a discussion with *Newsweek*'s Howard Fineman, who suggested that someone in the Democratic Party needed to "stop this thing" (the ongoing Democratic nomination contest), Olbermann replied, "Right. Somebody who can take her into a room and only he comes out."[5] (This example also reminds us that problematic comments can come from reporters or their sources, from show hosts or from their guests, but these distinctions are probably lost on the general public, who may take away from such moments simply a general impression of "the media.")

More outrageous, in the eyes of critics, were comments by MSNBC's Tucker Carlson that "when she [Hillary Clinton] comes on television, I involuntarily cross my legs" (a reflex that Carlson often told viewers he had to a variety of women) and commentator Mike Barnicle's observation on MSNBC's *Morning Joe* that "when [Clinton] reacts the way she reacts to Obama with just the look . . . looking like everyone's first wife standing outside a probate court, OK? Looking at him that way, all I could think of . . . was this fall, if it's McCain that she's facing, McCain is likable. She's not" (Media Matters 2008a, 2008i).

The collective behavior of the MSNBC commentators led one writer for the liberal *New Republic* (not a fan of Hillary Clinton himself) to charge the network with "using Hillary Hatred to fuel its coverage in a similar fashion to how Fox News uses Democrat Hatred to excite its viewers":

> MSNBC's coverage can lead to a perverse sort of cognitive dissonance in viewers like, well, me. Throughout the primary process, I often found myself much more bullish on the Illinois Senator's chances after watching MSNBC than I had any reason to be. After Obama's Iowa victory, for instance, I remember hearing Matthews' description of a giant "wave" of Obamamania sweeping across the nation; surely, the race was over. Likewise, during the month of February, when Obama won eleven straight primaries, I recall watching the network and occasionally convincing myself that Clinton was certain to drop out before Texas and Ohio because her chances had become so diminished. (Chotiner 2008)

This perspective on the 2008 nomination race—that Barack Obama was the inevitable nominee and that Clinton's choice to remain in the race was irrational and harmful—was one of the most pernicious patterns of media coverage in this campaign, a pattern, as we will show below, that extended across various media outlets. But it is important to remember that MSNBC is not "the media." It is one news outlet, albeit an influential one among those who watch politics closely.

In this Internet age, when virtually any kind of commentary can be easily disseminated and news consumers can feel flooded by the twenty-four-hour information tide, distinctions among different media outlets are easily lost, and examples of offensive speech can quickly "go viral" and take on a life of their own online. Similar to the dynamic in which a provocative political advertisement sets off a wave of news coverage that compounds the reach and the potential influence of the initial ad itself, certain moments captured and posted online could easily compound the average citizen's impressions of media bias. Perceptions of media sexism can be based upon these vivid viral moments that may not reflect patterns of coverage by an individual news outlet or across new outlets.

The *New York Times* public editor Clark Hoyt noted this dynamic in public reaction to the *Times'* coverage of the 2008 primary election. "Over the course of the campaign," Hoyt wrote in the fall of 2008, "I received complaints that *Times* coverage of [Hillary] Clinton included too much emphasis on her appearance, too many stereotypical words that appeared to put her down and dismiss a woman's potential for leadership and too many snide references to her as cold or unlikable. When I pressed for details, the subject often boiled down to [*Times* columnist Maureen] Dowd" (Hoyt 2008b). Indeed, like Chris Matthews, Dowd's biting commentary came in for bitter criticism among Clinton supporters (and feminists more generally), and we highlight throughout this book some of Dowd's columns that were, if not outright sexist, then certainly gendered. (In her own defense, Dowd argued, "From the time I began writing about politics, I have always played with gender stereotypes and mined them and twisted them to force the reader to be conscious of how differently we view the sexes"; in the 2008 campaign, she claimed, her critics "are asking me to treat Hillary differently than I've treated the male candidates all these years, with kid gloves" [Hoyt 2008b].) But just as MSNBC is not "the media," Maureen Dowd is not the *New York Times*. In the quantitative data reported below, we look for systematic patterns of coverage across traditional news outlets, both print and broadcast television.

Empirical Evidence: Amount of Coverage of Clinton's Campaign

Recall that a substantial media bias against women candidates often involves the amount of coverage they receive relative to male candidates, particularly in races for the Senate and, to an even greater degree, for the White House. Notably, this pattern did not seem to hold in the case of Hillary Clinton's presidential campaign, particularly in the early months of the campaign. As the presumed front-runner as the election season began, Clinton received substantial coverage in the fall of 2007, often more than her competitors (Project for Excellence in Journalism 2007a). As the race between her and Senator Obama tightened, however, the gap in media coverage, though not stark, more often than not favored Obama.

Our data are based upon a close analysis of a random sample of 437 news stories that appeared on the front pages of the *Los Angeles Times*, the *New York Times*, and the *Washington Post* (by definition, these were news items rather than editorial pieces) or aired on the evening news programs of ABC, CBS, and NBC.[6] Our sample is therefore geared toward measuring what the highest-profile mainstream news outlets highlighted in their campaign coverage. These three newspapers are among the top US news outlets in terms of their audience reach and resources for covering presidential campaigns, and in terms of their agenda-setting influence on the rest of the news media (see Bennett, Lawrence, and Livingston 2008, 57–58). The three broadcast TV evening news programs, though suffering (like virtually all mainstream news outlets these days) from declining audiences, still collectively reach approximately 25 million viewers each night and are a key source that many people in the United States report getting their political news from (Pew Research Center 2007a; Project for Excellence in Journalism 2007b).

We coded each story in our sample for a variety of variables related to the amount and content of coverage of the leading presidential candidates.[7] Our analysis focuses on coverage of Senator Clinton and of the two other candidates that offer her best available comparators: Senator Barack Obama (D-IL) and Senator John McCain (R-AZ). As in all real-world "experiments," this one is not perfect. For example, McCain's candidacy was evidently less newsworthy because he secured his party's nomination much earlier, creating fewer opportunities for the personalized, dramatized stories of conflict and competition that tend to dominate the news (Bennett 2008, 40–42). We should be careful, therefore, in drawing far-reaching conclusions based on these three particular candidates. Yet these three still offer the best available comparison for determining whether Clinton was treated differently in the media on account of her sex. Collectively, they were by far the three most newsworthy candidates in 2008 and, coincidentally, all senators (though obviously with different lengths of service); moreover, these two male candidates offer one comparator from each party and allow us to expand our comparison of Clinton's coverage beyond a single (and highly popular) Democratic opponent.

Our data show no significant Clinton disadvantage in terms of the amount of coverage she garnered overall. In fact, her coverage equaled or exceeded that of her main rivals. Looking at the full time period we analyzed, from mid-October of 2007 through mid-June of 2008, she was mentioned in an essentially equal number of paragraphs as Senator Obama and more paragraphs[8] than Senator McCain, and her name appeared as frequently as Obama's in the headlines and lead paragraphs of news stories and more frequently than McCain's. Table 6.1 summarizes these findings.

Table 6.1 also shows that the only measure of prominence on which Clinton's coverage did not equal her main Democratic rival's was television sound bites: On the evening news programs, Clinton was less frequently shown speaking in her own words than was Senator Obama, though she appeared in significantly more sound bites than did John McCain. This is a potentially important difference, given that sound bites represent an increasingly rare opportunity for candidates to speak for themselves (Patterson 1994), and given that female candidates often have greater difficulty gaining control over news presentations of themselves and their agenda (Kahn 1996).

Table 6.1   Media Prominence of Hillary Clinton, Barack Obama, and John McCain, October 2007–June 2008

	Average Number of Paragraphs Mentioning Candidate per Story		Percentage of Stories Mentioning Candidate in Headline/Lead		Average Number of Candidate Sound Bites per TV Story	
	Overall	March–June	Overall	March–June	Overall	March–June
Hillary Clinton	6.88	8.18	47.4	55.4	.39	.47
Barack Obama	6.97	9.41*	47.4	62.7	.54*	.75*
John McCain	3.89**	4.55**	22.0**	25.4**	.26*	.25*

Notes: Data are based upon front-page newspaper and prime-time network news stories.

*Paired-samples t-tests show the difference between Clinton and other candidates to be statistically significant at $p < .05$.

**Statistically significant at $p < .01$.

Crucially, Table 6.1 also indicates that Senator Clinton did fall behind Senator Obama in some measures of media prominence as Obama pulled ahead in the delegate count. Dividing our data into two time periods, one through the end of February 2008 (the month in which John McCain essentially clinched his party's nomination, many crucial Democratic primaries were held that established Obama's lead for that party's nomination, and the news media began to regularly refer to Obama as the leading or front-runner candidate), and the other from the beginning of March through the end of the primary season in June, tells a rather different story than the data overall. In the post-February period, Barack Obama received more coverage than Hillary Clinton, though Clinton still bested John McCain. In particular, Obama was mentioned in more paragraphs per story and in more headlines and leads per story

Figure 6.1 Percentage of Stories per Week Mentioning Hillary Clinton, Barack Obama, and John McCain, November 1, 2007–June 15, 2008

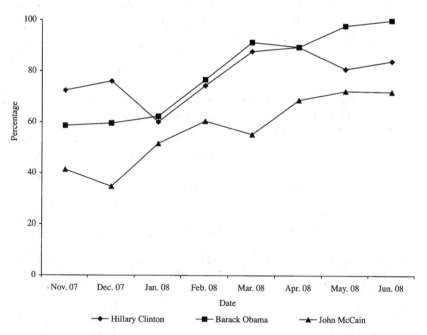

Note: Approximately two weeks in October 2007 were omitted from this figure because the very low number of stories during those two weeks artificially inflates the percentage.

than either Clinton or McCain, only the former difference is statistically significant. Figure 6.1 tracks the relative media prominence of Clinton, Obama, and McCain over the course of the primary season.[9]

The upshot of these data is that, just as Hillary Clinton overcame many of the institutional and fundraising barriers that have blocked other women presidential candidates, she also overcame the most basic media barrier, achieving rough parity in the amount of coverage her campaign garnered. Positioned as the front-runner at the opening of the campaign season, Hillary Clinton was indeed "The Get," as the online political news site the *Huffington Post* described her in the epigraph to this chapter. Unlike any female politician before her, Clinton was a main newsmaker—although in one respect (television sound bites), Clinton received significantly less exposure overall than her main Democratic rival. We will return later to the significance of the decline in her coverage after February.

Given the prominence of Senator Clinton from the very start of the election season and the long, close contest between her and Senator Obama, however, the real question is not the amount but rather the tone of the coverage each received. We consider next whether Hillary Clinton received more negative coverage than her opponents, and whether she was subjected to the kinds of gender-biased news coverage that have plagued other female candidates.

Tone of Coverage

As the research reviewed previously makes clear, news coverage of most presidential candidates—those who receive much coverage at all, that is—tends toward a negative tone. Generally speaking (though with one important exception in the case of "bandwagon" candidates), media negativity increases with increases in coverage and as the presidential campaign wears on (Patterson 1994; Johnston, Hagen, and Jamieson 2004). Thus, a basic dynamic of political campaigns is that all media coverage is not good coverage; often the media spotlight casts candidates in a harsh light. Thus, along with Clinton's rough parity in amounts of coverage came some predictable negativity. As the PEJ documented, during several of the weeks in which Hillary Clinton was a main newsmaker in the 2008 campaign, the tone of her media coverage was markedly negative. For example, she bested Obama by several percentage points in terms of media coverage during the week of February 11–17 (the same week that the media "vaulted Obama into the frontrunner spot"), but the coverage that week "raised serious questions about her campaign's capabilities and her viability" (Project for Excellence in Journalism 2008b).

While Hillary Clinton experienced considerable media negativity, Barack Obama largely managed, at least early in the campaign, to avoid this media pattern. Indeed, media critic Howard Kurtz observed in mid-February that Obama had so far "defied the laws of journalistic gravity" (Kurtz 2008d). [10] Several studies document the favorable treatment of Senator Obama lampooned by *Saturday Night Live*. According to the nonpartisan Center for Media and Public Affairs (CMPA), which has conducted content analyses of election coverage since the mid-1980s, Obama enjoyed a decided advantage in positive coverage early in the campaign. CMPA reported in early March of 2008:

> Since mid-December, five out of six on-air evaluations of Senator Obama (83%) have been positive, while Senator Clinton's coverage has been about evenly balanced (53% positive). Since Super Tuesday, however, Obama's proportion of good press has dropped to 67%, his worst performance during any phase of the campaign, while Clinton's coverage remained balanced (50% positive). For example, from the South Carolina primary (January 26) to Super Tuesday, a remarkable 96% of comments about Obama were positive. (Center for Media and Public Affairs 2008c; see also 2008a)[11]

Our coding of front-page newspaper and evening broadcast news stories about the campaign shows that negative comments were more frequently directed at Hillary Clinton than at her two main rivals. The stories in our sample were significantly more likely to contain at least one negative comment about Clinton than about either Obama or McCain, and the average number of negative paragraphs was greater for Clinton than for Obama or McCain (see Table 6.2). Moreover, when we filter our sample to include only stories that directly mentioned each candidate (not shown in Table 6.2), we find that the average number of paragraphs per story containing negative claims about Barack Obama was .30, for John McCain .35, and for Hillary Clinton .50. Overall, 30 percent of the 334 stories that mentioned Clinton contained at least one negative claim about her.

Front-Runner Status: The "Kiss of Death"

The relative absence of early negative coverage of Obama was a significant feature of the media environment in which Hillary Clinton waged her campaign. In the critical early months leading up to his important

Table 6.2 Tone of Coverage of Hillary Clinton, Barack Obama, and John McCain, October 2007–June 2008

	Percentage of Stories with at Least One Negative Comment About Candidate	Average Number of Paragraphs per Story with Negative Comments About Candidate
Hillary Clinton	23.1	.38
Barack Obama	15.8**	.24**
John McCain	13.3**	.20**

Notes: Data are based upon front-page newspaper and prime-time network news stories.

*Paired-samples t-tests show the difference between Clinton and other candidates to be statistically significant at $p < .05$.

**Statistically significant at $p < .01$.

victories in Iowa and other states, Obama was not treated as the media typically treat a front-runner, but rather as they typically treat an underdog "bandwagon" candidate: with generally positive coverage. But we also note that once Obama became the man to beat, his coverage became less positive—exactly the downward trajectory that the media and politics literature would predict for a front-runner.[12]

Indeed, the Pew/Shorenstein Center report found that "the year 2008 started off extremely well for Obama. Positive assertions commanded 77% of the [media] narrative studied about him from January 1–13. By March 9, the figure had dropped to 53%. During this time statements concerning his inexperience and youth more than doubled in prevalence" (Pew Research Center for People and the Press 2008a). Meanwhile, the report found that Clinton was no longer faring worse compared to Obama in terms of descriptions of her attributes—though largely because descriptions of Obama had become more negative, not because descriptions of Clinton had suddenly become more positive (Project for Excellence in Journalism 2008a).

Our own data, analyzed month by month, show that on average, 23 percent of news stories per month contained at least one negative claim about Hillary Clinton, compared with a monthly average of less than 16 percent for Barack Obama. As seen in Figure 6.2, even as early as November and December of 2007, her monthly negative coverage hit 27 percent and 24 percent, respectively; in contrast, Barack Obama was commented on negatively in less than 7 percent of stories in November, and less than 5 percent in December—though the two candidates were

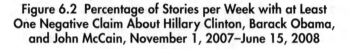

Figure 6.2 Percentage of Stories per Week with at Least One Negative Claim About Hillary Clinton, Barack Obama, and John McCain, November 1, 2007–June 15, 2008

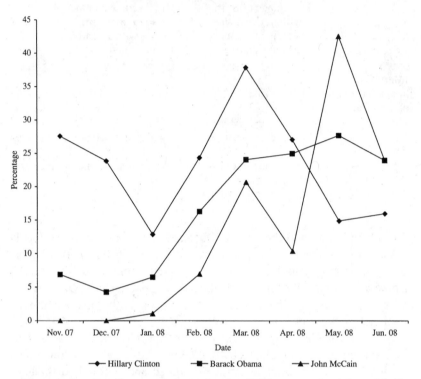

Note: Approximately two weeks in October 2007 were omitted from this figure because the very low number of stories during those two weeks artificially inflates the percentage.

featured in identical numbers of stories each month (in our sample, twenty-nine in November, forty-six in December). Hillary Clinton's best month in terms of the positive/negative ratio was January (the month in which she won New Hampshire), with negative coverage of just under 13 percent. That doubled to 24 percent in February and rose again to just under 38 percent negative stories in March, then dropped to 27 percent in April and down to the 15–16 percent range in May and the first half of June (when she suspended her campaign). In contrast, Barack Obama's negative percentage went from 6.5 percent in January to 16 percent in February and to Clinton-like ranges of 24 percent in March, rising to 25 percent and then to almost 28 percent in April and May.

(McCain's trajectory looked rather different, given that in late 2007 he was considered a political "dead man" but then bounced back to essentially clinch the Republican nomination in February.)

As noted earlier, Barack Obama's negative coverage increased during the month of the *Saturday Night Live* skit, seemingly confirming that the skit pricked journalists' conscience. But February was also the crucial month in which Obama clearly pulled ahead in the delegate count and clearly assumed the front-runner mantle.[13] These findings illustrate a fundamental media dynamic at work. As far back as 1980, scholars have found that "frontrunners . . . consistently experienced the least balanced, least favorable news coverage. Being at the head of the pack almost always means lots of access [to news coverage] but lots of bad press as well" (Robinson and Sheehan 1983, 138–139).

Hillary Clinton entered the race in 2007 as the designated front-runner, but her early, sizable advantage in resources and name recognition translated to only a mixed advantage (at best) in terms of media coverage. Her front-runner status made it almost inevitable that she would be subject to more critical coverage, along with higher expectations for her electoral performance (Patterson 1994; Kurtz 2007).[14] Internal memos from the Clinton campaign show that some members of her team understood the dangers of her front-runner status. Senior adviser Harold Ickes, for example, recognized "the asymmetric risk that accompanies overwhelming front-runner status: the collapse of momentum that would accompany an unexpected loss" (Green 2008b). This risk is why many candidates play the "expectations game," seeking to lower the media's expectations for how they will perform in upcoming contests (Iyengar and McGrady 2006). When asked why both the Clinton and Obama campaigns would try to present themselves as the underdog rather than be perceived as the front-runner, CNN political commentator Gloria Borger replied with a knowing laugh, "because it's a kiss of death" (Reliable Sources 2008a).

Thus, one reason for the more negative *tone* of Clinton's coverage was, ironically, the very thing that ensured that she received equal or superior *amounts* of coverage: her initial front-runner status. We explore this dynamic further in Chapter 7.

Titles, Emotions, and Other Patterns in Coverage of Clinton

Of course, what riled many people about media coverage of this election was not simply the general tone of the coverage, but the sense that there was a specifically gendered cast to the negativity. For example, in January of 2008, blogger John Cole, who stated flatly "I don't want Hillary as President," nevertheless observed,

> Quite frankly, I hate to say this, but I think what we are actually seeing is a double-standard here, and the feminists may be right. This is all about Hillary being a woman. John Edwards has been 150 times as angry the whole campaign, and has built his entire campaign around it. Howard Dean was angry, and people lapped it up. Here, Hillary isn't really angry, just matter-of-fact and frustrated, and people are giving her shit. (quoted in Cole 2008)

While he may not have been correct about Howard Dean, whose 2004 campaign was undone in part precisely by the press's characterization of him as too angry and out of control for the presidency (recall the infamous Dean "scream"), Cole did capture a sense among many observers of a subtle but pervasive double standard.

The women and politics literature yields testable expectations regarding some of the ways gender bias might have appeared in media coverage of Hillary Clinton's presidential campaign: that she would be addressed by her formal title less often than her male counterparts; that she would receive less substantive coverage of her qualifications for office and her issue stances than that given to her male competitors, and more coverage highlighting her (stereotypical) gender-related attributes, particularly emotionality, appearance, spouse, and children; and that her electoral viability would be more frequently questioned. Our random sample of newspaper and broadcast television campaign news offers only limited support for these predictions.

As Falk (2008) and others have shown, female candidates are more often referred to by their first names or as "Mrs." We coded every story in our sample for the title that accompanied each mention of Clinton's name, while also tracking the titles used for the other candidates. On one hand, the data show, Clinton was more likely to be addressed by the title of "Senator" than either of her main Senate colleague rivals. Yet she was also more likely to be addressed by her first name only (see Table 6.3). Uses of "Mrs." were not common and were seen only in the *Los Angeles Times* and the *New York Times*, the latter of which has a long-standing policy of using either "Mrs." or "Ms." depending upon the particular woman's preference—and according to the *Times,* Hillary Clinton prefers "Mrs." (Hoyt 2008a). While these findings would seem partially to confirm the predictions of the women and politics literature, the unique case at hand explains much: "Senator" served to distinguish one

Table 6.3   Titles Used in Coverage of Hillary Clinton, Barack Obama, and John McCain, October 2007–June 2008

	Average Number of Mentions of Surname Preceded by "Senator"	Average Number of Mentions of Candidate by First Name Only
Hillary Clinton	.66	.24
Barack Obama	.54*	.06**
John McCain	.38**	.04**

Notes: Data are based upon front-page newspaper and prime-time network news stories.

*Paired-samples t-tests show the difference between Clinton and other candidates to be statistically significant at $p < .05$.

**Statistically significant at $p < .01$.

famous Clinton from the other, as did "Hillary." Recall that this choice of names was in fact one of the strategic decisions candidate Clinton made when entering the presidential race—a decision apparently partly in response to gendered expectations that have plagued her identity since she first took the national stage—and that "Hillary" (not "Hillary Clinton") became a main logo of the campaign. Frequent uses of her first name, then, cannot be taken as prima facie evidence of gender bias. At the same time, the fact that Senator Clinton came to be referred to so often as simply "Hillary" illustrates how she was constrained by gender norms: Perhaps only a former First Lady who is viewed as "cold" might willingly choose to campaign on her first name.

Coverage of Hillary Clinton did show other of the gendered characteristics predicted by the literature, though not necessarily for the predicted reasons. Chelsea Clinton was mentioned slightly more often than Barack Obama's daughters, and more often than John McCain's children (only the Clinton-McCain difference is statistically significant—see Table 6.4). Clinton's daughter was mentioned in 4.6 percent of stories in our sample, compared with 2.5 percent mentioning Obama's daughters and less than 1 percent mentioning any of McCain's seven children. The news featured Clinton's husband far more often than the other candidates' spouses. Bill Clinton was mentioned in 30 percent of stories in our sample, compared with 4 percent mentioning Michelle Obama and less than 2 percent mentioning Cindy McCain—a difference that is substantively quite significant. Although the prominent discussion of Bill

Table 6.4   Coverage of Personal Characteristics of Hillary Clinton, Barack Obama, and John McCain, by Average Number of Paragraphs per Story, October 2007–June 2008

	Spouse	Children	Qualifications[a]	Appearance	Emotions
Hillary Clinton	.88	.08	.12	.04	.03
Barack Obama	.13**	.03	.03	.04	.03
John McCain	.04**	.01**	.04	.00**	.01

Notes: a. Data reflect the number of paragraphs in which candidate attributes were mentioned, coded according to the following scale: 0 = no mentions; 1 = mentioned in only one paragraph; 2 = mentioned in two to five paragraphs; 3 = mentioned in more than five paragraphs.

*Paired-samples t-tests show the difference between Clinton and other candidates to be statistically significant at $p < .05$.

**Statistically significant at $p < .01$.

Clinton, and the slightly greater discussion of Chelsea Clinton, would seem to confirm one prediction of the "hair, hemlines, and husbands" trilogy, again in this instance, the specific, unique profile of Hillary Clinton is also obviously at work. Bill Clinton, a former president and adept newsmaker in his own right, was a key figure in Hillary Clinton's campaign. Daughter Chelsea played a direct role in campaigning for her mother; so did one of McCain's adult children (Steinhauer 2007), but Meghan McCain had nowhere near the national name recognition of Chelsea Clinton. In these respects, it appears that the particulars of the case of Hillary Clinton, as a former First Lady trying to walk the delicate line of appropriate femininity while also symbolically showing herself distinct from her husband (and making the strategic choice to feature her articulate daughter and popular husband on the campaign trail), confound simplistic conclusions.

We find little support for other key predictions of the literature regarding coverage of candidates' electoral viability, qualifications, emotions, and appearance (again, looking at traditional news outlets only, not including cable news). A pervasive pattern found in media coverage of women candidates is speculation about the "viability" of their campaigns. Since Clinton entered the race with formidable resources that rendered moot the kinds of financial viability questions that plagued past candidates like Pat Schroeder and Elizabeth Dole, we coded our national media sample for a more specific type of viability discussion: whether each story contained any discussion of whether Clinton was "electable" given her gender or electoral challenges she faced in particular because she is a woman. We found almost nothing along these lines:

In our sample of 437 stories, only 6 (less than 3 percent) contained any such discussion, and only two contained more than one paragraph on that subject. (We explore more prevalent and pernicious forms of viability questioning that Clinton faced in Chapter 7.)

We also find that Hillary Clinton's qualifications were rarely featured in front page or evening broadcast news stories, with less than 5 percent of stories discussing this topic.[15] She fared better on this score, however, than either of her main rivals: John McCain's qualifications were discussed in just over 3 percent of stories, and Barack Obama's in just over 2 percent. Clinton's personal appearance, including her hair, clothing, attractiveness, stature, age, facial expression, eyes, voice, style of speech, or other physical characteristics, were mentioned in 3.2 percent of stories—more often than John McCain's (at less than 1 percent), but virtually as often as Barack Obama's (3.4 percent). Mainstream news thus did pay closer attention to Clinton's appearance than to McCain's, a difference that was significant in statistical terms (that is, a difference that was not likely simply due to chance) but substantively small; the news also paid equally small amounts of attention to the physical characteristics of both the main Democratic candidates. Meanwhile, none of these candidates' emotions were often discussed; less than 3 percent of articles in our sample mentioned emotions in regard to any of these candidates, with no significant differences among the three on this score (see Table 6.4).

To be sure that we were capturing the real texture of media references to Senator Clinton's personality characteristics—since this was the focus of considerable ire among some observers of the campaign— we conducted an additional search of our six main news outlets, adding two newsmagazines to the mix *(Newsweek* and *US News and World Report),* looking for negative emotion-related words in reference to Clinton throughout the campaign; importantly, this search included editorial items, since these harsher terms were unlikely to be found in front-page newspaper stories. Specifically, we searched the Nexis news database for all items appearing in these outlets containing both Hillary Clinton's name and any of the following words or roots of words: "mood," "hormone," "bitch," "hysteria," "nag," "frantic," or "shrill." We found that, even in this expansive search, such explicit negative references to Clinton's moods and personality characteristics were not very common: Between November 1, 2007, and June 15, 2008, we found only thirty-two news stories across all eight outlets specifically referencing Clinton's "mood" or other emotions (this among thousands of stories covering the campaign that were published or aired by these outlets during that time). Moreover, in most contexts, those words were often used to describe the "mood" among Clinton's campaign staff (twelve references, usually characterized as downcast) or to *critique* sexist characterizations of Hillary Clinton (ten references). Words like "bitchy" and "nagging" were thus actually more likely to appear in pieces defending Clinton against those characterizations and critiquing the sexist assumptions underlying them. For example, former New Jersey governor Christine Todd Whitman wrote an op-ed for the *New York Times* arguing, "Fifteen years after I was elected New Jersey's first female governor, women running for office continue to face huge obstacles. Indeed, watching Hillary Clinton these last few months, it's clear that voters and the news media still struggle with images and expectations of women as candidates. When Mrs. Clinton made points forcefully, people called her shrill, not bold and determined" (Whitman 2008).

There were some clear examples of sexist characterizations, however. A January *Los Angeles Times* story, for example, asked political consultants how they would advise Clinton as she headed into her first one-on-one televised debate with Obama. Their advice: "Don't get mean. . . . 'It's something a man can get away with easier than a woman can. That's unfair, but that's the way things are. If a woman does it, it seems bitchy. If a man does it, it seems masculine'" (S. Silverstein 2008). As in this example, characterizations of Clinton as "shrill" often occurred in the context of avoiding the danger of *"seeming* shrill." Finally, some examples of attributing shrillness and bitchiness to Clinton occurred when reporters and commentators repeated (usually wryly) sexist comments made in *other* venues. For example, *New York Times* columnist Maureen Dowd repeated comedian Penn Jillette's joke that Clinton's primary losses were "not fair, because they're being held in February, and February is Black History Month. And unfortunately for Hillary, there's no White Bitch Month" (Dowd 2008b).

Thus, over the many news stories these leading, noncable news outlets produced throughout the campaign, only a fraction contained the demeaning emotional characterizations of Hillary Clinton that so riled her supporters. Nevertheless, when that did occur, the moments arguably had an impact, and took on a life of their own—especially in a campaign in which parallel campaign universes played out in the mainstream media and on the Internet.

As we showed in Chapter 5, the news did pounce on Clinton's "schizophrenia" as the tensions and contradictions within her gender strategy became more pronounced. An especially noteworthy example followed Clinton's closing remarks at the end of the Texas Democratic debate on February 21. Clinton said, to the applause of the audience, "I think everyone knows I've lived through some crises and some challenging moments in my life. . . . You know, no matter what happens in this contest . . . I am honored to be here with Barack Obama. I am absolutely honored. Whatever happens, we're going to be fine."[16] Her closing remarks at the Texas debate were widely interpreted in the media as a "valedictory"—so much so that alarmed campaign staffers sent out an urgent press release and an e-mail alert to Clinton supporters asserting that she was not in fact ending her campaign. A few days later, Clinton held a press conference angrily denouncing the Obama campaign's misrepresentation of her stands on NAFTA and health care and challenged Obama to "meet me in Ohio." Since the media had interpreted the Texas debate comments as a preparatory farewell, they then interpreted her "shame on you Barack Obama" comments as a hormonally driven about-face, triggering a mini-flood of media "analysis" of Clinton's emotional stability. The *New York Times* television critic noted that MSNBC's subsequent Ohio debate opened with clips of "Mrs. Clinton in two starkly different moods that underscored expectations that she would display multiple personas: elegantly elegiac at the end of their last debate in Texas, then in 'Fight Club' ire ('Meet me in Ohio') over the weekend" (Stanley 2008a).

Key Moments That Weren't:
The Permissibility of Sexist Language

So far, we have looked for the frequency of various kinds of gendered news coverage and have found little in traditional news outlets, thus raising some doubt about the applicability of the women and politics literatures' predictions to the specific case of Hillary Clinton. But in one respect, a lack of coverage seems to speak loudly of gender bias. At various moments during the campaign, ugly comments about Hillary Clinton were met with a silence in the mainstream press that galled her supporters and other observers. Think of these as key moments that weren't: Instances of sexist speech that were not called out by the nation's leading media outlets.

As we watched the campaign unfold, several such moments illustrated a range of mainstream media responses to sexist speech—in some instances subtle and arguable, in others, outright and egregious—ranging from mild disapproval to total silence. The comment by MSNBC's David Shuster about Chelsea Clinton being "pimped out" by her mother evoked perhaps the strongest reaction of any such comment during the campaign, resulting in Shuster's temporary suspension from the air.

Similarly, as noted earlier, Chris Matthews apologized on the air for his comment that Clinton had won her Senate seat because Bill Clinton "messed around"—an apology prompted by a letter-writing campaign.

Anchoring the other end of the continuum are some comments that were not responded to at all in the mainstream news—presumably because they were considered too profane or tasteless to be discussed.[17] One example of this editorial filter occurred in early March 2008. While discussing the possibility that Barack Obama and Hillary Clinton would become running mates, radio personality Rush Limbaugh told his listeners "Let's say it is Obama and Hillary. . . . Let's put Hillary at the top— That's a position she's familiar with. Therefore, you've got a woman and a black for the first time ever on the Democrat ticket. Ahem. They don't have a prayer" (CNNPolitics.com 2008). While the racial overtones of Limbaugh's remark caught media attention—and a rapid response from political operatives such as Donna Brazile, who called it "un-American"[18]—the gendered overtones were met with silence. We searched our six mainstream news outlets and found no commentary on Limbaugh's aside that Senator Clinton would be "familiar" with being "on top"; though the CNN panel with Brazile did discuss the incident, its gendered or sexist aspects were not the topic of conversation.

Somewhere in between these two instances in terms of mainstream media reaction was the mid-November 2007 moment when a (female) McCain supporter at a campaign event was captured on video asking her candidate, "How do we beat the bitch?" Looking momentarily uncomfortable, McCain then responded, laughingly (to loud guffaws), "Can I give [sic] the translation? . . . But that's an excellent question." McCain then went on to discuss a recent poll showing him "three points ahead of Senator Clinton," making it clear that he understood to whom his supporter was referring.[19] (To be fair, McCain did say, later in his response, "I respect Senator Clinton.") We searched our sample of six mainstream news outlets and found five news items and one editorial that mentioned the moment explicitly.[20] While the editorial was quite critical,[21] the news stories were not. Four of these were campaign trail stories in the *New York Times* and one was a brief ABC story on the incident. In three of these news stories, the "bitch" incident was sandwiched between references to other candidates' gaffes, framed as one of several bad moments on the campaign trail for various candidates, including an incident in which a Clinton supporter asking a question about global warming later was revealed to have been planted by campaign staffers. In other words, the "bitch" incident was framed in the mainstream media as an "uncomfortable" campaign moment for John McCain among several uncomfortable and manipulative moments involving several candidates. None of these news stories put the question front and center of whether sexist language should be shrugged off (even laughed at) by a candidate.[22] Commenting on this and other incidents in the campaign, scholar Kathleen Hall Jamieson observed,

> Essentially what we say to the culture at large is that must be appropriate discourse to apply to a female candidate running for office—or at least this female candidate. . . . Was this a Hillary-specific comment? Or is this about women who get this far seeking the presidency? Or was this language that has been circulating in private circles for a very long time and now erupted into public? The people have heard it so often that they're not surprised by it? And as a result, they don't think we need to talk about it. (Jamieson 2008)[23]

Other problematic instances came from Clinton's main rival, Barack Obama, who engaged subtle digs at his opponent some observers interpreted as disrespectful and even sexist. Most notably, during the January 5, 2008, New Hampshire debate, Senator Clinton was asked by moderator Scott Spradling of WMUR-TV to respond to the public perception that she was not as "likeable" as Senator Obama. (Her response—"well, that hurts my feelings"—drew appreciative laughter from the audience.) In the follow-up exchange, Obama replied, without looking at Clinton, "You're likeable enough, Hillary" (Healy and Zeleny 2008a). Another Obama campaign trail statement in mid-February also raised questions: "I understand that Senator Clinton, periodically when she's feeling down, launches attacks as a way of trying to boost her appeal" (Tapper 2008b). This comment did receive some critical media scrutiny—at MSNBC, for example, where reporters Andrea Mitchell and Nora O'Donnell compared Obama's comment to allegedly racial remarks made during the campaign: "It's getting a little personal and, very frankly, you know how deeply we interpreted every comment to look for some sort of racial motivation before South Carolina." On his blog Political Punch, ABC's Jake Tapper argued, "I find it hard to envision Obama using the same language if he were facing, say, former Sen. John Edwards" (Tapper 2008b).[24]

Readers may fairly ask whether it is the media's responsibility to police sexist speech at all, and certainly, thinking people may disagree on this question; another question is whether reporters have a greater responsibility to cover perceived sexist speech uttered by or tacitly approved by candidates (as in the incidents involving McCain and Obama) than they do that made by other commentators (like Limbaugh). Without trying to settle these questions, we simply note that these and other moments of arguably sexist speech were met with a less vigilant reaction than greeted instances of allegedly racially charged speech during the campaign (many of those perpetrated by the Clinton campaign). To take just one comparison, the single remark by Bill Clinton comparing Senator Obama's South Carolina victory to Jesse Jackson's was mentioned in thirty-eight news stories in our six main news sources between January 27 (the day after Obama's victory) and February 15, a response that swamped that of the media's response to the remarks made against Clinton discussed here.

Indeed, we found evidence that "race card" talk was rather prevalent in campaign coverage and was framed in a way distinctly disadvantageous to Hillary Clinton's campaign. Across our six main news outlets between August 1, 2007, and June 15, 2008, we found almost twice as many mentions of the term "race card" (forty-eight articles) than the term "gender card" (twenty-three articles). Moreover, in most of these "race card" instances, Obama was framed as the victim of a race card played by someone else—often by Hillary Clinton or one of her surrogates. On the other hand, we found only two controversial gendered moments during the primary season—the October 30, 2007, "pile-on" debate, and the January 8 "teary" moment—that brought the term "gender card" into the news. In coverage of both of these moments, Clinton was not framed as the victim. In fact, articles that contained the term "gender card" consistently referenced *Clinton's* gendered campaign strategy. Clinton, in other words, was portrayed as playing both the race card (against Obama) and also the gender card (against her opponents more broadly).

We also note that while it may not be the job of reporters themselves to raise questions about sexist speech, the fact that stories about perceived racist speech abounded by comparison suggests that reporters' *sources* (campaign operatives, party leaders, pundits, strategists, and other experts) were not raising the issue of sexist speech as aggressively (see Mendelberg 2001 for analogies to calling out uses of the "race card"). And that is exactly what rankled some Clinton supporters: the sense that the party leadership and Clinton's opponents for the nomination were not speaking out on Clinton's behalf against perceived sexism, and indeed, that her main Democratic opponent was tacitly approving, even engaging in it.

Conclusion

Our analysis in this chapter suggests that, in the traditional media, Hillary Clinton escaped many, though certainly not all, of the patterns of media coverage predicted by previous research. In particular, we find that she received a great deal of news coverage (unlike previous female presidential contenders). Much of it, however, was not positive, and her coverage overall was more negative than that of her main opponents, but this negativity cannot be attributed solely to gender bias, for the trajectory and tone of her media attention were in many ways similar to coverage of previous (male) presidential front-runners. Meanwhile, particular gender biases found in media coverage of other female candidates do not appear to have been as prevalent in Hillary Clinton's case. According to our random sample of front-page and evening television news coverage, Clinton's appearance and emotions were not mentioned significantly more than those of her two main competitors; while she was called by her first name significantly more often than her main competitors, she was also addressed more often by her formal title; while her qualifications for office were rarely discussed, they were discussed more often than those of her main competitors; and the fact that her husband and, to a lesser degree, her child were mentioned more often than the families of the leading male candidates is at least in part attributable to the fame of those family members and their campaign activities on Clinton's behalf.

Ultimately, while Clinton did not face the same kinds of viability questions that have plagued previous female presidential contenders, her front-runner status at the beginning of the campaign proved a liability in terms of media coverage—a pattern also documented for other (male) presidential front-runners. In fact, one might argue, based on what we have presented so far, that Clinton suffered as much, or even more, from being the front-runner going into the campaign as from being a woman.

That conclusion, however, would have to overlook the flip side of the problem of gender bias: the relative silence of the media (and other key public spokespeople) when attacks on Hillary Clinton took sexist or gendered form. These "moments that weren't" illustrate, at least in several instances, relatively permissive bounds around sexist campaign language.

There are other questions lurking in the data presented here. We found, for example, that in one important respect, Clinton appears to have exercised less control over her own message, since she was granted fewer television sound bites on the evening news than was Barack Obama. To what degree does this pattern reflect the same hurdles found in studies of women candidates for lower offices, and to what degree does it reflect the unusual popularity and rhetorical skill of her main opponent? The more negative tone of Clinton's coverage raises another question: Does this kind of negativity harm the electoral chances of female candidates more than males (and, conversely, to what degree did it actually mobilize more voters to support her)? Even Clinton's relative media prominence comes with a question mark: Given her unprecedented (for a female candidate) fame and name recognition, should her success at winning comparable news attention during her campaign even be compared to the general pattern of lower media prominence for women candidates documented in many other elections?

Barack Obama's media prominence and the very positive tone of his early campaign coverage also raises a serious question about whether a female presidential candidate with a similarly slim governing record could have created a similar media sensation. Even as coverage of Obama did eventually turn to questions about his inexperience, the question remains whether "inexperience" is gendered such that, in men, it conveys notions such as "slim voting record" and "outside the Beltway," but for women, notions of political novelty and lack of viability. Again, the particular cases of Hillary Clinton and of Barack Obama caution us against drawing broad conclusions from these data.

Finally, the sanguine conclusion that Hillary Clinton was not treated in sexist terms by the mainstream media would also be too simplistic. We have not yet examined other, more qualitative ways in which the media playing field appears to have been tilted against her. The data presented above are in one sense the tip of an iceberg—the iceberg being the broader qualitative themes infused throughout campaign discourse in both the traditional media and on the Web. We turn now to a qualitative analysis of these themes each of which contributed significantly to the overall negative tone and the gendering of her media coverage.

Notes

1. Video of the *SNL* skit is widely available on the Internet; we accessed it at http://guerillawomentn.blogspot.com/2008/02/snl-spoofs-media-bias-for-obama-in-cnn.html.

2. The CBS/*New York Times* data were not broken down by the candidate the voter supported in the primary, making it impossible to judge from this poll whether Clinton supporters perceived this bias more strongly than did supporters of other candidates, though this would probably be a sound assumption.

3. This is a form of sexism that the campaign of Republican John McCain practically demanded from the media after it named Governor Sarah Palin as McCain's vice presidential running mate. Roughly two weeks after the Alaska governor was named as McCain's running mate, campaign manager Rick Davis announced on Fox News that Palin would not interact with reporters "until the

point in time when she'll be treated with respect and deference" (Lawrence 2008).

4. This is not to suggest that sexism in the newsroom has not been a significant problem. See, for example, Robertson (1992). As we discuss in the final sections of this chapter, the filtering of sexist commentary from mainstream news may actually have pernicious effects by tamping down public discussion of ugly and vulgar language and images that circulate freely in the online world.

5. The latitude granted these commentators seemed especially galling to feminist critics because, as the Women's Media Center (2008) charged, "sexism sells." Ratings data showed that "in the first quarter [of 2008] MSNBC's prime-time audience rose 63 percent over the previous year (compared with 12 percent for the Fox News Channel and 70 percent for CNN, though MSNBC still draws many fewer viewers overall)" (Leibovich 2008a).

6. To construct our news sample we employed systematic random sampling, choosing every *n*th day, stratified across news organizations (Neuendorf 2002, 84–87). Specifically, we drew our sample from coverage published/aired on two days of every week from October 29, 2007, through June 15, 2008, a thirty-three-week period, with the days sampled rotating across news organizations. (For example, the *Washington Post*'s coverage was sampled on Wednesday and Saturday of week 1, Tuesday and Friday of week 2, Monday and Thursday of week 3, etc., with different rotations for each news organization.) All items retrieved with the search term we employed (the words "campaign" or "election") for each day in the sampling schedule were examined to ascertain their relevance to the presidential campaign. Further examination found an additional four articles that were not truly focused on the campaign. After this culling, we arrived at a final sample size of 437.

7. The stories were coded by two graduate student coders; a subsample of stories was coded by both students to establish intercoder reliability, which ranged between 85 and 95 percent on various variables before any differences between the coders were resolved. In most cases, our coding did not rely on subjective judgments by the coders about qualitative aspects of the coverage, but rather on simply counting the number of paragraphs in which certain kinds of words appeared; differences between the two coders were greater than two paragraphs on less than 1 percent of the data points in the sample (5 out of 1,050). Within the data reported in this book, in no cases did coders disagree about the appearance or nonappearance of a particular variable within a story (merely on how many paragraphs contained it); some variables in the original coding protocol did result in these kinds of more fundamental disagreements, and no data involving those variables are used here.

8. "Paragraphs" in television coverage were as displayed in the Nexis database transcripts of these programs.

9. The Center for Media and Public Affairs (2008a) found a nearly identical pattern in their tracking of the amount of news coverage the candidates received throughout the primary season. The Project for Excellence in Journalism data also reveal an imbalance in coverage as the contest wore on. According to their study, during the seventeen weeks between the Iowa caucuses and the beginning of May, Obama received more coverage than Clinton from the major news outlets in nine of those weeks. The differences per week, according to PEJ, were often stark—during the week of April 28–May 4, for

example, Clinton was a "main newsmaker" in 26 percent of news stories, while Obama was a main newsmaker in 55 percent. Differences between our data and that of the PEJ may contribute to the differences in degree (though not in general direction) of our respective findings. Most notably, the PEJ's "main newsmaker" data reflect the person or group mainly focused on in each news story— the people discussed in at least 50 percent of the story's airtime or page space—whereas our study measures the precise number of times each candidate was mentioned by name; PEJ's data also include a wider range of news outlets and story placement, whereas our data strictly measure front-page and prime-time network news coverage.

10. Likewise, some commentators noted during the primary season that while Senator McCain struggled to win attention equal to that of the two Democratic contenders, he succeeded in winning largely positive coverage (Lizza 2008a; K. Silverstein 2008).

11. The Project for Excellence in Journalism also found, however, that

> Clinton had just as much success as Obama in projecting one of her most important themes in the media, the idea that she is prepared to lead the country on "Day One." She has also had substantial success in rebutting the idea that she is difficult to like or is cold or distant, and much of that rebuttal came directly from journalists offering the rebuttal. (Project for Excellence in Journalism 2008a)

While these secondary studies suggest that Clinton eventually drew even with Obama in the number of positive comments, coverage of the two candidates was dramatically imbalanced early in the campaign. Moreover, it is important to note that while the PEJ study measured positive comments made about the candidates, our study measures negative comments, and here, Clinton appears to have fared worse than her main competitors.

12. Even before the imbroglio over racially charged comments made by his former pastor, the Reverend Jeremiah Wright, the tone of Obama's media coverage had become less positive, as the PEJ study documented. In most recent presidential contests, the come-from-behind bandwagon candidate receives highly positive coverage—for a short while. But "when the bandwagon either sputters to a halt or carries the candidate into a safe lead, the press reverts to its more usual view of a candidate, and bad news begins to take precedence" (Patterson 1994, 119). Confirming this pattern, the CMPA found that, "Starting in mid-December, 90 percent of comments about Mr. Obama on the three broadcast networks were positive, and 61 percent about Mrs. Clinton were positive. . . . But as Mr. Obama became the front-runner, things evened out. . . . [B]y the time Mrs. Clinton suspended her campaign on June 7, they were getting about the same amount of positive coverage, with Mr. Obama at 48 percent and Mrs. Clinton at 45 percent" (Seelye and Bosman 2008).

13. Only six primaries and caucuses were held in January, awarding 358 delegates, but two of those that heavily favored Hillary Clinton—Michigan and Florida—were disputed (see the Appendix).

14. A vivid example of how front-runner status entails becoming the target of attack was provided by an interactive graphic in the *New York Times* in

December of 2007 (when Senator Clinton was still considered the clear front-runner). The graphic, which tracked the number of references to each Republican and Democratic primary candidate made by every other candidate in the candidate debates held to that point showed a rain of arrows showering on Hillary Clinton from both sides of the political aisle. Presumably, most of the references to Clinton by both her Democratic opponents and her would-be Republican challengers were not positive in nature. See www.nytimes.com/interactive/2007/12/15/us/politics/DEBATE.html#.

15. Candidate "qualifications" included any discussion of their professional experience, accomplishments, expertise, official duties, constituent service, and policymaking roles, and their *perceived* qualifications, such as in responses to polls about the candidate "best equipped" to deal with particular problems.

16. Clinton's closing remarks, February 21, 2008, www.youtube.com/watch?v=zwQ0W7B4qDI.

17. We were given a firsthand look at this phenomenon while doing research for this book, when we learned of a "527" political group campaigning on the Internet to mobilize opposition to Clinton's campaign (so-called 527s are nominally independent political groups designated by the section of the federal tax code that grants them tax-exempt status). The group called itself "Citizens United Not Timid," a name that creates an acronym spelling an offensive word—not a coincidence, since the group's tag line was "A 527 Organization to Educate the American Public About What Hillary Clinton Really Is." As it happens, at this same time, one of us (Rose) gave an interview to a writer for the *Oregonian* newspaper describing this group's efforts, among other developments in the campaign. The interview became news, but not "C.U.N.T.," because, as the writer explained, his editorial board would never allow that word, even as an acronym, to appear in their paper.

18. See, for example, http://politicalticker.blogs.cnn.com/2008/03/06/limbaugh-so-called-dream-ticket-doesnt-have-a-prayer.

19. November 13, 2007, www.youtube.com/watch?v=WLQGWpRVA7o.

20. We searched with the term "how do we beat the bitch" during the month of November 2007 (the incident was reported on November 14). We used that exact phrase in order to determine how readily the mainstream media would repeat verbatim this type of offensive language.

21. The single *Washington Post* op-ed piece on the incident raised direct criticism (as editorial pieces can do) of the sexism embedded in the situation. The author observed ruefully that "for Clinton, this episode has to be pretty much a case of another day, another insult" since "people who don't like Clinton have been throwing the slur at her since at least 1991" in "a hope that they can shut up not only one woman but every woman who dares to be assertive" (Zeisler 2007).

22. It bears mentioning here that McCain was also criticized during the general campaign for the sometimes vitriolic and even racist comments hurled by his supporters against Barack Obama at various Republican campaign events; again, it appears, McCain did little to suppress the vitriol.

23. We should note that not all media outlets were silent about Limbaugh's comment. CNN's Wolf Blitzer featured a panel that discussed it within the general topic of the campaign (the venue on which Brazile criticized Limbaugh's

comments as "un-American"). Indeed, in an interesting epilogue to the "how do we beat the bitch?" moment, the McCain campaign quickly featured it in a fundraising letter to supporters, singling out CNN's critical coverage of the moment in an effort to mobilize supporters. See, for example, www.alternet. org/blogs/peek/67991/mccain_trying_to_raise_money_over_hillary_%22bitch %22_flap.

24. Many took the comment to be malicious, though Obama claimed afterward it was a compliment, and that he thought Clinton was getting unfair attention on the likeability factor (Healy and Zeleny 2008a). Some also accused Obama of sexism toward Clinton, pointing to particular instances from the campaign: failing to take Senator Clinton's outstretched hand at the 2008 State of the Union address; pantomiming brushing Clinton off his shoulder at a campaign speech in Raleigh, North Carolina (Wiltz 2008); and, during the same speech, rubbing his face with his middle finger while discussing Senator Clinton (to the wild applause of the audience). The Obama campaign called these accusations "absurd and untrue" (Healy and Zeleny 2008a).

7

A Gendered Game?

The press will savage her no matter what. . . . They really have their knives out for her, there's no question about it.
—Dana Milbank, *Washington Post*
national political correspondent, December 2007

Beating on the press is the lamest thing you can do. It is only because of the utter open-mindedness of the press that Hillary can lose 11 contests in a row and still be treated as a contender.
—Maureen Dowd, *New York Times*, February 2008

On the night of the country's first victory for a female candidate in a major-party primary, journalists and other media personalities were taken by surprise. Public opinion polls leading into the New Hampshire primary had suggested that Senator Barack Obama was surging ahead of Senator Hillary Clinton in that state's contest for the Democratic nomination. When Clinton won New Hampshire by three points, many pundits reached for explanations. MSNBC's *Hardball* featured the following exchange between the show's anchor Chris Matthews and veteran journalist Tom Brokaw:

Brokaw: "You know what I think we're going to have to do?"
Chris Matthews: "Yes sir?"
Brokaw: "Wait for the voters to make their judgment."
Matthews: "Well what do we do then in the days before the ballot? We must stay home, I guess." (Steinberg and Elder 2008)

Brokaw's comment evoked what some observers of election 2008 found troubling: It seemed that the media had become quick to declare winners and losers in a historic primary season that had just begun—and that, in ways that were sometimes hard to pin down, the media were holding Clinton to different standards. Matthews' response, meanwhile, seemed to capture the dilemma for many pundits and reporters: If they did not handicap the horse race, relying on polls to forecast winners and losers, then how would they cover the election?[1]

In this chapter, we analyze some of the key themes and narratives that contributed powerfully to the negative tone of Clinton's media coverage—and to the perception of many observers that she was not being treated fairly. These themes, we argue, arose both from the media's standard routines for covering all presidential candidates, and from the ongoing, pervasive gendering of presidential politics that found a target in Hillary Clinton's campaign. Adding a perhaps fatal third ingredient to the mix was the poisoned relationship between Hillary Clinton and the national press corps stemming back to her days in the White House.

We begin by further analyzing our sample of mainstream front-page and prime-time news coverage to show the connection between the media's prevalent "game framing" of presidential politics and the negativity of coverage of Clinton's campaign. We then broaden the picture, moving beyond quantitative analysis of our mainstream news sample to show qualitatively how discourse about Clinton's campaign was infused with gendered themes in a variety of media venues. At the end of the chapter, we venture more fully into the online world—a world characterized by an astonishing number and array of websites offering everything from in-depth expert commentary and analysis to the crudest forms of political speech. If, as we argued in Chapter 6, Maureen Dowd is not the *New York Times* and MSNBC is not "the media," it is even harder to make generalizations about this online world occupied by thousands of news sites (Project for Excellence in Journalism 2007b) and literally millions of other politically oriented websites, particularly political "blogs" (a shorthand term for "weblogs," which are interactive web pages that allow anyone with Internet access and minimal skills to become a producer of "news" and commentary).[2] A thorough analysis of this complex online world is beyond the scope of this book, but we do construct a framework of themes regarding Hillary Clinton's campaign encountered in our monitoring of a variety of political websites and the popular video-sharing website YouTube. This framework, which we offer as a guide to further research, illustrates a broad range of media discourse about Clinton's presidential bid and suggests that the gendered and occasionally sexist commentary about Senator Clinton in the mainstream media morphed into explicit gendering and unbridled sexism, sometimes in ugly forms, in the parallel universe of the Internet.

Game-Framed Negativity

As discussed in Chapter 3, a prevalent pattern in media coverage of elections is a heavy emphasis on "who's up, who's down" and how the candidates are gaining (or losing) tactical advantage—what the Project for Excellence in Journalism describes as "the relentless tendency of the press to frame its coverage of national elections as running narratives about the relative position of the candidates in the polls and internal tactical maneuvering to alter those positions" (2008d, 3). The media filter campaign developments through the lens of who's winning and why, and tint their coverage of the candidates in tones that reflect those candidates' relative standing in the polls. Under these rules of the media game, it is difficult for the "losing" candidate to win positive coverage.

The Democratic primary election of 2008 will perhaps set a record for this horse-race and game-framed coverage. One report found that "fully 78% of the stories studied between January 1 and the first week of May have focused on political matters, such as who won the latest primary. By contrast, policy stories made up 7% of the stories, personal matters 7%, and the candidates' public record, 2%" (Project for Excellence in Journalism 2008c).

Game framing contributes substantially to negative media coverage of campaigns because it focuses so intently on the candidates' relative chances and setbacks, as well as on their tactics and tactical errors, thus casting the candidates' actions and statements in a cynical rather than substantive light (Cappella and Jamieson 1997; Lawrence 2000; Patterson 1994). When candidates do not perform as well as predicted, that light becomes particularly harsh, as Hillary Clinton learned firsthand. For example, a March 2008 study of television coverage by the Center for Media and Public Affairs found that "since Super Tuesday, 98% of comments about Sen. Obama's prospects for winning the Democratic nomination have been optimistic, compared to only 53% optimistic comments on Sen. Clinton's prospects." The CMPA also found that Senator Clinton held a tonal advantage over her competitors "on only one topic of debate: 67% of comments about her *policies* and her *record in politics* were positive, compared to 60% positive comments for Senator Obama. However, only one out of ten comments addressed these matters, an unusually low proportion" (Center for Media and Public Affairs 2008c, emphasis added). In other words, game framing rendered the coverage of Clinton more negative while it crowded out substantive coverage of policy issues—the very dimension upon which she scored the most positive coverage.[3]

One illustrative example occurred in mid-October 2007, when Senator Clinton gave a speech in New Hampshire unveiling her plans for helping middle-class families, including such policy proposals as guaranteeing wider access to paid family leave and sick leave. *New York Times* columnist Judith Warner observed that in terms of media coverage, "Clinton's family policy speech in New Hampshire all but sank like a stone. If it was covered at all, it was often packaged as part of a feature on her attempts to curry favor with female voters. ('Clinton shows femininity,' read a *Boston Globe* headline.)" (Warner 2007). Game-framed coverage emphasized Clinton's campaign tactics (the speech was presumably timed to coincide with her campaign's intensified focus on women voters) over the substance of her proposals.

Our sample of campaign stories from the front pages of the *New York Times, Los Angeles Times*, and *Washington Post* and from campaign coverage on the ABC, CBS, and NBC evening news programs also shows this lack of substance and heavy horse-race focus in coverage of campaign 2008. We coded each of the stories in our sample for the number of paragraphs[4] containing both a mention of one of the leading candidates (Clinton, Obama, or McCain) and some discussion of issue substance (i.e., policy or issue details, policy proposals, or current policy problems). To insure that we were indeed measuring substantive coverage, we stipulated that such discussion must be more than just a passing reference to "the economy," for example. The findings are stark. Issue-oriented coverage appeared so rarely that only 72 (less than 1 percent) of the 9,679 total paragraphs in our sample mentioned one of these three candidates in conjunction with substantive issue discussion. Measured at the story level, of the 437 stories in our sample, 95 percent (416) contained no substantive issue discussion in conjunction with Senator Clinton. The two other candidates fared even worse: 97 percent of the stories contained no detailed issue discussion in conjunction with either Senator Obama or Senator McCain. The lack of statistical significance of this small difference among the three candidates highlights the overwhelming predominance of nonsubstantive coverage of all three (see Table 7.1).

We also coded each news story for whether it was framed primarily in terms of policy issues; candidate character/personality; or the candidates' strategies, tactics, standing in the polls, and success or failure at winning votes. The data show that less than 4 percent of stories (16 out of 437) focused primarily on issues such as health care, the economy, national security, the war in Iraq, or immigration; 10 percent (44 stories) focused on the candidates' personal backgrounds and characteristics; and 81 percent (356 stories) focused primarily on the electoral game.[5]

Table 7.1 Percentage of Issue-Focused Paragraphs Mentioning Each Candidate, October 2007–June 2008

	Issue/Substantive Paragraphs
Hillary Clinton	4.8 ($n = 21$)
Barack Obama	3.2 ($n = 14$)
John McCain	3.0 ($n = 13$)

Notes: Data are based upon front-page newspaper and prime-time network news stories.

*Paired-samples t-tests show the difference between Clinton and other candidates to be statistically significant at $p < .05$.

**Statistically significant at $p < .01$.

Further analysis shows that only 1 percent of stories in which Hillary Clinton appeared in the headline or story lead[6] were issue-framed stories, while 89 percent (185 stories) were primarily focused on the horse race (see Table 7.2). Barack Obama fared no better, with virtually identical numbers: 184 stories featuring Obama in the headline or lead were game-framed. John McCain did slightly better, by this measure, at winning issue-oriented coverage: 81 percent of stories featuring McCain in the headline and/or lead were game-framed, while 6 percent focused primarily on issues—though as noted above, the actual substantive discussion of issues in these stories was generally limited.

Notably, we find no evidence that the traditional news media (excluding cable and online news) singled out Hillary Clinton for personal attacks. Table 7.3 shows that, measured by paragraph, the three main can-

Table 7.2 Percentage of Issue-, Character-, or Game-Framed Election Stories, by Candidate Appearing in the Headline/Lead, October 2007–June 2008

	Issue/Substantive	Character	Horse Race/Game
Hillary Clinton	1.0	5.3	89.4
Barack Obama	1.4	6.8	88.9
John McCain	6.2	12.5	81.2

Note: Data are based upon front-page newspaper and prime-time network news stories. Because some articles in our sample did not fit easily into these three categories, rows do not total to 100 percent. Chi-squares per candidate are all $p < .01$.

Table 7.3   Types of Negative Coverage of Hillary Clinton, Barack Obama, and John McCain, by Average Number of Paragraphs, October 2007–June 2008

	Criticism of Personal Characteristics	Criticism of Tactics and/or Strategies
Hillary Clinton	.03	.15
Barack Obama	.01	.07**
John McCain	.02	.08**

Notes: Data are based upon front-page newspaper and prime-time network news stories.

*Paired-samples t-tests show the difference between Clinton and other candidates to be statistically significant at $p < .05$.

**Statistically significant at $p < .01$.

didates were equally likely to be criticized for their personal attributes. Measured per story, only 4 percent of stories in our sample contained such criticism about any of these candidates. Negativity toward Clinton, in other words, was no more likely to be directed at her personal characteristics. Many more stories, however, criticized Clinton's strategies, tactics, advertising, and likelihood of winning as criticized Obama or McCain. In our sample, 12 percent of stories criticized Clinton on these tactical and horse-race grounds, while 6 percent of stories criticized Obama and McCain, respectively, on these grounds. As Table 7.3 shows, roughly twice as many paragraphs criticized Clinton than her opponents in tactical and "winning/losing" terms, and the difference is statistically significant.

Our data show that the media framed Hillary Clinton's campaign in heavily horse-race terms, though horse-race coverage dominated coverage of the primary contests across the board. We next show how deeply the game frame structured the news narratives around Clinton's campaign and how those narratives in some instances became highly gendered.

Calling the Game

If one candidate must be the front-runner, then according to the horse-race script, a second-place candidate has few available roles to play: either the "bandwagon" candidate who is gathering momentum, or the "losing ground" candidate who is falling behind. Thomas Patterson (1994) finds that bandwagon candidates (like Bill Clinton in 1992) win generally positively framed coverage, while those falling behind in the polls receive increasingly negative coverage.[7] These patterns appear most prominently during the nominating phase of presidential elections, in which "a candidate who catches fire can expect highly favorable news coverage for a brief period," but "a candidate who starts to slide is quickly written off as a loser in nearly every respect" (1994, 119). In the case of election 2008, in which two candidates waged an extraordinarily close protracted battle for the Democratic nomination, a pervasive "loser" theme contributed to negative coverage of Clinton—a theme sometimes shaded with a "death" motif.

Indeed, back in December of 2007, before a single primary vote had been cast, headlines were already declaring Clinton's candidacy ill, if not dead:

> "Slipping Away?" said a headline on ABC's "Good Morning America." "Hillary Clinton's campaign is teetering on the brink," [Howard] Fineman wrote in *Newsweek*. CBS's Jim Axelrod said her operation is "reeling." The *Los Angeles Times* said she is facing her "most serious crisis." And a banner headline on the Drudge Report asked: "Is It the End?" (Kurtz 2007)

Even earlier in the campaign, following the late-October 2007 debate that triggered the "gender card" imbroglio, critic Stanley Fish observed that "everyone was writing her political obituary ten seconds after the last word was spoken in the October 29 debate. . . . they were all standing over the body and taking bets on whether or not it could be revived" (Fish 2007).

Thus, before the first caucus was held, Hillary Clinton had been cast not simply as the front-runner, but as the stumbling front-runner. In breathless game-frame mode, the media and pundits relentlessly described the tightening of the preelection opinion polls in terms of Clinton losing her place in the race, though at the time she still held a commanding lead in most national polls (a reflection of her advantage as the candidate with superior name recognition and funding at that point in the campaign)—and even though a tightening of the race was a predictable development, given the crowded slate of contestants and the very early stage of the election year.

Of course, ultimately the Clinton campaign did not prevail in Iowa, taking a very close third place behind Barack Obama and John Edwards. That loss, which was often framed as a more decisive loss for Clinton than the actual vote tallies suggest (Bystrom 2008),[8] triggered a media theme that Hillary Clinton was no longer the "inevitable" nominee and further inscribed the death trope into the media narrative of the campaign. When Clinton and Obama each won some victories on Super Tuesday, the media's game-framed narrative continued: "Clinton and Obama Battle Through Super Tuesday Without a Knockout," read one representative headline. Then came the "Potomac Primary" one week later, in which Clinton lost four contests to Senator Obama. According to media critic Howard Kurtz, "The media floodgates opened after Obama swept [the] primaries in the District, Maryland, and Virginia. Never mind that the two Democratic candidates remain close in the delegate count, or that Clinton has been described as doomed once before, in New Hampshire." The media narrative that she was losing the nomination left Clinton "drowning in a sea of negative coverage" (Kurtz 2008d).

Though Clinton won the Texas and Ohio primary contests, the loser theme continued. On May 8, hours after Clinton won the Indiana primary by a narrow margin but lost North Carolina to Senator Obama by a resounding 14 percent, one reporter observed,

> Very early this morning, after many voters had already gone to sleep, the conventional wisdom of the elite political pundit class that resides on television shifted hard, and possibly irretrievably, against Senator Hillary Clinton's continued viability as a presidential candidate. The moment came shortly after midnight Eastern time, captured in a devastatingly declarative statement from Tim Russert of NBC News: "We now know who the Democratic nominee's going to be, and no one's going to dispute it," he said on MSNBC. (Rutenberg 2008b)

The pundits, led by Russert, thus declared her bid over a full month before Clinton actually suspended her campaign—and before all the primary voters had cast their ballots.[9]

In many respects, then, Clinton was treated almost from the beginning of the primary season as more of a loser than a winner—an ironic upshot of being the presumed front-runner at the beginning of the race. Especially once she did not decisively defeat her opponents in the early contests, media attention focused on voters' "rejection" of Clinton (Balz and Kornblut 2008)—even though, by the end of the primary season, she would win 21 primaries and amass over 17 million total votes, the closest second-place finish in modern presidential-nominating history.

Why Keep Running? Media Standards of Electoral "Success"

On April 27, after Senator Clinton won the Pennsylvania primary, media critic Howard Kurtz quipped, "We're the media, and a primary election means what we say it means. Got that?" Kurtz's acerbic quip captured what he saw as shifting standards of electoral "success" applied to Hillary Clinton versus Barack Obama by the national media—an observation echoed by some within the Clinton campaign. As one Clinton field organizer told us, "Every time we win, they [the media] talk about delegates. When he [Obama] wins, they talk about momentum" (J. Perez 2008). Anecdotal evidence suggests these perceptions are to some extent accurate.

On the eve of the Pennsylvania primary, another political reporter provided a window into the "battle of perception" being waged around Clinton's campaign:

> During those oh so many weeks before the Pennsylvania primary, television news commentators filled their face time by discussing the margin of victory Senator Hillary Rodham Clinton would need to justify her continued, uphill fight for the Democratic presidential nomination. . . .
>
> With no set rules dictating when a candidate should drop out of a presidential nominating contest that has been fought this hard—for this long—without an unquestionably presumed winner, it is public perception that rules the day.
>
> And while Mrs. Clinton's advisers knew she would most likely win on Tuesday, they also knew she would need a resounding chorus of instant analysts to say her victory was large enough to certify a sense that she still had at least the slightest chance to steal the nomination from Mr. Obama, that her candidacy was still credible.
>
> In the open borders of election-night, television talk—where pundits, paid campaign operatives and straight-news reporters mix comfortably in setting conventional wisdom for the next primary—a struggle for perceptions was under way. It played out in the open, in real time. (Rutenberg 2008a)

The game frame underlying this battle of perception is crucial to understanding why Hillary Clinton's wins were often treated as less significant than her losses—or than her competitor's wins. According to the implicit logic imposed by the game frame, if elections are all about winning, then second-place candidates have little reason to remain in the race.[10] As Clinton's mathematical chances of winning the needed number of delegates to secure the nomination became more remote, her victories were accordingly treated as less newsworthy, and the threshold for "meaningful" victories raised. The implicit logic of the game frame also helps to explain why the media so often framed Senator Clinton's primary victories as merely staving off ultimate defeat. When Clinton won the Ohio and Texas contests on March 4, for example, a *New York Times* lead illustrated this framing:

Senator Hillary Rodham Clinton's victories in Ohio and Texas on Tuesday night not only shook off the vapors of impending defeat, but also showed that—in spite of his delegate lead—Senator Barack Obama was still losing to her in the big states.

Those two states were the battlegrounds where Mr. Obama was going to bury the last opponent to his history-making nomination, finally delivering on his message of hope while dashing the hopes of a Clinton presidential dynasty.

Yet then the excited, divided American electorate weighed in once more, throwing Mrs. Clinton the sort of political lifeline that New Hampshire did in early January after her third-place finish in the Iowa caucuses. (Healy 2008d)

According to this narrative, Senator Obama's defeats were temporary setbacks to an inevitable victory; Clinton's victories were merely a "lifeline" keeping her afloat.

Shifting media-imposed standards of success were particularly clear in coverage before and after the April 22 Pennsylvania primary. The preceding Super Tuesday, Potomac, Ohio, and Texas primaries had, from one perspective, left the outcome of the race uncertain. By that point in the campaign, Obama had amassed 1,577 pledged delegates, while Clinton had won 1,420—a close margin, historically speaking.[11] Although Clinton had long been predicted to win the Pennsylvania primary, many reporters and pundits set the bar for "real" success—that is, a win that would "give her a rationale to go on"—at 10 percentage points. Anything less, many reporters and pundits tended to agree, would render a Clinton victory "murky" (Nagourney 2008c).

Clinton did win Pennsylvania, by a fraction of a percent shy of the 10 percent margin. Media coverage for the most part framed that victory as Pyrrhic, as in this *New York Times* lead: "Mrs. Clinton's margin was probably not sufficient to fundamentally alter the dynamics of the race, which continued to favor an eventual victory for Mr. Obama. But it made clear that the contest will go on at least a few weeks, if not more" (Nagourney 2008a).[12] The *Times* editorial page pronounced that "Mrs. Clinton did not get the big win in Pennsylvania that she needed to challenge the calculus of the Democratic race" (*New York Times* 2008) and called on Senator Clinton to leave the race.

It is important to be clear that reporters' evaluations of Clinton's electoral chances were not without merit. Every primary that Obama won put more pressure on Clinton to sweep the remaining contests—a challenging feat she was unlikely to pull off. In fact, as early as Super Tuesday but particularly after Pennsylvania,[13] Clinton had only a remote chance of securing the nomination through the usual process of amassing delegates awarded through the popular vote in each state (a fact due in large part to the way the Democratic Party awards delegates; see the Appendix). Indeed, while Obama appeared to have a razor-thin delegate lead over Clinton through much of the primary season, in reality the delegate gap became nearly impossible for Clinton to close because even her wins in big states were not winning her large numbers of delegates (Todd and Gawiser 2009, 14–15). It seems clear that, at a certain point, Senator Clinton's strategy became "to play for time, hoping that something would happen that might get uncommitted super delegates to think twice before supporting Mr. Obama" (Nagourney 2008a). It is also important to remember that some of the negative media assessment of Clinton's campaign was driven by key Democrats ostensibly concerned about the effects of her continued campaign on the party's chances in the general election—concerns skillfully reinforced by the Obama campaign[14] that reached a crescendo of calls for her to bow out of the race after Pennsylvania.

These dynamics were particularly evident on the evening of her May 6 Indiana victory (coupled with her North Carolina loss). As NBC commentator Rachel Maddow opined that evening, "Hillary Clinton has declared a post-rational approach toward getting this nomination. She has not had a clear path to the nomination for a very long time" (*NBC Nightly News* 2008b). Her Indiana win, in other words, became little more than a place-holder temporarily protecting Clinton from the inevitability of conceding defeat.

By the time of her lopsided victory (67 percent to Obama's 26 percent) one week later in the West Virginia primary, the notion that she "couldn't win" was so firmly in place that no conceivable rationale remained (in the eyes of most commentators) for her continuing in the race. When asked why Clinton's West Virginia win didn't get much news, *Washington Post* associate editor Kevin Merida answered that it "didn't change the dynamic of the race" (Reliable Sources 2008f). Similarly, in the aftermath of the Oregon and Kentucky primaries on May 20, which were crucial for Senator Obama to rack up the needed number of pledged delegates in order to clinch the nomination, Clinton's Kentucky victory (65 percent to 30 percent) received especially short shrift. The *New York Times* television critic, Alessandra Stanley, noted that "the shrinking candidacy of Senator Hillary Rodham Clinton all but vanished from the television set on Tuesday. . . ."

> Even her victory speech in Kentucky, shown live on cable news, was given perfunctory attention—a footnote to someone else's page in his-

tory. When MSNBC called the Kentucky primary early in the evening, Tim Russert, host of "Meet the Press," said her success with women and blue-collar voters "means Senator Obama has a lot of work to do" and sketched a rehabilitation plan. He did not mention Mrs. Clinton by name in that disquisition. (Stanley 2008b)

As these examples illustrate, along with this focus on Clinton's losses came a game-driven focus on the strategic reasons—or lack of reasons—for her to remain in the race, even when the strategic reasons became less compelling than her other stated reasons for staying in. Commenting on the election-night coverage of the Oregon and Kentucky primaries, the pundits "ticked through her talking points—among them that results from the disputed states of Florida and Michigan could change the dynamic; [and] that the race could swing her way with help from unaligned, party super delegates" (Rutenberg 2008c). Notably absent from those "talking points" were other points Clinton had been emphasizing to her supporters: That she was determined to stay in the race until all the Democratic primary votes had been cast on the principle that all voices should be heard, and that Clinton wanted to demonstrate that, as a female candidate, she would not be forced from the race. In fact, only one day before the article quoted above appeared, Patrick Healy of the *New York Times* reported, based on interviews with Clinton staff, this very rationale for Clinton's continuing campaign: "Advisers say that continuing her candidacy is partly a means to show her supporters—especially young women—that she is not a quitter and will not be pushed around" (Healy 2008b).[15]

While campaign messages like these should not necessarily be taken at face value, it is notable how rarely the media reported this alternative narrative of nonstrategic rationales. Focused through the prism of the game frame, the only "real" rationale for a candidate to stay in a race is to win the nomination. Because Clinton "couldn't" win, her continued campaigning was treated as irrational; because her other stated reasons for remaining in the race did not fit within the game frame, they were apparently difficult for the media to treat seriously.

Bringing Out the Hook: Calls for a Clinton Exit

A persistent theme of media coverage of Clinton's campaign—and, we suspect, a main reason that so many perceived her coverage as unfair—was whether and when Clinton would bow out of the race. This was a relatively prominent aspect of the coverage of Hillary Clinton's campaign: 50 stories in our sample of 437 (11 percent) contained discussion of a Clinton exit, ranging from explicit claims that she was obliged to step out of the race or mentions that she lacked a reason to remain in the race to discussion of when or if she might bow out. Measured as a percentage of all stories containing any direct mention of Hillary Clinton, 15 percent of her coverage included this exit theme.

One reason exit talk permeated the coverage was undoubtedly the calls for Clinton to bow out from various leading Democrats, including Ted Kennedy (D-MA) and Patrick Leahy (D-VT), and in more veiled form, from Democratic Party chairman Howard Dean (Bai 2008b).[16] News coverage of many political issues follows the lead of key political figures such as these (Bennett, Lawrence, and Livingston 2008; Sparrow 1999). Another factor that helped set Hillary Clinton's "losing" script in stone was the long campaign season that started in 2006 and was still "just getting warmed up," according to Clinton, in March of 2008, leaving reporters with a sense that they had precious little left to cover; unable or unwilling to break out of the well-established horse-race script, the story of the campaign became simply "when will it end?" Ana Marie Cox, reporter and blogger for *Time*, said of the 2008 campaign, "Of course it's historic, it's amazing, I feel lucky to be covering it. But how many more stories do I have to read, or be forced to write, about when Hillary will drop out?" Carl Cameron of Fox News reported that, in contrast to most elections in which reporters look eagerly for "comeback" stories to keep the election interesting to their audiences, "This is a really strange phenomenon in that you're seeing people who can't wait for it to be over. There's only so many stories you can write, and we're running out of them." A joke circulated among reporters that the Texas and Ohio primaries would be like Groundhog Day—"if Hillary didn't see the shadow of defeat, we'd have six more weeks of campaigning" (all quoted in Kurtz 2008c).

At the same time, it seems likely this exit talk stemmed from the demands of the horse-race script for a decisive early finish to the campaign.[17] The media's implicit script for a "normal" primary campaign hinges on the early emergence of a clear front-runner who quickly secures the nomination; in contrast, a conventional (pardon the pun) way of thinking about primary elections is that nominations are actually won at the convention, not before, and that the popular vote doesn't decide the nomination—delegates do, at the convention. Watching the media coverage of campaign 2008, one might have concluded that the 2008 nominating contest was a historical anomaly, and Hillary Clinton's continued campaigning until the final primary election was not only quixotic, but an unseemly aberration. In fact, while the 2008 race was unusual in some noteworthy ways, Clinton's refusal to exit the race before the final primary was not.

The (Forgotten) History of Nomination Contests

The 2008 Democratic nominating race was more protracted than many recent presidential campaigns, but only in certain respects. Historically speaking, presidential nominating campaigns not uncommonly extend into the summer months. What made the 2008 contest longer than others was not that it lasted until mid-June, but rather that it essentially began early in 2006—reflecting a trend in presidential politics toward a virtually continuous election cycle and the "front-loading" of primaries earlier in the season (see Menefee-Libby 2000; Ornstein and Mann 2000; Wayne 2008). Nor has it been unusual for second-place candidates to continue their campaigns even when their mathematical chances of securing the needed number of delegates have become remote. As one observer noted on the eve of the Democratic convention, in fact, "Hillary Clinton just became the first competitive candidate to ever endorse her opponent months before the party convention. Neither Gary Hart nor Jesse Jackson were *that* charitable" (A. Perez 2008).

Thus, far from being the exception to the rule, Clinton's determination to stay through the end of the contests makes her, ironically, just like many of her male predecessors who did not win as many delegates as she did. On the Republican side, Ronald Reagan vigorously challenged Gerald Ford's hold on his party's nomination in 1976, despite the fact that Ford was the sitting president, insisting, "I'm taking this all the way to the convention in Kansas City, and I'm going even if I lose every damn primary between now and then" (Kengor 1996; see also Cannon 2008). Despite a string of losses from January through March, Reagan kept his campaign alive, securing 1,070 delegates to Ford's 1,187 (1,130 were needed to nominate) (Ibid.). On the Democratic side, as historian David Greenberg argued in March of 2008,

> The calls to wrap up the Democratic primary race show . . . amnesia. To suggest that March 5 marks a late date in the calendar ignores the duration of primary seasons past. Indeed, were Hillary Clinton to have pulled out of the race this week, Obama would have actually clinched a contested race for the party's nomination earlier than almost any other Democrat since the current primary system took shape—the sole exception being John Kerry four years ago. Fighting all the way through the primaries, in other words, is perfectly normal. (Greenberg 2008a)

Indeed, in 1972 George McGovern won his nomination at the June 21 primary in New York. Four years later, Jimmy Carter faced a slew of contenders, including California's Jerry Brown, who did not even enter the race until May but won the huge California primary and forced Carter to fight on. Massachusetts Senator Edward M. Kennedy vigorously contested Carter's renomination effort in 1980 and took his campaign all the way to the convention (ironically, Senator Kennedy called for Senator Clinton to concede to Obama on June 7, 2008). In 1984, Gary Hart claimed right up to the July 16 convention that the nomination could go into "overtime." In the end, neither had the 2,023 delegates to be nominated, and the superdelegates brokered a deal at the convention for Hart's concession.

More recently, Michael Dukakis was not declared the presumptive nominee until late April of 1988; few called for Jesse Jackson, who trailed 1,400 delegates behind Dukakis, to bow out. Hillary Clinton's own husband remained plagued by opponents Paul Tsongas and Jerry Brown throughout the 1992 primary season, despite Brown carrying only 600 delegates. Only the most recent Democratic nominees, Al Gore and John Kerry, clinched their nominations early and handily. And though Hillary Clinton did suffer from a persistent delegate deficit following the Super Tuesday contests, Obama held "a much slimmer lead over Clinton than McGovern, Carter, and Mondale held over their closest challengers—or, for that matter, any of the nomination-bound front-runners in elections since" (Greenberg 2008a).

In other words, what was unusual in 2008 was the extraordinary closeness of the contest between Clinton and Obama, not the length of the contest. On the eve of Super Tuesday, Clinton trailed Obama by only 50 pledged delegates; after the final Democratic primary on June 3, Clinton still trailed by only 125 pledged delegates. By comparison, the last close contest occurred in the 1976 Republican battle, which ended with Reagan trailing Ford by 117 delegates.

From one perspective, that narrow margin was exactly why Clinton should have bowed out. A continuous theme of the coverage, driven in part by Obama supporters and some party leaders, was that her continued campaign (selfishly) endangered the Democrats' chances in the general election by dividing the party rather than uniting it behind a single candidate (a contention that is, by its nature, difficult to prove). But from another perspective, Clinton's narrow trailing margin was why she should not prematurely exit the race: Even if her mathematical chances of winning were declining, she clearly was a very strong candidate, not a distant second-placer.

Seen in this light, Clinton's decision to stay in the race and to fight hard may, as the quotes above suggest, be considered part of her gender strategy. Had she exited the race earlier, the historical significance of her feat would have been undermined; by remaining in the race, Hillary Clinton became the first woman to compete in all of her party's nominating contests. This significance appeared lost on the media—perhaps in part because, as we previously discussed, Clinton did not consistently present herself as a historic first. Columnist Gail Collins was one of the few journalists to capture the symbolism of staying in the race until her opponent actually won the requisite number of delegates: "Who do they think she is, the Clinton campaign mutters—some girl who'll give way so the guy can get what he wants?" (2008c). *Times* columnist Maureen Dowd captured, in contrast, the prevailing call for Clinton to concede, adapting the familiar Dr. Seuss *Marvin K. Mooney Will You Please Go Now!* cadence: "The time has come. The time has come. The time is now. Just go . . . I don't care how. You can go by foot. You can go by cow. Hillary R. Clinton, will you please go now!" (Dowd 2008f).

Once again, it is important to put comments like Dowd's, which were made on the editorial page and not in the straight news stories we have focused on so far, into perspective. In our sample of news stories, explicit calls for Clinton to exit the race were found in only 10 percent (11 of the 108) of the paragraphs that contained any "exit talk"; the rest were more general discussions, such as speculation about whether or when she would bow out. These findings suggest that some of the media critics we quote in this chapter may have exaggerated the extent of calls for Clinton to exit (at least in mainstream media venues). Yet our data also suggest that the exit theme was relatively common in Clinton's coverage, appearing more often than discussion of her qualifications for office, for example. Perhaps just as important, this exit talk was usually devoid of historical context—context that might have cast her decision to remain in the race in a less negative light.

Possibly undergirded by unexamined assumptions about proper "feminine" behavior, the media often cast Clinton in the spoiler role, rendering her more like a Ralph Nader in 2000 than a Ronald Reagan in 1976. The crescendo of "exit calls" might have been motivated by changes in journalism itself: "No longer content to be observers of the campaign," one blogger argued, "journalists now see themselves as active players in the unfolding drama, and they show no hesitation trying to dictate the basics of the contest, like who should run and who should quit. It's as if journalists are auditioning for the role of the old party bosses" (Media Matters 2008h). Others saw a more pointedly sexist bias at work. Andrew Stephen of the British publication the *New Statesman* observed,

> The massed ranks of male pundits gleefully pronounced that Clinton had lost the battle with Obama immediately after the North Carolina and Indiana primaries, despite past precedents that strong second-place candidates (like Ronald Reagan in his first, ultimately unsuccessful campaign in 1976; like Ted Kennedy, Gary Hart, Jesse Jackson and Jerry Brown) continue their campaigns until the end of the primary season and, in most cases, all the way to the party convention.
>
> None of these male candidates had a premature political obituary written in the way that Hillary Clinton's has been, or was subjected to such righteous outrage over refusing to quiesce and withdraw obediently from what, in this case, has always been a knife-edge race. Nor was any of them anything like as close to his rivals as Clinton now is to Obama. (Stephen 2008)

The Gendering of the Horse Race

Moving beyond a quantitative analysis of our mainstream news sample to the qualitative themes that emerged as we monitored campaign coverage in a variety of media venues, we find that the media often infused the stumbling front-runner theme, and later the story of Clinton as the second-placer who wouldn't go away, with gendered imagery. One vivid example was pointed out by columnist Timothy McNulty of the *Chicago Tribune* in the May 9 edition of that paper (McNulty 2008):

> The political horse race analogy went too far. The lead editorial "No photo finish for Clinton" in Thursday's *Tribune* played off Hillary Clinton's loss in the North Carolina primary and tied it to the fate of Eight Belles, the horse that was put down after breaking her front ankles in the Kentucky Derby. This was the beginning paragraph: "The only filly in the crowded field crossed the finish line second, but the fans who'd bet on her still had one last gasp of hope. Perhaps some fortuitous technicality would disqualify the first-place finisher. But things got worse instead of better. We're talking about Eight Belles, who was euthanized Saturday after almost winning the Kentucky Derby. But we're thinking about Hillary Clinton."

McNulty continued by noting that the *Tribune*'s editorial had ended with this sentence:

> "There's no reason to wait until August to put Clinton, and the rest of us, out of our misery." It made me queasy. The imagery would never

have been used if the linkage between the two events was not gender. You cannot imagine using a similar analogy about race in the case of Barack Obama or about age when referring to John McCain.

This anecdote illustrates in stark terms the intersection of game framing and gendering, in which the "loser" Clinton was admonished to bow out lest she become the (inappropriately unfeminine) "spoiler." Perhaps most pointedly, blogger and media commentator Craig Crawford advised Clinton to bow out of the race in mid-February rather than go on the offensive against Obama. She should opt to "lose pretty," Crawford advised, positioning herself "to pick up the pieces and rally the party if Obama loses the general election as the Democratic nominee," rather than "winning ugly" by "savaging" her opponent (Crawford 2008b). Maureen Dowd laid the gendering on thick, admonishing that Clinton "may want to take a cue from the Miss America contest: make a graceful, magnanimous exit and wait in the wings" (quoted in Hoyt 2008b).

Since according to game-framed standards, Clinton's continued bid for the nomination was by definition irrational, and since the history of similarly protracted nominating contests was largely ignored, commentators often explained Clinton's choice to remain in the race by recourse to a fundamental character flaw of overambition that has long been attributed to her. Writing for Salon.com, Walter Shapiro's May 12 essay, titled "Hillary Enters Death-with-Dignity Phase," wondered aloud about her motives:

> While everyone outside the Clinton family . . . knows *how* the Democratic donnybrook will end, almost no one has a confident theory about *when* it will end. Part of the uncertainty reflects the enduring mystery that has animated that academic discipline called Hillary Studies for the last 15 years: What motivates her? Is it ambition, pride, feminism, vindication, public service or ideology? Or is it some combination of all of them? (Shapiro 2008a)

The "Death" Motif

As the literal horse-race analogy equating Clinton with the euthanized Eight Belles suggests, this script and its gendered undertones invited reporters, pundits, and bloggers to anticipate a particular ending to the story that would echo the fate of many ambitious, destructive fictional feminine antagonists. "Death" and "zombie" imagery emerged persistently as the campaign wore on; though it did not appear regularly on the front pages of respectable newspapers, it did appear in the editorial pages and, with more frequency, in editorial cartoons and political blogs. In these venues, Clinton was sometimes portrayed as dying, often being slain by her competitors, but more often as something that would not die, the undead.

Perhaps the most frequent of such references in the mainstream media were to a comment made by Obama adviser Samantha Power calling Clinton a "monster,"[18] but reporters themselves also made death references. In addition to ongoing descriptions of her candidacy as being repeatedly "resuscitated" or "resurrected" (and, therefore, implicitly dead), some were more biting, such as this lead by *Washington Post* reporter Dana Milbank:

> It's Day 13 of the Clinton Campaign Death Watch, nearly two weeks since Tim Russert declared Barack Obama the Democratic winner.
> When last we caught up with our heroine, Hillary Clinton's plight was compared to the Monty Python routine in which a pet-shop owner insists that a dead parrot is still alive. Clinton loyalists disputed the comparison, while some scholars searched the literature and proposed a different Pythonian model: the Black Knight, who valiantly defends his bridge after losing all four of his limbs. (Milbank 2008b)

In a few instances, these "undead" references were framed rather positively, such as when *Newsweek* magazine reported that "some top [Clinton] staffers have laughed over the comparison between Hillary Clinton and the Hollywood movie monster Freddy Krueger: you can run her over, stab her, shoot her—and she still keeps coming" (Thomas 2008a). And several instances of "death" imagery were actually critiques of the language used to describe Clinton's campaign, such as one op-ed writer who mulled, "contemplating the 'Life's a Bitch, Don't Vote for One' T-shirts, the stainless-steel-thighed Hillary nutcrackers, the comparison to the bunny-boiling Alex Forrest of 'Fatal Attraction,' I struggle over how, when—even whether—to talk to girls truthfully about women and power" (Orenstein 2008). But for the most part, these references deliberately cast Senator Clinton in repellent roles. In part, this imagery reflected a media meta-narrative of press distrust of the Clintons, discussed earlier, that transcended the 2008 presidential campaign. (Indeed, Beasley [2005, xi] reports that during her first eight months as First Lady, at least 20 articles appeared in major newspapers and magazines drawing comparisons between Hillary Clinton and Lady Macbeth.) It also reflected the press's relentless search for a riveting story line: "While few in the media world will say so out loud, a Hillary collapse ('The Fall of the House of Clinton,' as a *Weekly Standard* cover put it last month) is a more dramatic outcome than a win by the woman originally depicted as inevitable" (Kurtz 2008c). While Kurtz noted that "there is considerable danger in writing that story prematurely," our findings suggest that the media inscribed the death theme into coverage of Clinton's campaign from the beginning of the primary season, when, as we explored previously, her victory in New Hampshire was shrouded in funereal imagery.

Hillary Clinton in the Wild West

The media environment in which candidates today must operate, and which shapes voters' impressions, is made up of a wide variety of media outlets. The "new media" world constitutes a kind of parallel political universe marked by a wide diversity and huge number of media outlets that reach, in most cases, relatively small (but politically attentive) audiences (Hindman 2008; Davis 2009). This universe is also characterized by freewheeling political speech that is in many cases outside the bounds imposed by editorial controls in the traditional news media—a wild west of edgy, sometimes incisive, sometimes offensive political speech. This cable news and online world exists in a symbiotic, even parasitic relationship with what many bloggers refer to as the "MSM" (mainstream media); political blogs often use mainstream media coverage as a jumping-off point for wide-ranging critiques of candidates, parties, ideologies (and, quite often, the MSM itself).

Gendered themes in media discourse around Clinton's campaign became more pronounced the further one moved beyond the confines of front-page, mainstream, straight news pages. The boundaries between "old" and "new" media are porous; in many cases, themes in the online world simply amplified themes voiced in more traditional news venues; meanwhile, with reporters for traditional media increasingly writing their own blogs, where editorial controls are more lax and reporters freer to speak in their own voice, the boundaries between "old" and "new" media become even harder to discern. In addition to examples that arose in our monitoring of mainstream news during the campaign, we include here portrayals of Clinton's campaign in other venues, including videos posted on YouTube, opinions expressed on political blogs, and the products and visual images peddled to anti-Clinton consumers through the commercial website Café Press;[19] from these sources, we often learned of additional examples occurring in the mainstream media, talk radio, and cable news.

We found in these venues four themes describing Clinton's candidacy that directly exploited earlier framings of Hillary Clinton popularized in the 1990s, and in some cases included tasteless and harsh depictions of the candidate. Our analysis is not intended to offer a complete picture of everything on the Internet pertaining to Hillary Clinton. The Internet featured a wide variety of discourse and debate about campaign 2008, including many defenders of Senator Clinton. In order to illustrate the range and nature of gendered and sexist depictions of Clinton, and to make clearer how certain comments and images took on a life of their own in the online world, we focus attention here on four narratives, all of which fed off of and back into mainstream discourse, all of which diminished the stature of Hillary Clinton.

Ambitious Woman as Man-Killer

Following the lead of mainstream news outlets, in which a key theme was Clinton's unseemly and unfeminine fight to the death for the Democratic nomination, a common theme in the world of the Web was Clinton as a power-hungry killer (a not-so-subtle return of the True Womanhood theme of the nineteenth century in which any outspoken or free-thinking woman undermines the home, family, and Christianity). The *Washington Post*'s Dana Milbank, blogging about then-president Bush's 2008 State of the Union address, observed that in the audience, "Hillary Clinton was situated immediately behind Barack Obama, making it easier for her to actually place the knife into his back, if that's what she was trying to do." At the *New York Times,* Maureen Dowd quipped that Senator Clinton, much like television thug Tony Soprano, "is so power-hungry that she can justify any thuggish means to get the prize" (Media Matters 2008k). MSNBC's Chris Matthews (whom the feminist blog Feministing described as a "semi-professional misogynist") played a key role in planting and reinforcing this theme, likening Clinton to a "sort of Madame Defarge of the left," a reference to Charles Dickens's murderous character from *A Tale of Two Cities;* calling her a "she-devil," complete with a behorned image on the screen behind him; accusing Clinton of trying to "strangle [the Obama campaign] in the crib before there's any chance he catches on"; and making multiple references to Clinton as a "Nurse Ratched," the infamous figure from *One Flew Over the Cuckoo's Nest* who takes pleasure from inflicting psychic pain on her patients (all quoted in Media Matters 2008f). Talk-radio personality Rush Limbaugh (a widely referenced figure in the blogosphere) favored this term as well, claiming that Clinton "reminds men of the worst characteristics of women they've encountered over their life: totally controlling, not soft and cuddly. Not sympathetic. Not patient. Not understanding. Demanding, domineering, Nurse Ratched kind of thing" (Media Matters 2008d).

Perhaps most glaring of the images and terms in this category were the references to Clinton as a "ball buster" or "castrator."[20] To make the point, one company produced a Hillary Clinton nutcracker sold at airports across the country and readily available online—a steel-thighed, pant-suited contraption that, according to its maker, "cracks the toughest nuts." Some women joined in the fray; conservative commentator Monica Crowley warned Clinton would "cut off your manhood." Others simply invented terms to convey that Clinton's power would be a direct assault on masculinity, as in the case of Limbaugh, who frequently claimed that Clinton possessed a "testicle lockbox . . . big enough for the entire Democratic hierarchy, not just some people in the media" (Media Matters 2008d). Tucker Carlson, Chris Matthews' MSNBC colleague, added, "There's just something about her that feels castrating, overbearing, and scary" (Media Matters 2008c). Limbaugh extended the "castrator" designation to Clinton's supporters in January, observing that Clinton was "in the Northeast . . . surrounded by her good old . . . white female new castrati male base" (Ibid.). Extending this theme to a general disempowerment of the public, one of the most-watched videos on YouTube during the campaign season, called "Vote Different," invoked both the famous Apple computer ad of the year 1984 and chilling Big Brother images from George Orwell's *1984*, picturing Hillary Clinton speaking mechanically and imperiously from a huge screen looming over an audience of (mostly male) zombie-like prisoners.[21]

Kill the Ambitious Woman

Notably, that video climaxed with a scene of a young blond athletic woman in running gear flinging a large hammer into Clinton's image on the oversized screen. Some blog posts and visual images offered on the Web also proposed to deal with the candidacy of Hillary Clinton through violence and even proposed her metaphorical murder. One of the more innocuous methods involved merely water: Said one CNN analyst regarding Hillary Clinton's January 21 debate performance, "if someone had splashed water on Hillary, she would have melted like the Wicked Witch of the West" (Media Matters 2008g). Others were more direct. A January 7 blog post by Joel Achenbach of the *Washington Post* declared that Clinton "needs a radio-controlled shock collar so that aides can zap her when she starts to get screechy" (Media Matters 2008j). Echoing this theme, the online magazine *Slate* launched a "Hillary Deathwatch," a daily assessment of Clinton's diminishing odds. With its inaugural post on March 27, *Slate* writers declared, "the question now is not just 'How dead is she?' but 'When will she realize it?'" (Beam, Matlin, and Wilson 2008). These kinds of comments often drew from commentary in the real world, such as comedian Chris Rock's observation, "It's going to be hard for Barack to be president. . . . Hillary's not going to give up. She's like Glenn Close in 'Fatal Attraction.'" Joining that theme, congressman and Obama supporter Steve Cohen (D-TN) told a television reporter that "Glenn Close should have just stayed in the tub" (Tapper 2008c).[22] A more extreme bumper sticker put it bluntly, "I Wish Hillary Had Married O.J.," a reference to the one-time National Football League star who was tried for the murder of his wife. Also available from Café Press were T-shirts announcing "Happiness Is Hillary's Face on a Milk Carton" (a reference to the practice of advertising abducted children), and products portraying the senator as half-donkey, half-woman, dodging rocks, while the tag line read, "Wanna See Hillary Run? Throw Rocks at Her."

She's Just a Woman

In comparison to the tropes described above, the most seemingly innocuous were simple statements that Hillary Clinton, *qua* woman, does not belong in politics. "Get Hillary Back in the Kitchen" bumper stickers and tote bags echoed this theme,[23] as did buttons featuring the phrase shouted out at a Clinton campaign event early in the season: "Hillary, Iron My Shirt!" An uglier version of this theme is evidenced in the 527 organization created to raise money to oppose Clinton's candidacy named Citizens United Not Timid. The group's website, whose acronym summons perhaps one of the most demeaning popular references to the female form, featured a buxom woman wearing a T-shirt with the group's name, on sale for only $25.00. Beneath a graphic depicting a woman's genitalia draped in the US flag, the slogan directly connected the senator to the group's acronym: "To Educate the American Public About What Hillary Clinton Really Is."[24]

Is She a Woman?

While the "Citizens United" group attempted to boil Clinton down to her biology, other efforts challenged the senator's womanhood. Efforts to undermine male presidential candidates routinely include attempts to feminize them, and we found that much of the online world's "Hillary hate" included challenges to her sexuality and questions about whether she is actually a woman at all. One genre cast Hillary as a lesbian; these posts and images generally depicted the candidate as *too manly* to be a woman in her stock pantsuit and practical shoes, but also sometimes included a tasteless tag line, such as one bumper sticker reading, "Hillary Stinks—Just Ask Her Girlfriend," or one showing Senator Clinton at a urinal with the tag, "She's Not What You Think." Often the images in these tropes included references to Bill Clinton and Monica Lewinsky, suggesting that had Hillary Clinton been a satisfying sexual partner, the president would not have strayed: "Hillary Clinton: Outsourcing Blowjobs Since 1995."

Alternatively, and less frequently, online sources depicted Clinton as *too womanly*—a temptress—another inappropriate role for a female president (though expressions of male presidents' libido are well known across the ages); in one version of this twist, a popular YouTube video showed a Hillary Clinton stand-in having sex with a stand-in Obama (an image that also plays to the racist trope of a black man as sexual aggressor).

In all of these tropes, Hillary Clinton runs afoul of the True Woman definition through her ambition and sexuality. One might also note that while male candidates are routinely undermined through feminization, it is hard to imagine a male presidential candidate being *too manly*. But, in the ultimate double bind for the female candidate, Hillary Clinton was portrayed as both too manly and too womanly to be president.

Conclusion

Taken together, the findings presented here suggest that the negative tone of Hillary Clinton's media coverage in the 2008 presidential campaign cannot be attributed to a single factor. Rather, media negativity toward Clinton was overdetermined, driven by a complex interaction of standard media framing of elections in "game" terms, a backdrop of gendered presidential politics and a wider societal backdrop of sex stereotypes, a preset (and gendered) script the press and punditry attached to this candidate, along with the candidate's own tactical decisions during the campaign. Moreover, it stemmed from the media's constant search for a riveting story within a lengthy and closely fought campaign, and from a long-running cycle of press antipathy toward Hillary Clinton, and Clinton antipathy toward the press.

Media coverage of the Clinton campaign affirms some of the findings of scholars who study women and politics, while also complicating the picture drawn by that literature. Though Senator Clinton overcame many of the barriers faced by previous female presidential hopefuls, particularly in terms of the amount of coverage her campaign received, many of the narrative themes running through coverage of Clinton's campaign—beginning in some cases long before the first vote was cast—were deeply gendered. As Erika Falk (2008) reminds us, "Both sexism and stereotypes have long been identified as playing a major role in American society. . . . [A]ny theories that attempt to explain news content relative to men and women candidates must take sexism and stereotypes into account" (157). It seems clear that stereotypes of female ambition, in particular, pervaded portrayals of Clinton's presidential campaign in the "old" media and particularly in the new.

At the same time, sexism (at least in the mainstream media) is only part of the explanation, for in many respects, Clinton was treated like one of the boys—particularly, like one of a long line of front-runners who have seen their media fortunes falter. Yet, the analysis presented here confirms that the horse-race and game-frame scripts are hardly gender neutral. Game-framing draws overtly from male-centered sports analogies that lean on football, baseball, and boxing metaphors rather than on, say, figure skating, gymnastics, or women's volleyball, and they emphasize "scores" and "knockouts" in ways that fit less comfortably with stereotyped femininity than masculinity. As Georgia Duerst-Lahti (2006) argues, presidential elections are a "gendered space." Given this standard media framing, Clinton perhaps faced little choice but to adopt the "fighter" stance—sometimes complete with boxing gloves—she assumed as the contest wore on.

Our findings lead us to new questions about the gendered game of media politics. For example, we know from previous research that viability themes can pervade news coverage of female candidates; in Hillary Clinton's case, incessant game-framing cast her in the "losing" role. Though, as we note above, there were very good reasons to wonder whether Senator Clinton could recover from her early electoral losses, we found evident themes of Clinton stumbling, losing, and even dying well before a single vote was cast—leaving us to wonder if "exit talk" is another form of viability talk, another way of casting doubt on the ability of women to rise to high political office.

We also find an intersection between Clinton's gender strategy and her news coverage. Most pointedly, the incessant exit talk pervading coverage of her campaign was not balanced by a recognition of her nonstrategic reasons for remaining in the race—in large part, perhaps, because Clinton had not presented herself primarily as a historic "first female." Having chosen not to be "damned if you do" with a gender difference strategy, Clinton arguably was "damned if you don't" by media coverage that overlooked the important symbolism of her staying in the race. We also find a troubling historic amnesia in the media coverage that implicitly portrayed Clinton's continued fight for the Democratic nomination as aberrational and unseemly. Further research will determine whether past male contenders who remained in the race even with diminishing chances of winning have been subject to similar levels of exit talk and calls to bow out. For now, we note that exit talk in the case of Hillary Clinton was often subtly, and sometimes disturbingly, gendered.

Finally, our qualitative venture into the new media world suggests that gendered themes were much more prominent and pointed, as one might expect from the less regulated realm of online media. Here, explicitly gendered attacks on Clinton mixed freely with commentary by mainstream media pundits, making it difficult for many in the audience to distinguish between the "respectable" and less explicitly sexist mainstream press and the more unruly discourse customary on the Internet. Indeed, we believe that the parallel universe of the online world served as an echo chamber in which moments of apparent sexist talk were amplified and served up in highly focused form to Clinton supporters, feminists, and others most likely to be offended. In particular, websites like Media Matters and NOW's "Hall of Shame" very effectively gathered multiple examples of denigrating comments against Hillary Clinton that quickly took on a life of their own in the online world.

As the 2008 Democratic primary dragged to a close, it was hard to escape the conclusion that the mainstream media had repeated its routine ways of covering presidential elections, only in larger doses, and possibly with more history-making effects. Elizabeth Edwards, wife of Democratic contender Senator John Edwards, wrote an op-ed piece for the *New York Times* in late April 2008 after the news media had focused intensively on the Pennsylvania contest for the past month (due to a primary schedule that placed Pennsylvania a full six weeks after the preceding primaries). Edwards asked, "Given the gargantuan effort, what did we learn? . . . the information about the candidates' priorities, policies and principles—information that voters will need to choose the next president—too often did not make the cut." The media had largely offered the public what she called "strobe-light journalism, in which the outlines are accurate enough but we cannot really see the whole picture" (Edwards 2008).

Hillary Clinton's campaign was arguably damaged by the press's perennial failures to cover politics—and particularly women politicians—more substantively. Illuminated through the media "strobe light," Hillary Clinton's candidacy became a caricature of itself: not merely losing but doomed to death; not simply a bid for power but a desperate, unseemly power grab. As *Time* magazine's editor at large, Mark Halperin (quoted in Kurtz 2007), observed months before the pattern would become clearer, "the press's flaws," including "accentuating the negative," were "magnified 50 times when it comes to her. It's not a level playing field."

Notes

1. Not insignificantly, it was this same evening on which Matthews reminded viewers that Hillary Clinton was a US Senator and therefore a viable candidate for the presidency simply because "her husband messed around" (see Chapter 4), further fueling the sense that Hillary Clinton was not getting a fair shake.

2. In April of 2007, as the presidential campaign was cranking up, trackers had detected over 70 million total blogs, with approximately 120,000 new blogs created daily. See www.sifry.com/alerts/Slide0002-6.gif.

3. Recall from the previous chapter, however, that Clinton actually gained more coverage of her qualifications for office—coverage related to her policy positions and experience—than did her main competitors. This media bias, in other words, extended across the main candidates, though an open question remains whether this erasure of policy coverage is ultimately more damaging to female candidates than male candidates.

4. "Paragraphs" in television coverage were as displayed in the Nexis database transcripts of these news programs.

5. Our coding instructions asked coders to choose which of these categories each story best fit into, looking at the headline and lead in particular to see which was emphasized: (1) predominantly substantive/issue focused, (2) predominantly focused on candidate personality/character/background, or (3) predominantly focused on the horse race and/or electoral strategies and tactics. Two coders coded a subsample of stories independently and the raw agreement between them on this variable was 86 percent. In most cases, the initial disagreements among the coders revolved around whether an article was more focused on the candidate's "character" or on the "game" frame; in no cases did the coders have trouble distinguishing an issue-framed article from the other two categories.

6. The story "lead" was defined as the first two paragraphs of each story.

7. Patterson identifies a fourth pattern: the "likely loser" candidate, represented by George H. W. Bush in his 1992 reelection bid in which he faced off against a charismatic "bandwagon" candidate (Bill Clinton). Given Hillary Clinton's formidable resources and advantages entering the primary season, this script was not applied to her.

8. Dianne Bystrom argues that "media coverage portraying Clinton's 'disappointing third-place finish' overemphasized the negative result of what was really a tie for second place. Also, many media reports failed to adequately report on coalitions that formed before and during the Iowa caucus on January 3, 2008. . . . Supporters of Bill Richardson were encouraged to caucus for Edwards if their candidate was not viable. Supporters of Obama were told to join the Edwards or Richardson camps to make them viable, as Obama could often spare a couple of supporters to make other male candidates viable." Often not reporting these backstage maneuverings, many news outlets followed the lead of the *Des Moines Register*, which "rounded these figures to headline the finishes as Obama first with 38%, Edwards second with 30%, and Clinton third with 29%—even though the difference between their 'state delegation equivalencies' were .28 points apart" (Bystrom 2008, 25–26).

9. It bears mentioning that Clinton seems to have succeeded in at least partially reframing herself as an underdog and a "fighter" (a key theme of her campaign's messaging after February), precisely because she remained in the race and continued to draw large numbers of votes to win key industrial states like Ohio and Pennsylvania. By early May, some of her negative coverage had been tempered with what one reporter described as a "grudging respect by continuing to forge on when she was down" (Reliable Sources 2008e). Clinton also succeeded in planting a story line that gained considerable coverage: Why, her campaign asked, could Obama not "close the deal" by winning key industrial and rural states with large numbers of working-class white voters? Nevertheless, it seems clear that Clinton carried on her fight burdened by the media's designation of her as a losing former front-runner.

10. The political science literature distinguishes between candidates who run to win and "issue" candidates who run to inject a favored issue into the election agenda (see, for example, Haynes et al. 2004). Issue candidates sometimes remain in a race they are losing in order to gain political leverage for their policy concerns. This distinction is often lost in media coverage that treats all candidates simply in terms of their chances for winning or losing. While it is a useful distinction for thinking about elections in general, it is not a category for thinking about Hillary Clinton, who was, as she liked to say, "in it to win it."

11. Delegate counts are according to the Associated Press's Delegate Tracker website (http://hosted.ap.org/specials/interactives/campaign_plus/delegate_tracker/delegate_tracker.swf). On the eve of the Pennsylvania primary, Senator Clinton trailed Senator Obama by an additional 236 unpledged superdelegates.

12. A different *Times* article was slightly more charitable: "If Mrs. Clinton did not emerge from the bruising six-week [Pennsylvania] campaign with a race-turning landslide—she still trails Mr. Obama in the popular vote and the delegate count—her victory nonetheless gives her a strong rationale for continuing her candidacy in spite of those Democrats who would prefer to coalesce around Mr. Obama" (Healy 2008b).

13. Pennsylvania, with its 158 delegates to be awarded, was the last sizable state other than North Carolina (115 delegates) to vote in the Democratic primary race.

14. As the *New York Times* reported, "to blunt any political damage from

losing in Pennsylvania, the Obama campaign distributed a memo to supporters late Tuesday [the evening of his Pennsylvania loss] titled, 'A Fundamentally Unchanged Race'" (Zeleny 2008b).

15. Clinton did occasionally try out her own game-frame metaphors to explain her continued campaigning. She told ABC News, "You don't walk off the court before the buzzer sounds," and said on CNN, "You never know, you might get a three-point shot at the end" (Associated Press 2008b).

16. For a poignant overview of key Democrats who "peeled away" from Clinton during the campaign, see Sheehy (2008).

17. Paradoxically, even while many media pundits called on Clinton to bow out, the long, close race was good for the news business economically speaking, particularly the cable news networks. The *Times'* Frank Rich observed: "As the Clinton-Obama marathon proved conclusively, a photo finish is essential to the dramatic and Nielsen imperatives of 24/7 television coverage" (Rich 2008b).

18. Samantha Power, foreign policy adviser to the Obama campaign, said in an interview with a Scottish newspaper after Obama lost to Clinton in Ohio, "We f***** up in Ohio. . . . In Ohio, they are obsessed and Hillary is going to town on it, because she knows Ohio's the only place they can win. . . . She is a monster, too—that is off the record—she is stooping to anything. . . . You just look at her and think, 'Ergh.' But if you are poor and she is telling you some story about how Obama is going to take your job away, maybe it will be more effective. The amount of deceit she has put forward is really unattractive" (http://thescotsman.scotsman.com/latestnews/Inside-US-poll-battle-as .3854371.jp). Power apparently thought her hasty "off the record" aside would keep her remark from becoming public. She subsequently resigned from the campaign.

19. Specifically, our methods were the following. We tracked all products related to Hillary Clinton being offered on the political products website Café Press (www.cafepress.com). We monitored YouTube by visiting that site once weekly (on Mondays, since in most cases primary elections occurred on Tuesdays) and searching it with the term "Hillary Clinton." Each week, we recorded the top-ten videos returned with that search and looked for patterns and themes among these most popular videos over the course of the campaign. For the political websites and blogs, we monitored the most-trafficked political sites (based on their continuously high ranking on traffic-measuring sites like The Truth Laid Bare's "Ecosystem"; see http://truthlaidbear.com/ecosystem .php), being sure to choose both liberal and conservative sites as well as feminist and media criticism sites pertinent to our study.

We monitored these sites by logging in once or twice weekly, particularly just before and just after primary election days, from late December 2007 until Clinton suspended her campaign in mid-June. For each site each day we checked in, we (1) looked at all links from the site's home page for that day's date that were relevant to the Clinton campaign; (2) took a screen shot of the home page, incorporating each item's "headline" into a list of that day's top stories and blog posts relevant to the campaign; (3) noted the topic of the post (e.g., new Clinton ad, new Iowa poll, etc.); and (4) read/viewed the material in each link. Blogs monitored in this way included: Michelle Malkin (conservative), http://michellemalkin.com; Redstate (conservative), www.redstate.com; Instapundit (conservative), www.instapundit.com; Daily Kos (liberal), www.dailykos.com; HuffPolitics at the *Huffington Post* (liberal), www .huffingtonpost.com/; Talking Points Memo (liberal), www.talkingpointsmemo. com; Media Matters (media/progressive), http://mediamatters.org; *Slate,* www.slate.com/; Tennessee Guerilla Women (feminist), http:// guerillawomentn.blogspot.com; Wonkette, www.wonkette.com; and feministing (feminist), www.feministing.com. Given the sheer size of the blogosphere, our sample of blogs cannot be considered random nor our findings generalizable; our aim with this analysis is qualitative, suggesting lines of inquiry to be followed in future research.

20. The larger culture was coincidentally invited to contemplate the quintessential castration myth in a film about the *vagina dentata* (Latin for "toothed vagina"), which is found in various folk stories and legends. The movie *Teeth* debuted at the 2007 Sundance Film Festival and was released for US audiences on January 18, 2008, just as the 2008 primary contests were under way. While on its surface the topic seems to coincide with sexist depictions elsewhere in the culture, the film's director had a more feminist intent: to show that this ancient myth "says only something about men, and their attitude toward women. It doesn't have anything to do with the qualities of women" (www.firstshowing .net/2008/01/15/sundance-interview-with-teeth-director-mitchell-lichtenstein).

21. Video viewed at www.youtube.com/watch?v=6h3G-lMZxjo. The video was not officially authorized by the Obama campaign and its creator remained unknown (Marinucci 2007).

22. National Public Radio's Ken Ruden and Andrew Sullivan, writer and blogger for *The Atlantic,* also both compared Clinton to the psychotic stalker character played by Glenn Close in the 1987 movie *Fatal Attraction.*

23. Given that the Clinton campaign itself wielded the "kitchen" metaphor at key moments in the campaign, this supposedly anti-Clinton message may have been interpreted differently, even co-opted, by Clinton supporters.

24. We were incredulous to find, in an etymological exercise on the term this group's acronym spells, that the Princeton University Press online dictionary contained the presidential candidate's name in that word's definition: "a person (usually but not necessarily a woman) who is thoroughly disliked; 'she said her son thought Hillary was a bitch'" (http://dictionary.reference.com/ browse/cunt; accessed September 2008).

8

The Future
Female Presidency

I met more discrimination as a woman than for being black.
—Congresswoman Shirley Chisholm,
on running for president in 1972

To paraphrase the feminist theorist Donald Rumsfeld, you don't try to make history . . . with the candidate you might want, you go with the one you have.
—Mark Halperin, political reporter, October 2007

In March 2008, as Senator Clinton struggled to gain ground in the 2008 primary, her surrogate and former vice presidential candidate Geraldine Ferraro gave an interview to *The Daily Breeze*, the local newspaper of Torrance, California. It was one of many appearances Ferraro made on behalf of Clinton, but this one proved explosive. When asked about the contest between Obama and Clinton, Ferraro commented, "I think what America feels about a woman becoming president takes a very secondary place to Obama's campaign—to a kind of campaign that it would be hard for anyone to run against," she said. "For one thing, you have the press, which has been uniquely hard on her. It's been a very sexist media. Some just don't like her. The others have gotten caught up in the Obama campaign." "If Obama was a white man," Ferraro concluded, "he would not be in this position. And if he was a woman he would not be in this position. He happens to be very lucky to be who he is. And the country is caught up in the concept" (Farber, 2008).

Ferraro's comments sparked an instantaneous firestorm. Several of her points were controversial, but by far the most inflammatory was Ferraro's claim that Barack Obama's race was a benefit to him rather than a burden. The notion that Senator Obama was "very lucky to be who he is" was widely interpreted as a thinly veiled slight, suggesting that Obama was an "affirmative action" candidate in the worst sense, unworthy of the office he sought. Illinois Congresswoman Jan Schakowsky, among others, objected to Ferraro's charge, stating, "It's disappointing that Clinton supporters have sought to diminish Senator Obama's candidacy to say that in some way he's been given special treatment because of his race. Any and all remarks diminishing Senator Obama's candidacy because of his race are completely out of line" (Jones and Rosado 2008). Ferraro stepped down from the Clinton campaign following this incident, though she continued to defend her comments in subsequent media appearances (Reliable Sources 2008c).

Lost in the controversy was the point that Ferraro claimed she was trying to make: That the historic presidential candidacy of a black man was more appealing to the public imagination than the historic candidacy of a white woman, and that Senator Obama might actually benefit from excitement about the possibility of turning a page on US history—an excitement Senator Obama captured on the evening of his victory in the Iowa caucuses: "On this January night, at this defining moment in history, you have done what the cynics said we couldn't do" (Associated Press 2008b).

Certainly, there was plenty to take offense at in Ferraro's comments, and the notion that a black man somehow was getting a "pass" due to his race was troubling to many whites and blacks alike. Aware of the minefield we enter, however, we take her observation about the baggage of being female as a starting point for the subject of this final chapter, underscoring one of the theoretical positions that forms the basis of this book's analysis: the candidate and her context affects a woman's race for the White House.

Our primary goal in this book has not been simply to understand why Hillary Clinton lost, but to illuminate the variety of factors that shape the electoral chances and strategies of female presidential candidates. We have argued that the presidential candidacy of Hillary Clinton, or of any female presidential hopeful, must be understood against a constellation of variables that shape the political opportunity structure and the candidate's strategic choices. Clinton's run for the White House was thus indelibly shaped not only by society's deeply held gender stereotypes and biases, but also by the media's professional norms and routines, and the candidate within her particular context.

In keeping with that last set of variables, we have explored various facets of Hillary Clinton's own political career, public persona, and long interactions with the national press corps that powerfully shaped her opportunities, liabilities, and strategic choices in the 2008 campaign. Until now, we have put aside perhaps the most consequential aspect of Clinton's context: the meteoric political career of Barack Obama. It seems clear that just as the particulars of Hillary Clinton matter to campaign 2008, so do the particulars of the man who would win that year's Democratic nomination—and, ultimately, the presidency. In this concluding chapter, we explore some of those particulars, which inevitably involves the challenging task of assessing how race, like gender, also mattered. As we will see, however, while race certainly shaped the context in which the nominating battle was fought, it was not the only factor associated with Senator Obama that contributed powerfully to the dynamics of the 2008 campaign.

Overall, the aim of this chapter is to assess what the campaign of 2008 teaches us about women in presidential politics and the importance of what we have called "gender strategy." Given the backdrop of androcentric notions of the presidency, and the necessity of negotiating the routines by which the national news media frame presidential elections, gender strategy looms as a crucial but underexplored aspect of how women run for high office. Hillary Clinton's gender strategy has offered us a rich case study for theory building, but her particular case leaves many questions unanswered. We explore in this chapter a variety of questions raised by our research for the future of women in presidential elections. Along the way, we briefly consider the vice presidential candidacy of Alaska governor Sarah Palin, who seems to have employed gender strategies and narratives nearly antithetical to Clinton's. Palin's role in the 2008 presidential campaign points to the many rich opportunities for future research on female candidates' gender strategies.

The Electoral Benefits of Being Male

A useful starting place is with the observation that Barack Obama arguably had a simple advantage over his main competitor for the Democratic nomination: the advantage of being a man. (We will complicate and question this simple notion below, but it serves as a familiar beginning point for this discussion.) Given the androcentrist notions of the presidency woven into the fabric of US political culture, most men enjoy a presumed advantage over most women in their ability to fit the unstated "qualifications" of that office. We have seen how Hillary Clinton tried to adopt her public persona to those androcentric demands by, for example, running television advertisements portraying her as tough enough to be commander in chief and implying that Senator Obama was not. Indeed, Clinton was accused of trying to demasculinize Obama. (With her usual acerbic wit, Maureen Dowd put this charge most pointedly: "Her message is unapologetically emasculating: If he does not have the gumption to put me in my place, when super delegates are deserting me, money is drying up, he's outspending me 2-to-1 on TV ads, my husband's going crackers and party leaders are sick of me, how can he be trusted to totally obliterate Iran and stop Osama?" [Dowd 2008f].) To the degree that this strategy worked with various voters, it proves the general point that *any* candidate for the White House must prove herself or himself "man enough" for the job—an easier task, generally speaking, for a male candidate than for a female. As one female Obama supporter observed simply, "He still looks more like every other president we've ever had than she does" (Kantor 2008a).

This gender advantage was keenly felt by many observers of campaign 2008 and was heightened by the fact that Senator Obama was relatively new to the national stage and lacked many of the bona fides often presumed essential for a presidential candidate. Dee Dee Myers, the first female White House press secretary (under Bill Clinton) and the author of *Why Women Should Rule the World*, stated the situation starkly: "No woman with Obama's résumé could run. . . . No woman [with that resume] could have gotten out of the gate" (quoted in Zernike 2008).

Being male also meant that certain strategic choices were available to Senator Obama that were not available to Senator Clinton. In particular, Obama could (and did) showcase his family as a way of establishing a sense of common identity with voters. "If I were to produce a spot for Obama," Democratic pollster Peter Hart observed early in the campaign, "I would take 100 photographs of everything that he does with his children and wife—that could range from Halloween to a picnic to everything we identify with as part of American life—so people could say, 'I relate to that, I understand it'" (Dowd 2008d). As this anecdote reveals, Senator Obama could mine whole veins of political symbolism in ways Hillary Clinton—whose marriage has been more publicly dissected than perhaps any in US history, and who has struggled to present herself as her own woman, not just a beneficiary of her husband's success—for the most part could not.

At the same time, we must also acknowledge that in some ways, Barack Obama's messaging and campaign style were more "feminine" than that of many male contenders for the presidency. Obama's emphasis on talk, negotiation, and personal connection with voters persuaded leadership expert Martin Linsky to declare him the "first serious woman candidate for president": "Clinton proposes policy solutions to every problem. . . . Obama can raise possibilities that are off the table for Clinton. She needs to tell us that she can solve our problems. Obama seems comfortable in what we think of as a female role: not overpromising what he can accomplish, and telling us that the work of change is ours as much as it is his" (Linsky 2008).

Indeed, while his candidacy is not the main subject of our work, it is important to acknowledge that Barack Obama had his own gender strategies to consider. Race and gender are not discrete categories, but rather, interlocking systems of oppression: race intersects with gender in powerful ways, deeply embedded in our nation's history, as black feminist theorists bell hooks (1981) and Patricia Hill Collins (1990) and others have so eloquently revealed with their scholarship. Old tropes of the black male conjure painful antebellum imagery of the African American man as animalistic and sexually threatening; more recent cultural history reveals public expectations that black men are prone to violence and crime (see Entman and Rojecki 2001 for an overview). For a black man to assume all the usual trappings of the masculinized presidency is therefore more challenging than it is for white men. Thus, without declaring gender an unalloyed advantage for Barack Obama, we can instead observe that gender offered Obama some symbolic and rhetorical advantages, while at the same time, the powerful intersection of gender with race complicated Obama's own strategies.

Racism vs. Sexism: "Which Is Worse?"

In media coverage of the campaign, another overly simplified starting point for discussing the contest between Hillary Clinton and Barack Obama was the question of whether racism or sexism constitutes the higher barrier to elective office, especially for the presidency. This question became particularly pointed at those moments when the Clinton campaign complained of sexist treatment by the media—complaints that sometimes provoked responses like this one from a blogger calling him- or herself "democrattotheend":

> I . . . think that Clinton has at times been the victim of sexism, just as Obama has at times been a victim of racism. However, I believe that Clinton's failure in this campaign has been a result of a poorly run campaign, not sexism. It insults me as a feminist to hear people say that she is losing because she is a woman and has received disparate

treatment. If anything, she has been propped up by her gender, making her (like Obama) a celebrity candidate who got more attention in the beginning than the other candidates and has been given more chances to bounce back. (quoted in A. Romano 2008)

Thus, not all Clinton supporters, nor all feminists, agreed that Hillary Clinton had faced pervasive sexism that had undermined her campaign; many believed that her gender had actually helped her. Interestingly, we came across few if any examples in mainstream or new media of these kinds of comments being met with the fierce reaction provoked by Geraldine Ferraro's suggestion that race had actually helped Barack Obama. Somehow the suggestion that gender might help the female candidate was not as explosive.

In media coverage, the question of which form of oppression is worse rarely drew upon the insights from scholarly research. That research teaches us that gender is neither an irrefutable benefit nor an absolute burden for female politicians. Gender stereotypes may help women who seek offices associated with the stereotypical female competencies, and being a woman may help a candidate with particular constituencies (particularly women voters) for particular offices (the case of the presidency notwithstanding). Moreover, even the literature that predicts difficulties for female presidential contenders is unavoidably based upon an extremely thin historical record; it may be that as more women enter presidential politics, we will learn that the gender strategies available to female presidential hopefuls are not as limited as is often assumed, nor the gendered barriers as fixed.

Discussion of sexism in the context of Hillary Clinton's presidential campaign rarely delved into these nuances, however, nor into the nuances of racial politics. Instead, "race versus gender" became a glib leitmotif of campaign coverage in ways that often forced candidates and voters into a facile dichotomy. That dichotomy led in turn to the unanswerable question, "Is it harder to be black or female?" While it is not our purpose to answer this question, it is important to acknowledge its impact upon the context in which the Clinton campaign was waged.[1]

One of the few examples of a more intelligent discussion of this question came in a *New York Times* column by Nicholas Kristoff entitled "Our Racist Sexist Selves" (Kristoff 2008). Published in the thick of racial controversies that cropped up during the campaign, Kristoff explained the cognitive science suggesting that gendered ways of thinking are harder to overcome—even though racial stereotypes lead to extremely ugly forms of bias, such as a quicker shoot-to-kill response when whites are confronted in experimental settings with images of threatening black men. According to Kristoff, "evolutionary psychologists believe we're hard-wired to be suspicious of people outside our own group, to save our ancestors from blithely greeting enemy tribes of cave men. In contrast, there's no hard-wired hostility toward women," although, he added, "men may have a hard-wired desire to control and impregnate them." However, the human brain makes sex categorizations more quickly and overlooks them less easily than racial categorizations; as one researcher explained it, "We can make categorization by race go away, but we could never make gender categorization go away." Moreover—and here Kristoff implicitly invoked the gender research discussed throughout this book—gender stereotypes make it difficult for women to be perceived as both "nice" (an expected female trait) and competent (a crucial leadership trait). Kristoff's point was not to ignore the persistence of racism as a factor in Obama's campaign, but rather to acknowledge that the gendering of human cognition and cultural stereotypes creates challenges for women presidential aspirants that males generally do not face.

Unlike Kristoff's column, most media discussion of sexism and racism did not distinguish the rather different ways that these forms of bias operate, or the interlocking relationship of race and sex. Nor did most discussion reflect an important distinction that scholars draw between the concepts of sexism, misogyny, and gendering. Public discussion often seemed to confuse "misogyny" with "sexism," muddling the picture that Kristoff captured concisely: "Americans don't hate women," he argued, "but they do frequently stereotype them as warm and friendly, creating a mismatch with the stereotype we hold of leaders as tough and strong"—precisely the double bind we have argued Hillary Clinton consistently found herself caught in. Drawing a simple equivalency between racism and sexism thus led to superficial comparisons between the hurdles each candidate faced and clumsily drew media attention to the one group apparently stuck in-between: black women. As political scientist Adolphus G. Belk Jr. told the *New York Times*, "They [black women] stand at the intersection of race, class, and gender. . . . Black men say to them 'Sister, are you with us?' And at the same time white women say, 'Sister, are you with us?'" (Seelye 2007, 2008c).

Transcending Race and Gender?

Despite all the simmering racial undertones of some aspects of this election, Barack Obama seemed to symbolize for many Americans a powerful way out of the ugly racial history of the United States and a way to move beyond present-day racial tensions and uncertainties. Obama's ability to seemingly glide past the race narratives that thwarted Jesse Jackson's presidential efforts in the 1980s may be explained by the way that group-based categories are understood in the United States. It seems clear that Obama's electoral strategy foregrounded the notion of him not as a "black" candidate, but as a "postracial" candidate to whom established racial categories and sentiments were not applicable. "Obama's campaign is . . . a bet on the ability of a black candidate to inspire voters across the lines that demarcate traditional racial, ethnic, and class divisions," wrote one liberal blogger (Sanders 2008).

It is interesting to consider whether Hillary Clinton's foregrounding of "equality" rather than "difference" claims represented a similar effort to transcend gender. Though there is certainly more research and debate to come on this question, our initial sense is that rather than transcending gender, Clinton played the more conventional strategy of suppressing it, relegating feminine appeals to particular contests and settings. A further possibility is that the nation does not see gender as something that needs transcending. Clinton's equality strategy may have in fact been a reflection of her pragmatic assessment that the nation is less receptive to gender change.

Our reading of campaign 2008 also suggests that race trumped gender in terms of public discussion. Uncomfortable questions about race relations in the United States formed the backdrop of much campaign coverage, while discussion of women's struggles in US society were more muted. As we noted in Chapter 5, for example, we found significantly less media discussion of the historic nature of Clinton's candidacy (and her primary victories) than of Obama's, and as we found in Chapter 7 and here in this chapter, instances of allegedly racially charged speech seem to have been met with a response more vigorous than instances of allegedly sexist speech. Overall, little mainstream media discussion indicated a need to move the nation beyond its sexist past and toward parity between men and women.

In making sense of these observations, we must consider whether Obama embodied and symbolized racial progress for many people in the United States (or at least many pundits and commentators) in a way that Clinton did not symbolize progress on sexual equality. As Hoover Institution senior fellow Shelby Steele noted in a *Wall Street Journal* op-ed piece, Obama presented a "blank screen" (Obama's own words) on which many Americans—and the media—projected their hopes for "racial innocence" (Steele 2008). Another writer, citing social critic John McWhorter, contended, "'What gives people a jolt in their gut about the idea of President Obama is the idea that it would be a ringing symbol that racism no longer rules our land.' He is the great white hope" (Greenberg 2008b). Perhaps many believed that an Obama presidency could proffer a national absolution of the country's racist past, what Secretary of State Condoleezza Rice described, in a March 2008 interview with the *Washington Times*, as our national "birth defect."[2] In our monitoring of media discourse throughout the primary season, we found the narrative of Obama as national absolution fairly common, which helps to explain why coverage of his candidacy was so positive. When he appeared on Jay Leno's *Tonight Show*, MSNBC's Chris Matthews famously effused on the night of Obama's Iowa victory that "if you're actually in a room with Barack Obama and you don't cry when he gives one of those speeches, you're not an American. It's unbelievable."[3] Reflecting on the tone of Obama's media coverage, the editor of the *American Journalism Review*, Rem Reider, described coverage of Obama as "euphoric" (Seelye and Bosman 2008). As Fox News's Brit Hume observed, Obama "steps into one of our national aspirations that, contrary to what some people say, that we love to see an African-American get ahead and do well because it satisfies us that we are a just and fair country" (quoted in Hart 2007).

Few, it seems, treated Clinton's candidacy as a similar opportunity for redemption for past (and current) wrongs against women. Nor did Clinton herself consistently foreground the historical nature of her own campaign, for reasons we have explored in prior chapters. Indeed, after Obama gave his now-famous televised speech on race (his first attempt to tamp down the Jeremiah Wright controversy), Clinton was urged by some supporters to give her own speech on gender. She declined.

Here, we return again to the fact that race and gender have operated in rather different ways in US history, culture, and politics. In her analysis of media coverage of female presidential contenders (prior to the Clinton candidacy), Erika Falk argues that the persistent theme that the country may not be "ready" for a woman president has "in no case" been described as the result of fundamentally un-American prejudice, discrimination, or injustice (2008, 48). In other words, Americans (or at least the US media) do not readily see the unspoken "qualifications" for the presidency that have subtly defined women out of contention as fundamentally violating national values. It is therefore perhaps not surprising that negative reaction against Clinton's campaign was rarely framed in mainstream news as an embarrassment or setback for US progress on equality. In contrast, this theme—or rather, its positive corollary—cropped up persistently in coverage of Obama's campaign.

Ultimately, for all of these reasons, the painful and public collective memory of struggles over race trumped the nation's more clouded memory of (often private) gender inequalities. During the campaign, a former speechwriter for Bill Clinton drew an analogy to something ex–heavyweight champion Floyd Patterson once said about Muhammad Ali:

> "I was just a fighter," Patterson had said, "but he was history." Obama, too, was, and is, history—the first viable African-American presidential candidate. Yes, Hillary Clinton was the first viable female candidate, but it is still different. Race is the deepest and oldest and most bitter conflict in American history—the cause of our great Civil War and of the upheavals of the 1950s and '60s. And if some voters didn't appreciate the potential breakthrough that Obama's candidacy represented, many in the Democratic primaries and caucuses did—and so did the members of the media and Obama's fellow politicians. And as Clinton began treating Obama as just another politician, they recoiled and threw their support to him. (Judis 2008)

The Importance of Candidate Messaging: "Experience" vs. "Change"

As the quote above suggests, the nation seemed more captivated by Obama's narrative than Clinton's. But this was also a campaign between two candidates with very different attributes *beyond* their respective race and gender. Indeed, to some degree, one could remove race and gender from the picture and still be left with key variables that help explain how Hillary Clinton narrowly lost a primary battle she had been predicted to win. Even apart from his unique "postracial" symbolism, Obama undercut several of Clinton's advantages and emphasized some of her negatives, casting the two candidates in stark relief.

Most notably, the message of "hope" and "change" resonated with many Democrats eager to make a clean break from the Bush years. As one study of media coverage found, "Over time, reaching more than half of the assertions studied by mid-February. Despite this, over time likely Democratic voters came to think of Obama, more so than Clinton, as best prepared to lead the country—a sign that perhaps they forgive his inexperience in favor of change" (Project for Excellence in Journalism 2008c). On a more critical note, conservative columnist George Will wrote that "people inebriated by 'hope' for 'change' are not smitten about issues, concerning which the differences between him [Obama] and her [Clinton] must be measured by ideological micrometers. Voters are attracted to him as iron filings are to a magnet" (Will 2008).

Indeed, voters' views of Obama, as a Pew Center survey discovered, were "more influenced by how he makes them feel ('hopeful' and 'proud') than by specific characteristics voters attribute to him," and "inspiring" was the main attribute connected to support for him. For Clinton, on the other hand, the strongest trait voters attributed to her was the perception that she is "a phony," and 43 percent of Democratic voters said Clinton was "hard to like" (though interestingly, that trait was not strongly linked to how people planned to vote) (Pew Research Center 2008d).

The public images of these two candidates were not merely a creation of campaign messages in 2008. Rather, each candidate's messaging possibilities were shaped by longer-running political narratives. The respective niches that Clinton and Obama occupied in the political environment prior to 2008 are (inadvertently) illustrated in the opening pages of the popular book *Culture War?* co-authored by political scientist Morris Fiorina. Describing the common perception of the highly polarized political scene of the 1990s marked in particular by talk of "angry white males," the book observes that the dominant story line of the time "held that white men under economic pressure were livid about gays, guns, immigration, affirmative action, and Hillary" (Fiorina, Abrams, and Pope 2005, 2). In contrast, the opening sentence of the chapter entitled "If America Is Not Polarized, Why Do So Many Americans Think It Is?" reads: "Barack Obama's speech to the Democratic National Convention [in 2004] was widely applauded, in part . . . because many heard it as a welcome call for reconciliation—a plea for Americans to overcome their differences and discover their commonalities" (Ibid., 11).

Perhaps to address these comparative image liabilities, as we have discussed in prior chapters, Clinton positioned herself as the candidate offering superior experience. But for many voters, Obama's message of "change" trumped Clinton's "experience":

> As the candidate running hardest on the platform of experience, Clinton was seen by a wide margin (61 percent to 22 percent) as the candidate possessing that quality. Obama, meanwhile, retained his ironclad aura as an agent of change: he holds an 8-point margin (47 percent to 39 percent) over Clinton as the candidate that Democratic voters believe is most able to "bring about the changes this country needs." On the issue of preparedness for office, more Democratic voters believe Clinton's plan for mending the nation is better than Obama's (45 percent to 37 percent). But by a 41-point margin the same voters laud Obama as the candidate who can inspire the country. Worse for Clinton, 58 percent of Democrats seemed to value aura over argument when they said that the ability to inspire people is more

important than having a winning plan of action. And the Illinois senator is seen by most Democrats as the candidate who can bring people together (53 percent to 32 percent for Clinton). (Dokoupil 2008)

Ultimately, candidate Obama captured the imagination of millions of Americans for a variety of reasons; race—or rather postrace—was arguably part of a larger symbolic appeal rooted in a range of attributes voters associated with him and his candidacy. These attributes were carefully stoked by a disciplined campaign that utilized emerging Internet technologies and fundraising strategies to impressive effect (Cohen 2008b; Green 2008a; Kuhn 2008). In contrast, Clinton excelled at "old school" politicking and fundraising. "What's amazing," observed Peter Leyden of the New Politics Institute, "is that Hillary built the best campaign that has ever been done in Democratic politics on the old model—she raised more money than anyone before her, she locked down all the party stalwarts, she assembled an all-star team of consultants, and she really mastered this top-down, command-and-control type of outfit. And yet, she's getting beaten by this political start-up that is essentially a totally different model of the new politics" (quoted in Green 2008a).

"The Real '08 Fight: Clinton vs. Palin?"

Of course, Hillary Clinton was not the only woman in the national political spotlight in 2008, as this headline in the *New York Times* indicates.[4] Our findings then beg the question: How do the Clinton lessons apply to Republican vice presidential nominee Sarah Palin? Palin's brief race for the vice presidency seemed to demonstrate different gender messaging strategies than we have identified in our analysis of Hillary Clinton's 2008 campaign. Indeed, the two candidates were virtually yin and yang. Rising from relative obscurity with a thinner resume than most national figures, and a generation younger than Clinton, Palin's case offers a puzzling counterpoint to the many pages we have dedicated to understanding Clinton's race and raises rich questions for future research.

One question involves the particulars of the vice presidency. Clinton's troubled campaign certainly casts doubt on whether a woman could succeed her husband's presidency via the East Wing; being First Lady presents significant hurdles in overcoming the independent/ dependent bind. With Governor Palin nominated as Senator McCain's vice presidential running mate, however, the possibility of succession through the vice presidency is more readily apparent. The gender binds and narratives that await the vice presidential candidate are necessarily distinct—perhaps more forgiving—than those applied to the presidential candidate. After all, a presidential nominee *campaigns for that office for years;* vice presidential hopefuls *are selected only months* before election day. Without years of news media scrutiny, perhaps the successful woman vice president can grow into the job—running for the top of the ticket after having served as the president-in-waiting. Perhaps the gender binds and strategies are less exacting, more pliable for a woman *vice president.*

Indeed, it would seem irrefutable that one's place on the ticket matters to one's opportunities and constraints. In running for the vice presidency, Governor Palin was chosen by her running mate Senator McCain—not by voters, which creates a profoundly different testing ground for gender strategy. While a presidential contender is unavoidably running from a foundation of ambition, a running mate can frame her ambition in the context of service: Sarah Palin could argue that she did not seek power, but rather that she was called to it. No modern presidential candidate can credibly make such a claim, and as we have shown, ambition is problematic for female candidates.

Moreover, Palin's messaging leads us to wonder about the role of party in gender strategy options. While Clinton positioned herself within the equality frame, and mainly argued her viability through political experience and policy mastery, Palin's message was in some respects more overtly feminine and in many respects appealed to a more traditional notion of womanhood. Clad in the (expensive[5]) trappings of femininity—stiletto heels, silk skirts, and pearls—Governor Palin embraced that most traditionally feminine justification for power: motherhood. She commonly introduced herself to audiences by explaining that she "never really set out to be involved in public affairs," and described herself as having been an "average hockey mom" who went from the local parent-teacher association to the governorship (Palin 2008).

Yet Palin also gestured toward feminine solidarity, at least on one occasion, in terms more stark than Hillary Clinton employed. Speaking in California, she invoked the words of former secretary of state Madeleine Albright, the first woman to serve in that office, to suggest that gender loyalty should cross party lines: "There's a place in Hell reserved for women who don't support other women" (Pitney 2008).[6] Palin also overtly highlighted her feminine "difference," perhaps most famously when she called upon Clinton's own language to draw attention to her historic role on the Republican Party's ticket, offering to finish the fight Clinton had begun. "It was rightly noted in Denver this week that Hillary left 18 million cracks in the highest, hardest glass ceiling in America," she told the crowd who attended the announcement of her selection. "But it turns out the women of America aren't finished yet, and we can shatter that glass ceiling once and for all" (Eilperin and Kornblut 2008). Defending his running mate's credentials, Senator McCain burnished Palin's gender qualification during the final presidential debate, announcing that Palin was "a role model to women and reformers all over America" (CNN Political Ticker 2008).

While so many of Palin's visual gender cues (from the clothing to the winking and kiss-blowing and many photo ops surrounded by her beautiful children) and campaign-trail sound bites appeared to embrace the difference model of gender strategy, there were distinct signs of masculinity, as well. Indeed, Palin melded Clinton's masculinized fighter image with her own indelibly feminine style, declaring while campaigning in Carson, Nevada, "The heels are on, the gloves are off!" (Hair 2008). As David Carr of the *New York Times* explained, Palin is "a Rachael Ray with a 4x4, who can not only make a meal in under 30 minutes but hunt and kill the main course" (Carr 2008). Perhaps her ability to seamlessly invoke the most feminine alongside the most masculine images—Palin was widely pictured holding guns, including a semiautomatic weapon, and discussing her hunting practices—results from her party affiliation or rural background. Perhaps Republican women—particularly of Palin's generation and beyond—will find it possible, as Palin did, to occupy a longer stretch of the gender continuum.

Though a thorough exploration of Palin's messaging style must await further research, her candidacy signals the importance of gender strategy to contemporary presidential politics. Georgia Duerst-Lahti notes that "much of the heat around gender performances, or the way individuals 'do gender,' derives from contests to make one version of gender the hegemonic form, the form that is recognized as right, just, proper, and good. It is the form most able to control all other forms, and therefore it becomes most 'normal'" (2006, 28). In this vein, we suggest that Sarah Palin's entrance onto the national stage did not simply usher another woman to within striking distance of the White House. Palin brought with her an almost utterly different "version of gender" that signals a contemporary struggle for the "proper" articulation of female power. In another pithy observation, Carr (2008) summed up the difference between Clinton and Palin this way: "Senator Clinton is a politician who also happens to be a wife and mother. Ms. Palin is a wife and mother who also happens to be a politician." Palin's gender strategy was clearly enormously appealing to some voters, especially social conservatives, who lauded her stand on abortion and her personal decision to carry her

Down-syndrome baby to term, and among many Republican men, who could be seen at campaign events carrying signs reading "Palin Is a Fox." Yet just as clearly, Palin came in for heavy criticism and negative media coverage (Center for Media and Public Affairs 2008b), at least in part, it seems, because of her highly feminine style, and the early evidence suggests that unlike Hillary Clinton, Palin did not escape the "hair and hemlines" coverage so often trained on female candidates.

What Can We Learn from the Clinton Candidacy?

It is well worth remembering as we conclude this book that Hillary Clinton nearly secured the Democratic nomination and won close to 18 million votes along the way. While she may not have single-handedly normalized the image of a woman running for president, Clinton certainly debunked the notion that a woman could not run a viable presidential campaign. As Clinton said herself as she closed down her campaign on June 7, "From now on it will be unremarkable to think a woman could be president of the United States—and that is truly remarkable." Children coming of political age during the 2008 election cycle have been treated to an inspiring and groundbreaking experience: A woman nearly won a major party nomination, and a black man won the presidency.

Nevertheless, of course, many were deeply disappointed by Clinton's defeat, and many of her supporters took the lesson of 2008 to be the intractability of sexism in US politics. Some organized themselves as PUMA ("Party Unity My Ass") to protest Clinton's treatment during the campaign, saying they would "stay home or vote for John McCain in November to protest the way Democratic leaders 'allowed the primary campaign to go forward with the sexism in the media going unchecked by the party'" (Collins 2008b). Many believed, like Marilu Sochor, a 48-year-old real estate agent in Columbus, Ohio, that "women felt this was their time, and this has been stolen from them. . . . Sexism has played a really big role in the race" (Kantor 2008c). Many who had hoped to see a woman president in their lifetime were crushed by Obama's ability to snatch away from their candidate what they believed she had earned through years in service to the Democratic Party and the nation.

The fallout of Clinton's loss may be more lasting than personal disappointment. Erika Falk warns, "The most important consequence [of gender bias in media coverage of campaigns] is that the press coverage may make women less likely to run" (2008, 14). Given the apparently widespread perception of media bias among Clinton's supporters, Falk's concern is a serious one. Women who follow Clinton will inevitably be studying her path, fearing landmines. And yet, the argument of this book is that gender and media bias provide an illuminating but incomplete perspective on the difficulties Clinton faced. Thus, one danger in drawing lessons from 2008 lies in overemphasizing the role played by sexism in her defeat.

At the same time, if many of Clinton's difficulties stemmed from the particular context of 2008, then it is tempting to conclude that her candidacy teaches us little about future female candidacies. Moreover, if, as we have argued, Hillary Clinton brought particular liabilities to her quest that were unique to her, then it becomes more tempting to treat her as "sui generis"—an anomaly with little light to shed on future women who will run for the White House. The framework presented in this book also argues against that conclusion. For example, even as Clinton faced unique challenges, her messaging strategies seemingly mined the literature on women and politics and, to a significant degree, followed its counsel. Indeed, Clinton's gender strategy seemed premised on walking the tightrope of gendered double binds that presumably will face women politicians for the foreseeable future. We therefore have much to learn from how Clinton's strategies were crafted and conveyed, and in ascertaining how well they worked.

Future female candidates can learn not just from the gendered aspects of Clinton's strategy, but from the nongendered aspects as well. Indeed, given how close the final delegate count was, if Clinton had chosen a different battle plan we might well be telling a different kind of story in this book. For instance, the Clinton team reportedly focused its attention exclusively on primary rather than caucus states, declining to train campaign workers in the intricacies of caucus strategy. In part, this decision must have been guided by the daunting task of caucus work: it is far more labor- and time-intensive to bring voters to a caucus than a primary. More important, perhaps, Clinton appeared to have believed the nomination would be settled by Super Tuesday, spending vast sums of money leading up to February 5 and leaving herself little for battles in the remaining four months (on these and other errors see Cottle 2008; Kuhn 2008; Nagourney 2008a). As one postmortem account described it, "The campaign was built on the assumption of overwhelming force" (Baker and Rutenberg 2008). While this strategy worked, in that "in just about every state in which she spent serious time organizing and campaigning, she won" (Todd and Gawiser 2009, 14), the early primary states did not generate the delegates needed to win.

Indeed, one could argue that the party's use of proportional representation to award delegates was the single biggest hurdle Clinton faced in the context of 2008. By our own projections and those of some other observers (see Schnur 2008), had the Democrats operated under a win-ner-take-all system, Clinton would have clinched the nomination fol-lowing her Pennsylvania win because of her successes in larger, more delegate-rich states. Other Democratic Party rules, such as the party's primary schedule in 2008, also played a role in Clinton's defeat. While the practice of front-loading the nominating contests ostensibly helps any candidate possessing her considerable war chest and significant name recognition, it gave Clinton little time to remake her image with the press and the public, which had been deeply entrenched for some time. The role of superdelegates also made a difference to the 2008 race. The fact that, after Super Tuesday, Clinton could not hope to claim the nomination without winning a sizeable portion of the superdelegates meant that she could not win without being portrayed as having "won ugly." That is, her win would likely have been described as "theft" of the nomination from Obama.[7]

These rule-bound features of the 2008 campaign help to explain (if not to excuse) the sometimes aggressive tactics employed by the Clinton campaign, including several of the notable missteps described in previ-ous chapters. Clinton's gaffes, such as her "Bosnia fairy tale," her "hard-working white Americans" comment, and other missteps, were part of a larger strategic decision (made haltingly by the Clinton team [see Green 2008b, 2008c]) to go on the attack against Obama once her initial strate-gy of winning the big states proved inconclusive. By the end of the cam-paign, some simple poll numbers told a damning story of how dearly these campaign mistakes had cost her. A Gallup poll taken in late April found that while the number who described Clinton as "qualified/capa-ble of being president" was essentially unchanged from the beginning of the race, the two biggest characteristics voters spontaneously attributed to Clinton were "dishonest/don't trust" at 15 percent, up from 6 percent before the campaign began, and "past baggage associated with Bill" at 13 percent, up from 3 percent (Jones 2008).

Thus, the task for analysts is to keep the more enduring features of gender politics, presidential politics, and media politics simultaneously in focus even as we zoom in on the single, highly important and rather unique case of Hillary Clinton.

Three Interlocking Factors: Implications for Future Research

No campaign occurs in a vacuum—and Clinton's is no exception. We have analyzed Hillary Clinton's race for the US presidency within the context of her electoral circumstances, as well as media routines and gender bias. We therefore write at the interstices of two literatures: political communication, and women and politics. We have argued that the Clinton candidacy is best understood with a unique method of accounting for the gender bias embedded in a culture that sees presidential leadership as inherently male, the norms and practices of the news media for covering presidential politics, and the candidate and her particular context, and we have employed the literatures of our two fields to shine a bright light on the Clinton candidacy. Simply by analyzing the 2008 Democratic nominating race in this particular way, we hope we have advanced knowledge about how women have, and will, run for the White House.

In particular, by expanding the analyst's repertoire of "double binds," we have been able to consider more thoroughly many of the cultural and messaging hurdles faced by contemporary female presidential candidates. Two of these binds, equality/difference and femininity/competence, previously identified by communication expert Kathleen Hall Jamieson (1995), proved powerful constraints on Clinton's 2008 strategy. We have also argued that each candidate, and the political climate she faces, will raise additional and possibly unique binds. In her case, Clinton confronted an independence/dependence bind as a consequence of her partnership with the former president, as well as an experience/change agent bind that reflected both the political winds of 2008 as well as Clinton's unique challenges to articulate a message of change through experience.

Meanwhile, with (at the time of this writing) no women vice presidents or five-star generals, and the ranks of women governors and US senators quite thin, other binds loom for the immediate future. As one reporter observed after 2008, "there is no Hillary waiting in the wings. Except, of course, Hillary" (Zernike 2008). While it may be Clinton herself who emerges (again) as the next female presidential candidate, the bind of age/invisibility would seem to weigh heavily on her prospects. Jamieson (1995) warns that the aging US woman is dogged by a culture dismissive of mature women whose physical beauty has begun to fade. We found some of that tendency in media discourse around Senator Clinton in 2008; by the time she could launch her next attempt at the White House, she will have aged more. While age for some men conveys distinction, professional accomplishment, even wisdom (a benefit that did not always accrue to Republican presidential candidate John McCain, who was often portrayed as "too old" for the presidency), the aging woman faces irrelevance and erasure. Couple this with the fact that women must have a full resume in order to establish viability, and the reality that women enter electoral politics on average a decade later than men in order to balance their professional and personal responsibilities, and the age/invisibility bind looms large before Senator Clinton and those of her generation.

The case of Clinton in 2008 also leaves open a very fundamental question of gender strategy: Should she have run more explicitly "as a woman"? Should she have more consistently highlighted her history-making candidacy and what that might mean for US politics? Even during the "gender card" episode of October 2007, when Clinton was roundly accused of trying to deploy gender to her benefit, Clinton did not make the case that the United States needed a woman president, though she did at times suggest that there are hurdles to women who seek that post: "I am a woman . . . and like millions of women I know there are still barriers and biases out there, often unconscious" (quoted in Sheehy 2008). It appears that Clinton tended to raise gender at times and in ways that played right into the news media's obsession with campaign strategy and Clinton's ambition, so that gender talk during campaign 2008 became mostly talk about whether Clinton was benefitting politically from being a woman. Whether the country might benefit from electing a woman was rarely discussed.

The News Media and Female Presidential Candidates

Meanwhile, Clinton's 2008 campaign has offered a rich case study in how the contemporary national news media, within an increasingly complex media environment, portrayed the most serious female presidential candidate in US history. We have argued that Senator Clinton leapfrogged over some of the most enduring barriers to national office: neither fundraising nor name recognition proved her undoing, and the mainstream news media did not repeat some of the habits women and politics scholars have come to expect. Clinton received as much coverage (and early in the campaign, more) as her male competitors and was not particularly treated to the appearance-driven coverage found in earlier studies of women running for high office. Her qualifications and issue stands were covered more than those of her opponents (though were almost entirely overshadowed by horse-race coverage). Perhaps most interestingly, she was not marginalized as a "first" as were previous female presidential contenders (though it is an open question whether Ms. Clinton might have actually *benefited* from greater attention to her historical place among "firsts"). We leave open for now the question of whether the news media's routines for covering women politicians are changing—or perhaps Clinton is seen as a unique subject and therefore has not been treated qua woman as much as have lesser-known female politicians.

Our study therefore contributes to the women and politics literature by showing the limitations of earlier findings that are based largely upon research on women running for other offices, leaving us to wonder whether the media "rules" that often apply to campaigns for the Senate and governorships have less authority in the presidential context than previously assumed. But our study also cautions that even the politically viable female candidate will be treated to the media's relentless game-framing, which male candidates also face, and the negativity that framing entails, particularly if she falls behind in the polls.[8]

One thing unlikely to change is the fact that modern presidential campaigns run through the newsroom (even if they also increasingly run through the likes of Facebook). For candidate Clinton, we argue, the newsroom contained particular landmines. But one significance of Clinton's run for the White House (and Obama's) may simply have been to burst open the assumptions that seem to have structured news in the past. Based upon 2008, we can no longer just assume that a woman candidate is not viable, and we can no longer assume that the female candidate will be overlooked by the news media. Still, we find that the media imposed distinct and gendered burdens on candidate Clinton. While she bolted out of the gate toward her party's nomination, we have documented the many subterranean ways in which media coverage hindered her race. The news media's emphasis on the campaign "horse race" disadvantaged the lone filly on the track, both because she strategized poorly and did not perform as expected, and because the horse-race narrative lent itself to insidious gendering. For example, the mainstream media habit of zooming in on moments at which a candidate's fate may be decided, whether it is Edmund Muskie's cheek dabbing or Howard Dean's scream—or Hillary Clinton's misty eyes—highlighted the most controversial moments from Clinton's campaign. Again, this is an aspect of presidential politics that has sunk many a male candidacy; what was unique in 2008 was the way that key moments suddenly hinged on gender in a way rarely seen on our national stage—and many of those moments ultimately did not play to Clinton's benefit (beyond the particular voters who may have been mobilized by what they saw as her unfair treatment).

Meanwhile, the horse-race framework that dominated the 2008 primary election coverage crowded out the issue coverage that was

Clinton's strong suit. Because women regularly face a public that harbors doubts about female competence, any substance deficit in electoral coverage may be particularly debilitating to the female candidate. If the counsel of the women and politics literature is for women candidates to drive home their policy expertise and issues-based appeals, the lesson of the political communication literature, and of our findings, is how difficult it is for any presidential candidate to get their issues-based messages through the media filter. The game frame may amplify female candidates' particular challenge in getting out their policy messages— or, as Duerst-Lahti puts it, establishing "presidential timber" (Duerst-Lahti 2006, 22).

As we also saw in the case of Hillary Clinton, the game frame lends itself neatly to assumptions about the candidates' motives and personal failings—assumptions that are likely to be grounded in gendered stereotypes and gender norms. As Clinton continued her fight for the nomination rather than opting to "lose pretty" by bowing out early, exit talk and the "death" motif pervaded coverage and commentary, casting Clinton as a distinctly unfeminine spoiler who, by some accounts, needed to be forcibly removed from the scene. As feminist constitutional scholars might put it, game-framing may be neutral on its face, but discriminatory in its impact.

One final lesson from Clinton's campaign most assuredly is that "the next woman who decides to run . . . better have the hide of a rhinoceros" (Pollitt 2008). But it must also be said that a simple but crucial lesson of Clinton's candidacy for future female candidates is the importance of cultivating good relations with the national news media. By all accounts, Clinton's team did not cultivate reporters, but instead relied on message control and, failing that, intimidation. This was especially consequential because she more than most other candidates had to try to reframe the public's established image of her. We should therefore be careful in drawing too many conclusions from Clinton's case regarding prospects for future women in presidential politics. It remains to be seen whether a female presidential candidate possessing Hillary Clinton's resume and fundraising advantages but also possessing a different set of personal attributes and a different public persona leading into the campaign, and employing a different press management strategy, might fare better in gaining positive news coverage.

Ultimately, we are left with the proverbial $64,000 question: Had these patterns of coverage not prevailed in the media, would Hillary Clinton have won the Democratic nomination? If the media had not relentlessly game-framed the coverage, ignoring substance over politics and focusing on Clinton's "dying" campaign, would more Americans have given Hillary Clinton their votes? If individual news outlets like MSNBC had not drummed up anti-Hillary sentiment among viewers, would more voters have felt comfortable supporting her—even liking her? And if the news media overall had not downplayed the significance of Clinton's campaign victories, would her delegate count have reached the mark necessary to seal the nomination?

These are fascinating and important questions that we must leave to future studies to answer. For now, we are left with a conundrum. On the one hand, we may try to imagine what might have happened had the tone of Clinton's coverage been as positive, in the early months of the campaign in particular, as Barack Obama's. On the other hand, Clinton's long-established public image and her long-running troubles with the national press corps make such a thought experiment difficult: As the new, exciting (and male) candidate on the scene, Obama faced an entirely different set of opportunities and challenges than did Clinton.

Ultimately, it seems likely that media coverage of the 2008 election only partly accounted for public attitudes toward Hillary Clinton. The Project for Excellence in Journalism, whose report "Character and the Primaries of 2008" released in the waning weeks of the primary season found Clinton receiving as much or more positive coverage than her main rival, contended that "the public seemed to have developed opinions about her that ran counter to the media coverage, perhaps based on a pre-existing negative disposition to her that unfolded over the course of the campaign" (2008c). Given Clinton's long time in the public eye and the various controversial aspects of her political career, it would not be surprising if more positive media coverage would have failed to help her to secure the nomination.

Yet we cannot conclude that media negativity did not matter. In the aftermath of her Super Tuesday disappointments, campaign spokesman Doug Hattaway dismissed the media's "Clinton is doomed" theme, saying, "The 'momentum' story is just not all that real. People aren't led around by the nose by the national media narrative" (quoted in Kurtz 2008d). But decades of media research show that even though the media are unlikely to lead many voters by the nose, they certainly shape voters' perceptions of who the candidates are, why they are seeking power, and whether they are likely to win. And the media play a powerful role in creating gendered narratives during a campaign of such historic proportions, particularly in the arena of presidential politics. In the final analysis, though charges of rampant media sexism may be overwrought or simplistic, it does seem clear that the qualitative themes prominent in mainstream news wre markedly and negatively gendered—themes amplified greatly in the online world. It is unremarkable to conclude that this negative tone likely had *some* impact on the election.

Research also suggests that negative media coverage, particularly in the early months of the primary season, can contribute to candidates deciding to exit the nominating race (Haynes et al. 2004). While this obviously did not occur in Clinton's case, it is a disturbing irony that the portrayals of Clinton's "death" and the calls for her to exit seemingly became more pronounced the more votes she won. As Clinton biographer Gail Sheehy observed, Clinton's decision to remain in the race defied the press's expectation of her political "death," even though "in the last few months, she was winning" (*Talk of the Nation* 2008).

"Liking" Madam President

One of the nagging conclusions we draw from this research is that any woman running for president may confront certain "likeability" challenges. Hillary Clinton had particular challenges along these lines, which coincided with years spent in the public eye, many of them as a role-defying First Lady. Still, many aspects of Clinton's circumstances will likely be shared by future candidates: It is hard to imagine, for instance, a woman running for president who lacks prior media exposure and political experience, given the challenges of establishing viability. And although a majority of people in the United States report to pollsters that they would consider a "qualified" woman for the office, they are reporting on an abstraction, not a real woman with a voting record, time spent in the bright light of publicity, and a past. Moreover, any actual woman running for president is likely to be strong-willed, vocal, and ambitious. We thus should "consider . . . whether we would like *any* woman who works her way through the pipeline" (Zernike 2008). We are centuries past the model of the reluctant president who finds himself in office through political duty alone (Barber 1977). The current structure of presidential elections, relatively weak political parties, and televised competition requires personal ambition, but also "likeability." The contemporary "personal president," as Lowi (1986) calls it, may be a particularly challenging role for women to fill.

Future studies may consider the role that political party plays in the ability of female candidates to access the White House—and whether the challenges of gender strategy and media coverage take on particular qualities based on the candidate's party label. So too future scholars will have opportunities to consider the role of race: How will the next black woman candidate run? Will she face the same challenges and opportunities as Clinton did? And if the next woman to run wins her party's nomination, what awaits her in the months following the convention? Are the gender strategy demands distinct from the nominating phase to the general election? These are questions scholars did not have the opportunity to test with Hillary Clinton's 2008 campaign.

Conclusion

In 2008, Senator Hillary Rodham Clinton came closer than any woman in history to the US presidency. Governor Sarah Palin became only the second woman in our nation's history, and the first Republican woman, to be nominated for the vice presidency. For those citizens concerned with the status of women in the United States, the 2008 election proved many things: that women can be viable national candidates, that they can overcome at least some gendered barriers in media coverage, and that they can assume different gender strategies. There is reason to see 2008 as another milestone in the transformation of gender politics. As Jamieson suggests:

> as women have conquered the no-win situations confronting them, they have marshaled resources and refined aptitudes that have made them more and more capable of facing the next challenge, the next opportunity. At the same time, they have systematically exposed the fallacious constructs traditionally used against them, and changed and enlarged the frame through which women are viewed. Although the result is not a steady move toward equitable treatment of women, it is a world in which progress is certainly sufficient to justify optimism. (1995, 7)

This optimism should hearten those who read the academic study released at the end of October 2008, shortly before election day, which revealed that a full quarter of US school children ages five to ten believe it is *illegal* for a woman or a minority to be president of the United States (Bigler et al. 2008). With increasing images of women on the national stage, the public perception of the female contender will certainly evolve. As Jamieson reminds us, double binds are not immutable. But in the meantime, perhaps the biggest lesson of Clinton's 2008 quest for the White House—and our analysis of it—is that "nobody knew how to run a woman as leader of the free world" (Sheehy 2008).

Notes

1. As many scholars of race and/or gender know, there have long been tensions between the causes for racial and sex-based freedom and equality.

Unfortunately, some have seen these movements at odds with one another. The case is made most famously through a reminder of the falling-out between the abolition and women's suffrage movements of the mid-nineteenth century. Suffragist Elizabeth Cady Stanton, having advocated initially for both African American and women's rights, grew increasingly frustrated by the treatment of white women in the abolition movement. Spurred by the refusal of the 1840 World's Slavery Convention in London to seat her and other women delegates, Stanton increasingly argued on behalf of women's rights, calling for the historic Seneca Falls Convention, where she penned the Declaration of Sentiments in 1848. Ultimately, she abandoned her support of African Americans by opposing ratification of the 14th and 15th "civil war amendments" to the US Constitution. Though she had previously forged a unique political partnership with African American abolitionist Frederick Douglass, Stanton was incensed particularly by the 15th Amendment's overt institutionalization of male power in the constitution, which creates suffrage rights for freed black *men*. Stanton's language became racially charged, and she represents a deep schism in the causes of civil and women's rights.

2. Quoted in NPR's news blog, March 28, 2008, www.npr.org/blogs/news/2008/03/sec_of_state_rice_us_has_birth_1.html.

3. Video January 17, 2008, at hotair.com/archives/2008/01/17/video-chris-matthews-emotes-over-obama/.

4. This was the title of a *New York Times* article, analyzing the distinct messaging of these two female candidates (Healy 2008e).

5. Palin was roundly criticized, when, two weeks before election day, the *New York Times* revealed the campaign had spent $150,000 for the vice presidential candidate's wardrobe. The expenditures came from high-end designer retailers, which appeared to undermine the candidate's "every woman" message (Healy and Luo 2008).

6. Much was made in the media of the observation that Palin learned of the Albright quote by reading it from her Starbucks cup, and that she misquoted the former secretary of state, who actually said, "There's a place in Hell reserved for women who don't *help* other women" (Pitney 2008).

7. The role of Democratic superdelegates in the election was, to our reading, persistently framed in ways that made Clinton's reliance upon their votes highly problematic. This pervasive framing rested on two assumptions, at least one of which was factually wrong. First, as the candidates headed into the final leg of the nominating race before Pennsylvania, neither candidate could have won the 2,025 delegates required to secure the nomination without winning more of the superdelegates than the other. Second, the historical fact is that superdelegates were instituted by the party with the expectation that they would vote their conscience, not their constituency. Yet media coverage overlooked that role and consistently framed the question as whether the superdelegates would "follow the will of the voters," or whether Clinton would win by "overturning" that will.

8. Kahn (1996) has reasoned that women candidates are subjected to greater horse-race coverage because reporters doubt their political viability. According to this logic, reporters preoccupied with women's viability will write even more stories analyzing their political ups and downs. Our findings, coupled with the general political communication literature, suggest that horse-race and game-framed coverage are an endemic feature of how the media cover presidential politics.

APPENDIX
Democratic Party Rules in 2008

D emocratic Party election rules played a key role in the outcome of the 2008 nomination. We highlight here four factors that, combined with Clinton's strategic responses, contributed to her loss.

Michigan and Florida

Since 1972, and implementation of the McGovern-Fraser reforms (Crotty 1978; Shafer 1983),[1] the Democratic Party has allowed states to use either caucuses or primaries as their mode of selecting delegates to the national convention. The rules surrounding these electoral processes are rather complicated, but several facets had lasting implications for the 2008 candidates.

Perhaps most evident was the Democratic National Committee's decision under the leadership of Chairman Howard Dean to punish any state other than Iowa or New Hampshire that held its nomination contest before February 5 by stripping its delegates and rendering its primary elections "unofficial." Dean's action was a response to the long pattern of "frontloading," whereby more states have been setting earlier primary dates each successive presidential election in an effort to wield greater influence over the outcome. Many voters watched in confusion as both Michigan and Florida proceeded to vote before February 5 and then were punished by the party; surely, many voters in these states did not understand Dean's warning.[2] Further adding to the confusion, Senator Obama had withdrawn his name from the Michigan ballot in observance of the party's rule, leading many of his followers only the option to cast a vote for "uncommitted" delegates, or expressing their preference through the "other" category. In Florida, both Senators Obama and Clinton remained on the ticket, though national party rules prohibited them from campaigning there.

Clinton ostensibly won both states, and though she initially supported the party's decision to enforce its February 5 rule, as the primary contest dragged on and the competition for delegates tightened, she demanded the votes be counted and Michigan and Florida delegates be seated at the convention.[3] The party's Rules and Bylaws Committee met on May 31 to consider the controversy and decided to seat a reduced number of delegates.[4] The Clinton team objected to the committee's distribution of the Michigan delegates; their candidate had won 55 percent of the Michigan vote, and while Senator Obama was not on the ballot, "uncommitted" (most of whom were presumably Obama supporters) accounted for 40 percent of the votes cast. Clinton's representatives argued that she should take 55 percent of the Michigan delegates, while Obama's team advocated for splitting them 50-50 (in part because, in their view, their candidate had followed party rules by neither campaigning nor appearing on the ballot in that state). The resulting 69 for Clinton and 59 for Obama represented the party's compromise; in effect, it rendered Clinton's victories in those states "hollow" (Todd and Gawiser 2009, 14).

The impact on Clinton of the party's initial decision to render these two primaries unofficial, and then the Rules Committee's allocation of the delegates, was significant, for if the popular vote had been official, or if those delegates had been fully counted, Clinton would have had a clear claim to the majority of Democratic primary votes. Indeed, winning those primaries outright "might have given Mrs. Clinton a burst of momentum going into the 'Super Tuesday' primaries of February 5, and possibly allowed her to emerge that day with a significant lead in delegates, not to mention the popular vote" (Nagourney 2008e).

It also must be noted that the distinction between primaries and caucuses was relevant to the outcome of the 2008 nominating process. In broad terms, primaries are elections that occur in secrecy (the voting booth), while caucuses employ a more complex system of community discussion and publicly expressed preferences. The Clinton campaign decided to focus its attention and resources on states holding primaries rather than caucuses, and that decision was costly (see Cottle 2008; Kuhn 2008; Sheehy 2008). As master campaign strategist Joe Trippi observed after Clinton suspended her campaign, "Keep everything else the same and add that she competed in the caucus states, she would have won," adding that the ultimate outcome of her loss was "actually fairly amazing" (quoted in Kuhn 2008). As another observer noted, "by mostly neglecting these small contests, Clinton conceded delegates that effectively canceled out her gains in larger states. In Minnesota, for example, Obama beat Hillary by 24 delegates, twice as many delegates as Clinton gained on her rival in the much larger Pennsylvania primary" (Kuhn 2008). The fact that Obama largely won the caucus states underscores the shortsightedness of the Clinton campaign's lack of caucus organizing.

The Democratic Primary Calendar

The Democratic calendar of primaries and caucuses for 2008 was designed in part to offset the disproportionate effect that Iowa and New Hampshire have had for many years on the presidential selection process. But the 2008 calendar, which came about less through an orderly process than through a series of maneuvers by states seeking to increase their influence over the nomination, created a haphazard, illogical schedule for the candidates. And ultimately, the disproportionate influence of Iowa, at least, was not curbed, because Barack Obama's decisive win in that (largely white) state immediately gave him tremendous media coverage and momentum. (As we discussed in this book, Hillary Clinton's historic victory in New Hampshire was not granted similar significance by the media and pundits.) Shortly after those early primaries, twenty-three other contests were lumped together on February 5—a date that pundits dubbed "Super Duper Tuesday."[5] The Clinton campaign's decision to focus its resources on the February 5 contests turned out to be fateful, for when she lost fourteen of those contests, her campaign had few resources left and no clear plan in place for fighting the protracted battle to come (Kuhn 2008; Sheehy 2008).

The 2008 season also featured "a calendar of contests that had candidates rushing around the country for one week and settling down in another for weeks at a time"—"a recipe for the candidates getting embroiled in increasingly nasty . . . arguments as they sought to fill the vacuum. It also meant that gaffes that might normally have flared and subsided for a day lingered on" (Nagourney 2008d). More important, the schedule may have particularly disadvantaged Clinton by the simple fact that the states she would do best in came later in the schedule, after the notion of Obama as the front-runner had hardened and his delegate count mounted. NBC political analyst Chuck Todd has argued that Barack Obama's ability to win the Democratic nomination was largely "a matter of timing," since "primaries in February featured states that were dominated by Obama's coalition, while Clinton's coalition really didn't dominate any state primaries until much later when the campaign was all but over. Had the Kentucky, West Virginia, and Pennsylvania contests been held in February, and Virginia, Wisconsin, and Mississippi in May, there may have been another nominee" (Todd and Gawiser 2009, 13). Indeed, while Obama won eleven straight contests early in the primary season, he then lost nine of the final fourteen primaries. By then, however, his delegate lead had solidified, due largely to way the Democratic Party allocates delegates.

Proportional Representation

The Democratic Party distributes states' delegates to candidates based on proportional representation of the state vote. Republicans, on the other hand, use the winner-takes-all model that allocates all a state's delegates to the candidate who wins the popular vote in that state. The Democrats' proportional representation system for allotting delegates, as one observer noted, means that "sometimes the loser gets more":

> Proportional allocation of delegates in most Democratic contests means that, for instance, a candidate who wins with 49 percent of the vote might still have to evenly split the rewards, sharing the delegate take with a candidate who gets 45 percent.
> That same split—49 percent to 45 percent—represents Obama's current lead [by the end of the primary season] over Hillary Rodham Clinton among all nominating delegates going to the party's August convention. (Crawford 2008)

The tightness of this race, intensified by proportional distribution of delegates, pushed the contest on through the spring and into June, forcing candidates to raise and spend record amounts of money. Had the Democrats used the winner-takes-all rules—or had the Clinton team strategized more effectively with the existing rules in mind—Hillary Clinton may well have become the Democrat nominee, by virtue of her success in larger states. By one measure, had the Democratic delegates been assigned on the basis of the Republican winner-take-all rules, Clinton would have cinched her party's nomination the night of the Pennsylvania primary (see Schnur 2008). And in that scenario, the so-called superdelegates would not have become virtually a household word.

The Superdelegates

The final rule that shaped the outcome of the primary contest, and the one that received the most attention, is the role of the now (in)famous superdelegates. Following the failed Democratic candidacy of George McGovern in 1972, and the 1980 election, in which the incumbent Democratic president Jimmy Carter nearly lost his nomination to Senator Ted Kennedy (D-NY), Democratic Party leadership revisited nomination rules. Intending to offer a counterweight to democratic participation in the nomination process, party leaders added "noncommitted," or super delegates, in 1984. Democrats have used superdelegates to moderate the impact of popular minorities ever since, though until 2008, the role of superdelegates has been little known and carried little influence (*Congressional Quarterly* 1992). While many called on the superdelegates to affirm the 2008 majority popular vote in their states, the history of the creation of the superdelegate role shows it was explicitly created as a countermajoritarian influence, not as an affirmation of the democratic process.

One lesson of 2008 is that the quest for the Democratic nomination is a two-stage process of popular voting followed by the party leadership process. With her considerable political establishment network, Clinton carried an advantage in already-pledged superdelegates through much of the primary season, though the momentum of new superdelegate endorsements was Obama's, not hers. At the end of the season, after former candidate Senator John Edwards endorsed Senator Obama, a surge of superdelegates endorsed Obama as well, and the overall delegate calculation (regular plus superdelegates) grew insurmountable for the Clinton campaign.

The role of these rules in 2008 loomed larger than usual because of the closeness of the contest: A tight race brings the underlying rules of the game (and the tactical decisions induced by those rules) into sharp relief. Given the trajectory of the nomination process in 2008, it would be no surprise to see party leaders reconsider some of these practices. In the meantime, all candidates live by them, and Hillary Clinton's bid for the White House died, in part, because of them.

Notes

1. The media-dominated electoral system that is a main topic of this book came about in part because the political parties (first the Democrats and later

the Republicans) became disenchanted by the elite-driven system for choosing presidential nominees that prevailed from the mid-nineteenth century until 1972. That system, commonly described as involving behind-closed-doors negotiations among party elites in "smoke-filled rooms," allowed far less role for rank-and-file voters in choosing a nominee—and thus, far less of a role for the media. The rise of primaries and caucuses brought greater potential for voter involvement, but also made the media an essential conduit of information between all those voters and the candidates who now required ways of reaching the voters efficiently (see Patterson 1994).

2. Florida Democrats appealed to Chairman Dean and filed an unsuccessful lawsuit claiming that punishing the change in primary date, which was determined by the Republican-controlled state legislature, was unconstitutional (Kaczor 2007).

3. She also included the votes from those states in her frequent claims to having won 18 million votes (CNN Election Center 2008b).

4. The Rules Committee allocated 105 Florida pledged delegates and 69 Michigan pledged delegates to Senator Clinton, for a total of 87 official votes. Senator Obama received 67 Florida and 59 Michigan pledged delegates, resulting in a total of 63 total convention votes.

5. Super Tuesday included nineteen states, plus American Samoa, the District of Columbia, the Virgin Islands, and US citizens abroad.

References

ABC News. 2008. "Rivals Reacts to Teary Clinton." January 7. http://blogs .abcnews.com/politicalradar/2008/01/rival-reacts-to.html.

Abrams, Dan. 2008. "Media Matters?" No date given. www.msnbc.msn.com/id/ 21134540/vp/22581293#22581293.

Aday, Sean. 2004. "Reinventing John Kerry." AlterNet. July 19. www.alternet.org/story/19280/?ses=d157f4a4578c157fc18cbda670bbd6c9.

Aday, Sean, and James Devitt. 2001. "Style over Substance: Newspaper Coverage of Elizabeth Dole's Presidential Bid." *Harvard International Journal of Press and Politics* 6, no. 2: 52–73.

Aldrich, John H. 1992. "Presidential Campaigns in Party- and Candidate-Centered Eras." In Mathew D. McCubbins, ed., *Under the Watchful Eye: Managing Presidential Campaigns in the Television Era*. Washington, DC: CQ Press, 1992.

Alexovich, Ariel. 2008a. "Clinton Aspires to Be an Amiga." *New York Times*, February 29. http://thecaucus.blogs.nytimes.com/2008/01/29/clinton-aspires-to-be-an-amiga.

———. 2008b. "Clinton's National Security Ad." *New York Times*, February 29. http://thecaucus.blogs.nytimes.com/2008/02/29/clintons-national-security-ad/index.html?nl=pol&emc=pol.

———. 2008c. "New Clinton Ad: 'Night Shift.'" *New York Times*, February 19. http://thecaucus.blogs.nytimes.com/2008/02/19/new-clinton-ad-night-shift/?ex=1204088400&en=6fd1fb202b06.

Alter, Jonathan. 2008. "Is Penn Mightier Than Axe? A Look at the Chief Strategists Behind Clinton and Obama." *Newsweek*, January 21. www.newsweek.com/id/91666.

Ambinder, Mark. 2007. "Teacher and Apprentice." *The Atlantic Monthly*, December. www.theatlantic.com/doc/200712/clinton-obama.

Americans for Democratic Action. 2008. *ADA Today* 63, no. 1 (February).

Argetsinger, Amy, and Roxanne Roberts. 2008. "Down Pa. Avenue, a Farewell Toast." *Washington Post*, June 9, C3.

Associated Press. 2008a. "Clinton Says She Regrets Comment About Race." May 14. www.msnbc.msn.com/id/24633826.

————. 2008b. "Transcript of Barack Obama's Iowa Victory Speech." www .newsday.com/news/local/politics/ny-usobam0105-transcript,0,7073760. story.

Bai, Matt. 2008a. "The Change Versus Experience Pitfall." *New York Times,* February 5. http://thecaucus.blogs.nytimes.com/2008/02/05/the-change-vs-experience-pitfall.

————. 2008b. "Obama and Clinton Brace for Long Run." *New York Times,* February 7.

Baker, Peter. 2007. "Hold the Crumpets." *Washington Post,* December 27. http://blog.washingtonpost.com/the-trail/2007/12/29/hold_the_crumpets .html.

Baker, Peter, and Jim Rutenberg. 2008. "The Long Road to a Clinton Exit." *New York Times,* June 8. www.nytimes.com/2008/06/08/us/politics/ 08recon.html?th&emc=th.

Balz, Dan. 2007a. "Taking Absolutely Nothing for Granted." *Washington Post Online,* October 18. http://blog.washingtonpost.com/the-trail/2007/10 /18/post_135.html.

————. 2007b. "Victim or a Party Crasher in the 'All-Boys Club'?" *Washington Post Online,* November 2. http://blog.washingtonpost.com/thetrail/2007/ 11/02/post_172.html.

Balz, Dan, and Anne Kornblut. 2008. "Obama Claims Nomination." *Washington Post,* June 4. www.washingtonpost.com/wp-dyn/content/ article/2008/06/03/AR2008060300888.html.

Barber, James David. 1977. *The Presidential Character: Predicting Performance in the White House,* 2nd ed. Englewood Cliffs, NJ: Prentice-Hall.

Beam, Christopher, Chadwick Matlin, and Chris Wilson. 2008. "The Hillary Deathwatch: Gauging the Odds that Clinton Will Win the Nomination." *Slate,* March 27. www.slate.com/id/2187558.

Beasley, Maurine H. 2005. *First Ladies and the Press: The Unfinished Partnership of the Media Age.* Evanston, IL: Northwestern University Press.

Bennett, W. Lance. 2008. *News: The Politics of Illusion,* 8th ed. New York: Longman.

Bennett, W. Lance, Regina G. Lawrence, and Steven Livingston. 2008. *When the Press Fails.* Chicago: University of Chicago Press.

Berke, Richard L. 1999. "As Political Spouse, Bob Dole Strays from Campaign Script." *New York Times,* May 17, A1.

Bernstein, Carl. 2007. *A Woman in Charge: The Life of Hillary Rodham Clinton.* New York: Alfred A. Knopf.

————. 2008. "Hillary Clinton: Truth or Consequences." *CNN.com,* March 26.

Bigler, Rebecca S., Andrea E. Arthur, Julie Milligan Hughes, and Meagan M. Patterson. 2008. "The Politics of Race and Gender: Children's Perceptions of Discrimination and the U.S. Presidency." *Analyses of Social Issues and Public Policy,* October 3. www3.interscience.wiley.com/journal /121429416/abstract.

Blumenthal, Mark. 2007. "What's in a Name?" *Pollster.com,* August 24. www .pollster.com/blogs/whats_in_a_name.php.

Bombardieri, Marcella. 2007. "Clinton Shows Femininity to Court Key Constituency." *The Boston Globe*, October 18. www.boston.com/news/nation/articles/2007/10/18/clinton_shows_femininity_to_court_key _constituency/.

Brown, Tina. 2008. "Hillary and the Invisible Women." *Newsweek*, March 8. www.newsweek.com/id/120064.

Burrell, Barbara C. 1994. *A Woman's Place Is in the House: Campaigning for Congress in the Feminist Era*. Ann Arbor: University of Michigan Press.

———. 1997. *Public Opinion, the First Ladyship, and Hillary Rodham Clinton*. New York: Garland.

———. 2005. "Campaign Financing: Women's Experience in the Modern Era." In Sue Thomas and Clyde Wilcox, eds., *Women and Elective Office: Past, Present, and Future*, 2nd ed., 26–37. New York: Oxford University Press.

———. 2006. "Political Parties and Women's Organizations: Bringing Women in the Electoral Arena." In Susan Carroll and Richard Fox, eds., *Gender and Elections: Shaping the Future of American Politics*, 143–68. New York: Cambridge University Press.

Bystrom, Dianne. 2003. "On the Way to the White House: Communication Strategies for Women Candidates." In Robert P. Watson and Ann Gordon, eds., *Anticipating Madam President*, 95–106. Boulder: Lynne Rienner Publishers.

———. 2008. "Gender and U.S. Presidential Politics: Early Newspaper Coverage of Hillary Clinton's Bid for the White House." Paper presented at the annual meeting of the American Political Science Association, Boston, MA, August 28–31.

Bystrom, Dianne G., Mary Christine Banwart, Lynda Lee Kaid, and Terry A. Robertson. 2004. *Gender and Candidate Communication: VideoStyle, WebStyle, and NewsStyle*. New York: Routledge.

Bystrom, Dianne G., Terry A. Robertson, and Mary Christine Banwart. 2001. "Framing the Fight: An Analysis of Media Coverage of Female and Male Candidates in Primary Races for Governor and US Senate in 2000." *American Behavioral Scientist* 44, no. 12: 1999–2012.

"Campaign Essentials: Unraveling of a Candidate." 2004. Discovery Channel. www.cosmeo.com.

The Campaign Spot. 2007. "Hillary's 'The Politics of Pile-On' Video: Digging the Hole Deeper." November 1. http://campaignspot.nationalreview.com/post/?q=YmQwZDA4MjRiZTk3N2VmMDU0ZjUxNDIxOTY2YmM5NWM=.

Campbell, Karlyn Kohrs. 1998. "The Discursive Performance of Femininity: Hating Hillary." *Rhetoric & Public Affairs* 1, no. 1: 1–19.

Cannon, Lou. 2008. "Reagan's Choice: From 1976, a Question for Obama and Clinton." *Washington Post*, June 3. www.washingtonpost.com/wpdyn/content/article/2008/06/02/AR2008060202599.html.

Cappella, Joseph N., and Kathleen Hall Jamieson. 1997. *Spiral of Cynicism: The Press and the Public Good*. Chicago: University of Chicago Press.

Carr, David. 2008. "The Media Equation: Drawing a Bead on the Press." *New York Times*, September 8. www.nytimes.com/2008/09/08/business/media/08carr.html.

Carroll, Susan J. 2009. "Reflections on Gender and Hillary Clinton's Presidential Campaign: The Good, the Bad, and the Misogynic." *Politics & Gender* 5: 1–20.

Center for American Women and Politics. 2004. "The Gender Gap and the 2004 Women's Vote: Setting the Record Straight." October 28. Advisory.

———. 2006. "Women's Votes Pivotal in Shifting Control of US Senate to Democrats." November 9, Press Release.

Center for Media and Public Affairs. 2004. "Campaign 2004 Final." *Media Monitor* 18, no. 6 (November/December). www.cmpa.com/files/media _monitor/04novdec.pdf.

———. 2008a. "Election Watch '08: The Primaries." www.cmpa.com/files/ media_monitor/08marapr.pdf.

———. 2008b. "Obama Leads the Media Race as Well." Press release, October 14. www.cmpa.com/media_room_press_8.htm.

———. 2008c. "Study Finds Obama's Media Momentum Slows." March 3. www.cmpa.com/Studies/Election08/election%20news%203_3_08 .htm.

The Charlie Rose Show. 2008. February 8. PBS.

Chotiner, Isaac. 2008. "Dangerous Liaisons." *The New Republic*, May 27. www.tnr.com/politics/story.html?id=b48a6936-fb3c-42b0-83c1-f91d1cb3a3dc.

Chozick, Amy, and Nick Timiraos. 2008. "Campaign Notebook: How Clinton Won." *Wall Street Journal*, March 5.

Clift, Eleanor. 2008. "Showing His Mettle." *Newsweek*, May 2. www .newsweek.com/id/135157.

Clift, Eleanor, and Tom Brazaitis. 2003. *Madam President: Women Blazing the Leadership Trail.* New York: Routledge.

Clinton, Hillary. 1995. "Women's Rights Are Human Rights." Speech delivered September 5. Beijing, China.

———. 2002. *Floor Speech of Senator Hillary Rodham Clinton on S.J. Res. 45, A Resolution to Authorize the Use of United States Armed Forces Against Iraq.* October 10. http://clinton.senate.gov/speeches/iraq_101002.html.

———. 2005. *Remarks by Senator Hillary Rodham Clinton to the NYS Family Planning Providers.* January 24. http://Clinton.senate.gov/~clinton/ speeches/2005125A05.html.

———. 2007. Video Transcript: Presidential Exploratory Committee Announcement. January 30. Press Release. www.hillaryclinton.com/news/ release/view/?id=1234.

CNN Election Center. 2008a. Primary and caucus information. www.cnn.com/ELECTION/2008/primaries.

———. 2008b. "Clinton Says She Leads in Popular Vote." April 24. http://www.cnn.com/2008/POLITICS/04/24/campaign.wrap/#cnnSTCText.

CNN Political Ticker. 2008. "McCain Praises Palin as 'Role Model' and 'Reformer.'" October 15. http://politicalticker.blogs.cnn.com/2008/10/ 15/mccain-praises-palin-as-role-model-and-reformer/.

CNN Politics.com. 2008. "Limbaugh: So-Called 'Dream Ticket' Doesn't Have a Prayer." March 6. http://politicalticker.blogs.cnn.com/2008/03/06/ limbaugh-so-called-dream-ticket-doesnt-have-a-prayer/.

Cohen, Noam. 2008a. "Is Obama a Mac and Clinton a PC?" *New York Times*, February 4. www.nytimes.com/2008/02/04/technology/04link.html.

————. 2008b. "The Wiki-Way to the Nomination." *New York Times*, June 9. www.nytimes.com/2008/06/08/weekinreview/08cohen.html?nl=pol&emc= pol.

Cole, John. 2008. "Thin-Skinned, Much?" Balloon Juice, January 6. http://www.balloon-juice.com/?p=9421.

Collins, Gail. 2008a. "The Battle of the Baggage." *New York Times*, April 17. www.nytimes.com/2008/04/17/opinion/17collins.html?emc=eta1.

————. 2008b. "The Denver Accords." *New York Times*, August 16. www.nytimes.com/2008/08/16/opinion/16collins.html?ex=1219636800&e n=d9c6c7ea6341f2aa&ei=5070&emc=eta1.

————. 2008c. "The Uncle Al Election." *New York Times*, March 27. www .nytimes.com/2008/03/27/opinion/27collins.html?_r=1&hp&oref= slogin.

————. 2008d. "What Hillary Won." *New York Times,* June 7. www.nytimes .com/2008/06/07/opinion/07collins.html?scp=3&sq=gail+ collins&st=nyt.

Collins, Patricia Hill. 1990. *Black Feminist Thought: Knowledge, Consciousness, and the Politics of Empowerment.* New York: Routledge.

Congressional Quarterly Almanac. 1992. "Superdelegates: 'Window Dressing.'" 18.

Conversation between Carol Gilligan and Catharine MacKinnon. 1984. Mitchell Lecture Series, State University of New York at Buffalo School of Law. November 20. In "James McCormick Mitchell Lecture: Feminist Discourse, Moral Values, and the Law—A Conversation." *Buffalo Law Review* 34, no. 1: 11–87.

Cook, Charlie. 2008a. "The Race to the White House." Manship School of Mass Communication, Louisiana State University. October 16.

————. 2008b. Personal conversation with the author. Baton Rouge, Louisiana, October 16.

Cottle, Michelle. 2008. "What Went Wrong?" *The New Republic*, May 16. www.tnr.com/politics/story.html?id=f7a4a380-c4a4-4f84- b653-f252e8569915.

Countdown with Keith Olbermann. 2007. "Up Close and Personal with Sen. Hillary Clinton." October 11. www.msnbc.msn.com/id/21255520.

Couric, Katie. 2008. "Katie Couric's Notebook: Sexism and Politics." CBS News, June 11. www.cbsnews.com/blogs/2008/06/11/couricandco/entry 4174429.shtml.

Crawford, Craig. 2008a. "Dem Rules Say Winners Don't Take All." *CQ Politics*, June 3. http://blogs.cqpolitics.com/trailmix/2008/06/dem-rules- say-winners-dont-tak.html.

————. 2008b. "Losing Pretty or Winning Ugly." *YouTube*. www .youtube.com/watch?v=mbSUURZUXwc (accessed October 15, 2008).

Crotty, William J. 1978. *Decision for the Democrats: Reforming the Party Structure*. Baltimore: The Johns Hopkins University Press.

Dalton, R. J., Beck, P. A., and Huckfeldt, R. 1998. "Partisan Cues and the Media: Information Flows in the 1992 Presidential Election." *American Political Science Review* 92, no. 1: 11–26.

Davies, Dave. 2008. Interviewed on *Fresh Air*. April 17. www.npr .org/templates/player/mediaPlayer.html?action=1&t=1&islist=false&id=89 687774&m=89728065.

Davis, Richard. 2009. *Typing Politics: The Role of Blogs in American Politics.* Oxford: Oxford University Press.

"The Democratic Debate in Cleveland." 2008. *New York Times*, February 26. www.nytimes.com/2008/02/26/us/politics/26text-debate.html.

Devitt, James. 2002. "Framing Gender on the Campaign Trail: Female Gubernatorial Candidates and the Press." *Journalism and Mass Communication Quarterly* 79, no. 2: 445–463.

Dokoupil, Tony. 2008. "The Stalemate Continues." *Newsweek*, March 7. www.newsweek.com/id/119953.

Dolan, Kathleen A. 1998. "Voting for Women in the 'Year of the Women.'" *American Journal of Political Science* 42: 272–293.

———. 2004. *Voting for Women: How the Public Evaluates Women Candidates.* Boulder: Westview Press.

———. 2008. "Is There a 'Gender Affinity Effect' in American Politics?" *Political Research Quarterly* 61, no. 1: 79–89.

Dowd, Maureen. 1999. "Freudian Face-Off." *New York Times*, June 16. http://query.nytimes.com/gst/fullpage.html?res=9405E1DB1E38F935A257 55C0A96F958260.

———. 2007. "Gift of Gall." *The New York Times*, November 4. www.nytimes.com/2007/11/04/opinion/04dowd.html?pagewanted=print.

———. 2008a. "Can Hillary Cry Her Way Back to the White House?" *New York Times*, January 9.

———. 2008b. "A Flawed Feminist Test." *New York Times*, February 13, 25.

———. 2008c. "She's Still Here!" *New York Times*, June 4. www.nytimes.com/ 2008/06/04/opinion/04dowd.html?em&ex=1212724800&en=82513e4995f 35fab&ei=5087%0A.

———. 2008d. "Surrender Already, Dorothy." *New York Times*, March 30. www.nytimes.com/2008/03/30/opinion/30dowd.html?hp.

———. 2008e. "Two Against One." *New York Times*, January 23. www.nytimes.com/2008/01/23/opinion/23dowd.html.

———. 2008f. "Wilting Over Waffles." *New York Times*, April 23. www.nytimes.com/2008/04/23/opinion/23dowd.html.

Downs, Anthony. 1957. *An Economic Theory of Democracy.* New York: Harper.

Duerst-Lahti, Georgia. 2004. "Masculinity on the Campaign Trail." In Lori Cox Han and Caroline Heldman, eds., *Rethinking Madam President.* Boulder: Lynne Rienner Publishers.

———. 2006. "Presidential Elections: Gendered Space and the Case of 2004." In Susan Carroll and Richard Fox, eds., *Gender and Elections: Shaping the Future of American Politics*, 12–42. New York: Cambridge University Press.

———. 2007. "Masculinity on the Campaign Trail." In Lori Cox Han and Caroline Heldman, eds., *Rethinking Madam President: Are We Ready for a Woman in the White House?* 87–112. Boulder: Lynne Rienner Publishers.

Duerst-Lahti, Georgia, and Rita Mae Kelly, eds. 1995. *Gender Power, Leadership, and Governance.* Ann Arbor: University of Michigan Press.

Edwards, Elizabeth. 2008. "Bowling 1, Health Care 0." *New York Times*, April 28. www.nytimes.com/2008/04/27/opinion/27edwards.html?ex=120996 0000&en=42cf9ad2ef539bb3&ei=5070&emc=eta1#.

Eilperin, Juliet, and Anne Kornblut. 2008. "An All-Out Battle for Women's Votes Begins." *Washington Post*, August 30, A01.

Entman, Robert. 2003. *Projections of Power*. Chicago: University of Chicago Press.

Entman, Robert, and Andrew Rojecki. 2001. *The Black Image in the White Mind: Media and Race in America*. Chicago: University of Chicago Press.

Estrich, Susan. 2005. *The Case for Hillary Clinton*. New York: HarperCollins.

Fahey, Anna Cornelia. 2007. "French and Feminine: Hegemonic Masculinity and the Emasculation of John Kerry in the 2004 Presidential Race." *Critical Studies in Media Communication* 24, no. 2: 132–150.

Falk, Erika. 2008. *Women for President: Media Bias in Eight Campaigns*. Urbana: University of Illinois Press.

Falk, Erika, and Kathleen Hall Jamieson. 2003. "Changing the Climate of Expectations." In Robert P. Watson and Ann Gordon, eds., *Anticipating Madam President*, 43–52. Boulder: Lynne Rienner Publishers.

Falk, Erika, and Kate Kenski. 2006. "Sexism Versus Partisanship: A New Look at the Question of Whether America Is Ready for a Woman President." *Sex Roles* 54: 413–428.

Fallows, James. 1997. *Breaking the News: How the Media Undermine American Democracy*. New York: Vintage.

Faludi, Susan. 2007. "Hillary Clinton Plays the Winning Gender Card." *Los Angeles Times*, November 9. www.latimes.com/news/opinion/la-oefaludi9nov09,0,4001222.story?coll=la-opinion-center.

Farber, Jim. 2008. "Geraldine Ferraro Lets Her Emotions Do the Talking." *The Daily Breeze*, March 7. www.dailybreeze.com/lifeandculture/ci_8489268.

Farnsworth, Stephen J., and S. Robert Lichter. 2007. *The Nightly News Nightmare: Television's Coverage of U.S. Presidential Elections, 1988–2004*, 2nd ed. Lanham, MD: Rowman & Littlefield.

Ferraro, Susan. 1990. "The Prime of Pat Schroeder." *New York Times*, July 1. http://query.nytimes.com/gst/fullpage.html?res=9C0CE3DA103CF932A35754C0A966958260&sec=&spon=&pagewanted=5.

Fiorina, Morris, Samuel J. Abrams, and Jeremy C. Pope. 2005. *Culture War? The Myth of a Polarized America*. New York: Longman.

Fish, Stanley. 2007. "It Depends on What the Meaning of 'Makes Sense' Is." *New York Times*, November 11.

Fishbowl.com. 2008. "Couric Gets Honored in D.C." June 11. www.mediabistro.com/fishbowlDC/television/couric_gets_honored_in_dc_86823.asp.

Fox, Richard L. 2006. "Congressional Elections: Where Are We on the Road to Gender Parity?" In Susan Carroll and Richard Fox, eds., *Gender and Elections: Shaping the Future of American Politics*, 97-116. New York: Cambridge University Press.

Freeman, Jo. 2000. *A Room at a Time: How Women Entered Party Politics*. Lanham, MD: Rowman and Littlefield Press.

———. 2008. *We Will be Heard: Women's Struggles for Political Power in the United States*. Lanham, MD: Rowman and Littlefield Press.

Gallup, George Jr. 2000. *The 1999 Gallup Poll: Public Opinion*. SR Books.

Gandy, Kim. 2008. "Ignorance and Venom: The Media's Deeply Ingrained

Sexism." National Organization for Women, February 14. www.now.org/news/note/021408.html.

Gerth, Jeff, and Don Van Natta Jr. 2007. *Her Way: The Hopes and Ambitions of Hillary Rodham Clinton.* New York: Little, Brown and Company.

Gidengil, Elisabeth, and Joanna Everitt. 2000. "Filtering the Female: Television News Coverage of the 1993 Canadian Leaders' Debates." *Women & Politics* 21, no. 4: 105–131.

———. 2003. "Talking Tough: Gender and Reported Speech in Campaign News Coverage." *Political Communication* 20, no. 3: 209–232.

Gilligan, Carol. 1982. *In a Different Voice: Psychological Theory and Women's Development.* Cambridge: Harvard University Press.

Glass, David. 1985. "Evaluating Presidential Candidates: Who Focuses on Their Personal Attributes?" *Public Opinion Quarterly* 49, no. 4 (Winter): 517–534.

Graber, Doris. 1976. "Press and TV as Opinion Resources in Presidential Campaigns." *Public Opinion Quarterly* 40: 285–303.

———. 2001. *Processing Politics: Learning from Television in the Internet Age.* Chicago: University of Chicago Press.

Green, Joshua. 2006. "Take Two—Hillary's Choice." *Atlantic Monthly,* November. www.theatlantic.com/doc/200611/green-hillary.

———. 2008a. "The Amazing Money Machine." *Atlantic Monthly,* August. www.theatlantic.com/doc/200806/obama-finance?ca=8icrvpjQp3%2BuFgKxkWZIezzVy%2BpScbOtVgDJOhSazEI%3D.

———. 2008b. "The Front-Runner's Fall." *Atlantic Monthly,* September. www.theatlantic.com/doc/200809/hillary-clinton-campaign.

———. 2008c. "The Hillary Clinton Memos." *Atlantic Monthly,* August 11. www.theatlantic.com/doc/200808u/clinton-memos.

———. 2008d. "Inside the Clinton Shake-Up." *Atlantic Monthly,* February. www.theatlantic.com/doc/200802u/patti-solis-doyle.

Greenberg, David. 2008a. "The Long Goodbye: It's Too Early to Talk About Hillary's Withdrawal." *Slate,* March 5. www.slate.com/id/2185831.

———. 2008b. "Why Obamamania? Because He Runs as the Great White Hope." *Washington Post,* January 13, B4.

Guy, Mary Ellen. 1995. "Hillary, Health Care, and Gender Power." In Georgia Duerst-Lahti and Rita Mae Kelly, eds., *Gender Power, Leadership, and Governance,* 239–256. Ann Arbor: University of Michigan Press.

Hair, Connie. 2008. "The Heels Are On, the Gloves Are Off." *Human Events,* October 6. www.humanevents.com/article.php?id=28882.

Halperin, Mark. 2007. *The Way to Win: Taking the White House in 2008.* New York: Random House.

Hamby, Peter. 2008. "Clinton Explains RFK Assassination Comment." CNN, May 23. www.cnn.com/2008/POLITICS/05/23/clinton.comments.

Han, Lori Cox. 2007. "Is the United States Really Ready for a Woman President?" In Lori Cox Han and Caroline Heldman, eds., *Rethinking Madam President: Are We Ready for a Woman in the White House?* Boulder: Lynne Rienner Publishers.

Han, Lori Cox, and Caroline Heldman, eds. 2007. *Rethinking Madam President: Are We Ready for a Woman in the White House?* Boulder: Lynne Rienner Publishers.

Hansen, Susan B., and Laura Wills Otero. 2006. "A Woman for U.S. President? Gender and Leadership Traits Before and After 9/11." *Journal of Women, Politics, and Policy* 28, no. 1: 35–60.

Harper, Liz. 2004. "Poll Crazy in Campaign Coverage." *NewsHour Extra*, October 20. www.pbs.org/newshour/extra/features/july-dec04/polls_10-20.html.

Hart, Peter. 2007. "Obamania: How Loving Barack Obama Helps Pundits Love Themselves." FAIR *Extra!* March/April. www.fair.org/index.php?page= 3094.

Hart, Roderick. 1998. *Seducing America: How Television Charms the Modern Voter*. Thousand Oaks, CA: Sage.

Hart/McInturff. 2008. NBC News/*Wall Street Journal* Survey. Study #6080. March 12. http://msnbcmedia.msn.com/i/msnbc/sections/news/080312_NBC-WSJ_Poll_Full.pdf.

Haynes, Audrey A., Paul-Henri Gurian, Michael H. Crespin, and Christopher Zorn. 2004. "The Calculus of Concession: Media Coverage and the Dynamics of Winnowing in Presidential Nominations." *American Politics Research* 32: 310–337.

Healy, Patrick. 2007a. "Clinton Gives War Critics New Answer on '02 Vote." *The New York Times,* February 18.

———. 2007b. "In Elderly Women, Clinton Sees an Electoral Edge." *New York Times,* November 27. www.nytimes.com/2007/11/27/us/politics/27ladies.html.

———. 2008a. "Clinton Clearly Outduels Obama in Pennsylvania." *New York Times*, April 23, A1.

———. 2008b. "Clinton Sees Many Reasons to Stay In." *New York Times*, May 21. www.nytimes.com/2008/05/21/us/politics/21clinton.html?nl=pol&emc=pol

———. 2008c. "Clinton's Message, and Moment, Won the Day." *New York Times*, January 10. www.nytimes.com/2008/01/10/us/politics/10clinton.html?th&emc=th.

———. 2008d. "In 2 Battlegrounds, Voters Say, Not Yet." *New York Times*, March 5, A1.

Healy, Patrick, and Michael Cooper. 2008. "Clinton Is Victor, Defeating Obama." *New York Times*, January 9. A1.

Healy, Patrick, and Michael Luo. 2008. "$150,000 Wardrobe for Palin May Alter Tailor-Made Image." *New York Times,* October 23. www.nytimes.com/2008/10/23/us/politics/23palin.html.

Healy, Patrick, and Jeff Zeleny. 2008a. "At Debate, Two Rivals Go After Defiant Clinton." *New York Times,* January 6. www.nytimes.com/2008/01/06/us/politics/06dems.html?partner=rssnyt&emc=rss.

———. 2008b. "Obama and Clinton Tangle at Debate." *New York Times*, January 22. www.nytimes.com/2008/01/22/us/politics/22dems.html.

———. 2008c. "Obama Extends Streak to 10, Makes Inroads Among Women." *New York Times*, February 20. www.nytimes.com/2008/02/20/us/politics/20cnd-campaign.html?_r=2&nl=pol&emc=pol&oref=slogin&oref=slogin.

Heith, Diane. 2003. "The Lipstick Watch: Media Coverage, Gender, and Presidential Campaigns." In Robert P. Watson and Ann Gordon, eds.,

Anticipating Madam President, 123–130. Boulder: Lynne Rienner Publishers.

Heldman, Caroline. 2007. "Cultural Barriers to a Female Presidency in the US." In Lori Cox Han and Caroline Heldman, eds., *Rethinking Madam President: Are We Ready for a Woman in the White House?* 17–42. Boulder: Lynne Rienner Publishers.

Heldman, Caroline, Susan Carroll, and Stephanie Olson. 2005. "'She Brought Only a Skirt': Print Media Coverage of Elizabeth Dole's Bid for the Republican Presidential Nomination." *Political Communication* 22, no. 3: 315–335.

Herbert, Bob. 2008. "Some Perspective on 'Bitter.'" *New York Times,* April 15. www.nytimes.com/2008/04/15/opinion/15herbert.html.

Hernandez, Raymond, and Patrick D. Healy. 2005. "The Evolution of Hillary Clinton." *New York Times,* July 13. http://www.nytimes.com/2005/07/13/nyregion/13hillary.ready.html?_r=1&oref=slogin.

Herrick, Rebekah. 2004. "The Gender Gap in Early Congressional Retirements." *Politics and Policy* 32, no. 3: 397–411.

Herrnson, Paul J., Celeste Lay, and Anita Stokes. 2003. "Women Running as 'Women': Candidate Gender, Campaign Issues, and Voter-Targeting Strategies." *Journal of Politics* 65: 244–255.

Hindman, Matthew. 2008. *The Myth of Digital Democracy.* Princeton, NJ: Princeton University Press.

Hoogensen, Gunhild, and Bruce O. Solheim. 2006. *Women in Power: World Leaders Since 1960.* Westport, CT: Praeger.

hooks, bell. 1981. *Ain't I a Woman: Black Women and Feminism.* Boston, MA: South End Press.

Horowitz, Jason. 2008. "The Hillary Haters." *GQ Magazine,* February 6. http://men.style.com/gq/features/full?id=content_6249.

Hoyt, Clark. 2008a. "Getting Past the Formalities." *New York Times,* September 22. www.nytimes.com/2008/09/14/opinion/14pubed.html?ei=5070& emc=eta1.

———. 2008b. "Pantsuits and the Presidency." *New York Times,* June 22. www.nytimes.com/2008/06/22/opinion/22pubed.html?_r=2&ref= opinion&oref=slogin&oref=slogin.

Huddy, Leonie. 1994. "The Political Significance of Voters' Gender Stereotypes." *Research in Micropolitics* 4: 169–193.

Huddy, Leonie, and Nayda Terkildsen. 1993. "Gender Stereotypes and the Perception of Male and Female Candidates." *American Journal of Political Science* 37, no. 1: 119–147.

Hunt, Albert R. 2008. "Clinton's Loss Not Driven by Sexism." *Bloomberg.* http://bloomberg.com/apps/news?pid=20601070&sid=aF8xEqtSXbiQ& refer=politics.

Iyengar, Shanto, and Jennifer McGrady. 2006. *Media Politics: A Citizen's Guide.* New York: W. W. Norton.

Iyengar, Shanto, Nicholas A. Valentino, Stephen Ansolabehere, and Adam F. Simon. 1997. "Running as a Woman: Gender Stereotyping in Women's Campaigns." In Pippa Norris, ed., *Women, Media, and Politics,* 77–98. Oxford: Oxford University Press.

Jalalzai, Farida. 2006. "Women Candidates and the Media: 1992–2000 Elections." *Politics & Policy* 34, no. 3: 606–633.

———. 2008. "Women Rule: Shattering the Executive Glass Ceiling." *Politics & Gender* 4, no. 2: 205–231.

Jamieson, Kathleen Hall. 1993. *Dirty Politics: Deception, Distraction, and Democracy*. New York: Oxford University Press.

———. 1995. *Beyond the Double Bind: Women and Leadership*. New York: Oxford University Press.

———. 1998. *Eloquence in an Electronic Age*. Oxford: Oxford University Press.

———. 2008. Interviewed on *Bill Moyers Journal*. May 2. www.pbs.org/moyers/journal/05022008/watch2.html.

Johnston, Richard, Michael G. Hagen, and Kathleen Hall Jamieson. 2004. *The 2000 Election and the Foundations of Party Politics*. Cambridge: Cambridge University Press.

Jones, Jayson K., and Ana C. Rosado. 2008. "Obama Campaign Criticizes Ferraro Comments." *New York Times*, March 11. http://thecaucus.blogs.nytimes.com/author/jayson-k-jones-and-ana-c-rosado.

Jones, Jeffrey M. 2007. "Hillary Edges Out Oprah as Most Admired Woman in '07." *Gallup*. December 26. www.gallup.com/poll/103462/Hillary-Edges-Oprah-Most-Admired-Woman-07.aspx.

———. 2008. "Top-of-Mind Candidate Perceptions in Depth." *Gallup,* April 30. www.gallup.com/poll/106909/TopofMind-Candidate-Perceptions-InDepth.aspx.

Judis, John B. 2008. "The Autopsy Report: Exploring the Political Reasons for Hillary Clinton's Defeat." *The New Republic*, May 21. www.tnr.com/politics/story.html?id=f1281d27-d950-4dfd-a59b-66e905918d20.

Just, Marion R., Ann N. Crigler, Dean E. Alger, and Timothy Cook. 1996. *Crosstalk: Citizens, Candidates, and the Media in a Presidential Campaign*. Chicago: University of Chicago Press.

Kaczor, Bill. 2007. "Florida Democrats Lose on Primary." Tampa Bay Online. December 6. http://www2.tbo.com/content/2007/dec/06/me-florida-democrats-lose-on-primary/.

Kahn, Kim Fridkin. 1996. *The Political Consequences of Being a Woman*. New York: Columbia University Press.

Kantor, Jodi. 2008a. "Gender Issue Lives on as Clinton's Hopes Dim." *New York Times*, May 19. www.nytimes.com/2008/05/19/us/politics/19women.html?ex=1211860800&en=d681ab86406ac15f&ei=5070&emc=eta1.

———. 2008b. "A Show of Emotion That Reverberated Beyond the Campaign." *New York Times*, January 9. www.nytimes.com/2008/01/09/us/politics/09moment.html.

———. 2008c. "Women's Support for Clinton Rises in Wake of Perceived Sexism." *New York Times*, January 10. www.nytimes.com/2008/01/10/us/politics/10women.html?pagewanted=print.

Kaufman, Jonathan, and Carolyn Hymowitz. 2008. "At the Barricades in the Gender Wars." *Wall Street Journal*, March 29, A1.

Keeter, Scott. 1987. "The Illusion of Intimacy Television and the Role of Candidate Personal Qualities in Voter Choice." *Public Opinion Quarterly* 51, no. 3 (Autumn): 344–358.

Kellerman, Barbara, ed. 1984. *Leadership: Multidisciplinary Perspectives*. Englewood Cliffs: Prentice-Hall.

Kengor, Paul. 1996. "A Pair for History: Presidents Ford and Reagan." *National*

Review. http://article.nationalreview.com/?q=OWQ1NzJjZmViNTRkOWY
3ZDZjMWQ5YzFjNjBiYjAyYzc=.

Kennicott, Philip. 2007. "Sooner or Later, Candidates Will Surely Look Lost."
Washington Post, December 26, C1.

Kerber, Linda K. 1998. *No Constitutional Right to Be Ladies: Women and the
Obligations of Citizenship.* New York: Hill and Wang.

Kincaid, Diane. 1978. "Over His Dead Body: A Positive Perspective on Widows
in the U.S. Congress." *Western Political Quarterly* 31: 96–104.

Klein, Ezra. 2007. "The Polarizing Express: Is It Hillary Clinton Who's Too
Divisive, or Is It the Political Process?" *Los Angeles Times*, December 16,
M1.

Kolbert, Elizabeth. 2008. "The Tyranny of High Expectations." In Susan
Morrison, ed., *Thirty Ways of Looking at Hillary: Reflections by Women
Writers,* 9–15. New York: HarperCollins.

Kornblut, Anne E. 2008. "Clinton Urges Backers to Look to November: 'We
Will Someday Launch a Woman Into the White House.'" *Washington Post*,
June 8, A1.

———. 2009. Telephone interview. February 16.

Kornblut, Anne E., and Perry Bacon, Jr. 2008. "Clinton's King Comment 'Ill-
Advised,' Obama Says." *Washington Post*, January 14, A1. www
.washingtonpost.com/wp-dyn/content/article/2008/01/13/
AR2008011303624.html?hpid=topnews.

Kovach, Bill, and Tom Rosenstiel. 2001. "Campaign Lite: Why Reporters
Won't Tell Us What We Need to Know." *Washington Monthly*,
January/February. www.washingtonmonthly.com/features/2001/0101
.kovach.rosenstiel.html.

Kramer, Jane. 2008. "My Generation." In Susan Morrison, ed., *Thirty Ways of
Looking at Hillary: Reflections by Women Writers,* 65–71. New York:
HarperCollins.

Kramnick, Isaac. 1977. "Religion and Radicalism: English Political Theory in
the Age of Revolution." *Political Theory* 5, no. 4 (November): 505–534.

Kristoff, Nicholas. 2008. "Our Racist, Sexist Selves." *New York Times*, April 6.
www.nytimes.com/2008/04/06/opinion/06kristof.html?_r=1&ref=
opinion&oref=slogin%3E.

Kuhn, David Paul. 2008. "Hillary Clinton's 5 Mistakes." *Politico.com*, June 7.
www.politico.com/news/stories/0608/10911.html.

Kurtz, Howard. 1998. *Spin Cycle: How the White House and the Media
Manipulate the News.* New York: Simon & Schuster.

———. 2007. "For Clinton, A Matter of Fair Media." *Washington Post*,
December 19, C01.

———. 2008a. Email interview with the author. June 1.

———. 2008b. "For Political Reporters, A Never-Ending Story." *Washington
Post*, March 6, C1.

———. 2008c. "It's All Uphill from Here." *Washington Post.* February 18,
2008. C1.

———. 2008d. "Washington Times Names Post Reporter Its Top Editor."
Washington Post, January 15, C1.

Ladd, Carl Everett. 1997. "Media Framing of the Gender Gap." In Pippa Norris,
ed., *Women, Media, and Politics.* New York: Oxford University Press.

Lang, Kurt, and Gladys Engel Lang. 1968. *Politics and Television*. Chicago: Quadrangle Books.

Lawless, Jennifer L. 2004. "Women, War and Winning Elections: Gender Stereotyping in the Post September 11th Era." *Political Research Quarterly* 57: 479–490.

Lawless, Jennifer L., and Richard L. Fox. 2005. *It Takes a Candidate: Why Women Don't Run for Office*. New York: Cambridge University Press.

Lawrence, Jill. 2007. "Fight Is on to Capture Women's Votes." *USA Today*, July 22. www.usatoday.com/news/politics/election2008/2007-07-22-women-votes_N.htm?POE=click-refer.

Lawrence, Regina G. 2000. "Game-Framing the Issues: Tracking the Strategy Frame in Public Policy News." *Political Communication* 17, no. 2: 93–114.

———. 2008. "Will Palin Ride Press Deference to the White House?" The Chicago Blog, September 18. http://pressblog.uchicago.edu/2008/09/18/will_palin_ride_press_deferenc.html.

Leibovich, Mark. 2008a. "The Aria of Chris Matthews." *New York Times Magazine*, April 13. www.nytimes.com/2008/04/13/magazine/13matthews-t.html?nl=pol&emc=pol.

———. 2008b. "Black Leader in the House Sharply Criticizes Bill Clinton." *New York Times*, April 25. www.nytimes.com/2008/04/25/us/politics/25clinton.html?ref=politics.

———. 2008c. "Clinton Goes Face to Face with the Public as Obama Plays Not to Lose." *New York Times*, January 20. www.nytimes.com/2008/01/08/us/politics/08style.html?n=Top/Reference/Times%20Topics/People/L/Leibovich,%20Mark.

———. 2008d. "Rights vs. Rights: An Improbable Collision Course." *New York Times*, January 13. www.nytimes.com/2008/01/13/weekinreview/13leibovich.html.

Levy, Ariel. 2008. "Cheating." In Morrison, Susan, ed., *Thirty Ways of Looking at Hillary: Reflections by Women Writers,* 87–93. New York: HarperCollins, 2008.

Linsky, Martin. 2008. "The First Woman President? Obama's Campaign Bends Gender Conventions." *Newsweek*, February 26. www.newsweek.com/id/115397.

Lipset, Seymour Martin. 1990. *Continental Divide: The Values and Institutions of the United States and Canada*. New York: Routledge.

Lizza, Ryan. 2008a. "Can John McCain Reinvent Republicanism?" *The New Yorker*, February 25. www.newyorker.com/reporting/2008/02/25/080225fa_fact_lizza.

———. 2008b. "The Iron Lady." *The New Yorker*, March 17. www.newyorker.com/reporting/2008/03/17/080317fa_fact_lizza.

Lovaglia, Michael. 2008. "Leadership Study Suggests Age May Have Helped Obama, Hurt Clinton." University of Iowa News Release, July 30. http://newsreleases.uiowa.edu/2008/july/073008leadership-age.html.

Lowi, Theodore J. 1986. *The Personal President: Power Invested, Promise Unfulfilled*. Ithaca, NY: Cornell University Press.

Malkin, Michelle. 2008. "Hillary Exploits the Ghost of Ann Richards." February 27. http://michellemalkin.com/2008/02/27/hillary-exploits-the-ghost-of-ann-richards-over-sons-objections.

Mann, Robert. 2008. "Who Was More Important, the President or the Preacher?" *Boston Globe*, January 15. www.boston.com/news/nation/articles/2008/01/15/who_was_more_important_the_president_or_the_preacher.

Marinucci, Carla. 2007. "'Hillary 1984': Unauthorized Internet Ad for Obama Converts Apple Computer's '84 Super Bowl Spot into a Generational Howl Against Clinton's Presidential Bid." *San Francisco Chronicle*, March 18. http://www.sfgate.com/cgi-bin/article.cgi?f=/c/a/2007/03/18/MNGHNONEPS1.DTL.

Matthews, Donald R. 1978. "'Winnowing': The News Media and the 1976 Presidential Nomination." In James David Barber, ed., *Race for the Presidency*, 55–78. Englewood Cliffs, NJ: Prentice-Hall.

McNulty, Timothy J. 2008. "Horse Analogy Impolitic, Unsettling." *Chicago Tribune*, May 9. www.chicagotribune.com/news/columnists/chi-oped0509mcnultymay09,0,6895454.column.

Media Matters for America. 2008a. "All-Male *Morning Joe* Panel Laughed as Barnicle Compared Clinton to 'Everyone's First Wife Standing Outside a Probate Court.'" January 23. http://mediamatters.org/items/200801230004.

———. 2008b. "Kristol: 'White Women Are a Problem, That's, You Know—We All Live with That.'" http://mediamatters.org/items/printable/200802030002 (accessed August 4, 2008).

———. 2008c. "Limbaugh: Clinton, 'The Most Cheated-On Woman in the World,' Now 'Surrounded' by Her 'White Female New *Castrati* Male Base.'" http://mediamatters.org/items/printable/200801240014 (accessed August 4, 2008).

———. 2008d. "Limbaugh Returned to 'Testicle Lockbox'; Claimed Clinton 'Reminds Men of the Worst Characteristics of Women.'" http://mediamatters.org/items/printable/200802150004 (accessed August 4, 2008).

———. 2008e. "Media Diagnose Hillary 'Sybil' Clinton with 'Mood Swings,' Depression, and 'Multiple Personality Disorder.'" http://mediamatters.org.items.printable/200802270010 (accessed August 4, 2008).

———. 2008f. "More Violent Imagery from Matthews: If Clinton Beats Obama, 'What Does She Do with the Body?'" http://mediamatters.org/items/printable/200801050005 (accessed August 4, 2008).

———. 2008g. "On CNN, Jeffrey Said 'It Looked Like, If Someone Had Splashed Water on Hillary, She Would have Melted Like the Wicked Witch of the West.'" http://mediamatters.org/items/printable/200801230011 (accessed August 4, 2008).

———. 2008h. "So Now the Press Tells Candidates When to Quit?" http://mediamatters.org/items/printable/200804300001 (accessed August 4, 2008).

———. 2008i. "Tucker Carlson on Clinton: '[W]hen She Comes on Television, I Involuntarily Cross My Legs.'" July 18. http://mediamatters.org/items/200707180009.

———. 2008j. "*Wash. Post*'s Achenbach: Hillary Clinton, 'Needs a Radio-Controlled Shock Collar So That Aides Can Zap Her When She Starts to Get Screechy.'" http://mediamatters.org/items/printable/200801080007 (accessed August 4, 2008).

———. 2008k. "Maureen Dowd Repeatedly Uses Gender to Mock Democrats." June 10. http://mediamatters.org/research/200806100002.

Mendelberg, Tali. 2001. *The Race Card: Campaign Messages, Implicit Messages, and the Norm of Equality*. Princeton, NJ: Princeton University Press.

Menefee-Libby, David. 2000. *The Triumph of Campaign-Centered Politics*. New York: Chatham House Publishers.

Meyrowitz, Joshua. 1992. "The Press Rejects a Candidate." *Columbia Journalism Review*, March/April. http://backissues.cjrarchives.org/year/92/2/opinion.asp.

Milbank, Dana. 2007. "Hillary, We Thoroughly Knew Ye." *Washington Post*, December 19, A2.

———. 2008a. "She Lives." *Washington Post*, January 9, A1.

———. 2008b. "Still After the Holy Grail." *Washington Post*, May 20. www.washingtonpost.com/wp-dyn/content/article/2008/05/19/AR2008051902369.html.

———. 2008c. "Team Clinton: Down, and Out of Touch." *Washington Post*, February 26, A2.

Milligan, Susan. 2008. "Iraq Returns as Prime Debate Issue." *Boston Globe*, February 1. www.boston.com/news/nation/articles/2008/02/01/iraq_war_returns_as_prime_debate_issue.

Moore, Lorrie. 2008. "Boys and Girls." In Morrison, Susan, ed., *Thirty Ways of Looking at Hillary: Reflections by Women Writers*, 29–36. New York: HarperCollins, 2008.

Morris, Dick. 2008. "Who's to Blame? It Was Mark Penn." *Real Clear Politics*, June 11. www.realclearpolitics.com/articles/2008/06/whos_to_blame_it_was_mark_penn.html.

Morrison, Susan, ed. 2008. *Thirty Ways of Looking at Hillary: Reflections by Women Writers*. New York: HarperCollins.

MSNBC. 2008a. "Clinton Says She Regrets Comment About Race." May 14. www.msnbc.msn.com/id/24633826.

———. 2008b. "Hillary's New 'Do'—Senator Clinton Moves from Left to Right—Her Part, Not Her Positions." July 17. http://news.spreadit.org/hillary-clinton-new-hairdo-photo.

Mueller, James E. 2008. *Tag Teaming the Press: How Bill and Hillary Clinton Work Together to Handle the Media*. Lanham, MD: Rowman & Littlefield.

Myers, Dee Dee. 2008. *Why Women Should Rule the World*. New York: HarperCollins.

Nagourney, Adam. 2008a. "The Bruising Will Go On for the Party, Too." *New York Times*, April 23. www.nytimes.com/2008/04/23/us/politics/23assess.html.

———. 2008b. "Clinton's Options Seem to Dwindle." *New York Times*, May 7. www.nytimes.com/2008/05/07/us/politics/07assess.html?th&emc=th.

———. 2008c. "In Pennsylvania, What Constitutes a Win?" *New York Times*, April 22. http://thecaucus.blogs.nytimes.com/2008/04/22/in-pennsylvania-what-constitutes-a-win/index.html?8au&emc=au.

———. 2008d. "A Primary Calendar Democrats Will Never Forget." *New York Times*, June 2. www.nytimes.com/2008/06/02/us/politics/03nagourney.html?nl=pol&emc=pol.

———. 2008e. "A Series of Unfortunate Events." *New York Times*, May 20. www.nytimes.com/2008/05/20/us/politics/20nagourney.html.

Nagourney, Adam, and Marjorie Connelly. 2000. "In Poll, Mrs. Clinton Makes Gain Among Women from the Suburbs." *New York Times,* September 21, A1.

Nagourney, Adam, and Patrick Healy. 2007. "Different Rules When a Rival Is a Woman?" *New York Times,* November 5. www.nytimes.com/2007/11/05/us/politics/05memo.html.

Nather, David. 2008. "The Space Between Clinton and Obama." *Congressional Quarterly Weekly* 124, January 14. http://public.cq.com/docs/cqw/weeklyreport110-000002654703.html.

National Organization for Women. 2008. "NOW's Media Hall of Shame: 2008 Election Edition." www.now.org/issues/media/hall_of_shame.

National Public Radio. 2008a. "Female Journalists on Clinton's Fighting Chance." January 10. www.npr.org/templates/player/mediaPlayer.html?action=1&t=1&islist=false&id=18070805&m=18070798.

———. 2008b. "30 Women Writers Pen 'Ways of Looking at Hillary.'" January 24. www.npr.org/templates/story/story.php?storyId=18382003.

NBC Nightly News. 2008a. "Barack Obama, John Edwards, Hillary Clinton Preparing for New Hampshire Primary Tonight." January 8.

———. 2008b. "North Carolina and Indiana Called." May 6. www.msnbc.msn.com/id/3032619/#24494766.

Neuendorf, Kimberly A. 2002. *The Content Analysis Guidebook.* Thousand Oaks, CA: Sage.

Newport, Frank. 2007. "Hillary Clinton's Big Lead in Democratic Race Unchanged." *Gallup,* November 7. www.cawp.rutgers.edu/Facts/Elections/pres08_polls/Gallup_HClinton_leadunchanged.pdf.

New York Times. 2008. "The Low Road to Victory." April 23, A20.

New York Times/CBS Poll. 2008a. February 20–24. http://graphics8.nytimes.com/packages/pdf/politics/20090226poll.pdf.

———. 2008b. March 28–April 2. http://www.nytimes.com/2008/04/04/us/politics/04campaign.html.

Nicholas, Peter. 2007. "Clinton Says Change Better with Experience." *Los Angeles Times,* September 3. http://articles.latimes.com/2007/09/03/news/na-hillary3.

Norris, Pippa, ed. 1997. *Women, Media, and Politics.* New York: Oxford University Press.

O'Connor, Karen, Bernadette Nye, and Laura Van Assendelft. 1996. "Wives in the White House: The Political Influence of First Ladies." *Presidential Studies Quarterly* 26, no. 3 (Summer): 835–853.

October 30th Democratic Debate Transcripts. 2007. MSNBC online. www.msnbc.msn.com/id/21528787.

Ohlemacher, Stephen. 2008. "Obama Used Party Rules to Foil Clinton." *Breitbart.com,* May 30. www.breitbart.com/print.php?id=D91018RO0&show_article+1.

Orenstein, Peggy. 2008. "The Hillary Lesson." *New York Times Magazine,* May 18. www.nytimes.com/2008/05/18/magazine/18wwln-lede-t.html?ref=magazine.

Ornstein, Norman, and Thomas Mann, eds. 2000. *The Permanent Campaign and Its Future.* Washington, DC: American Enterprise Institute.

Paglia, Camille. 2008. "Hillary's Race Against Time." Salon.com. March 12. http://www.salon.com/opinion/paglia/2008/03/12/red_phone/print.html.

Palin, Sarah. 2008. "Remarks Accepting Senator McCain's Nomination as the Republican Nominee for Vice President in Dayton, Ohio." The American Presidency Project. www.presidency.ucsb.edu/ws/index.php?pid=78574& st=hillary+clinton&st1=.

Palmer, Barbara, and Dennis Simon. 2008. *Breaking the Political Glass Ceiling*, 2nd ed. New York: Routledge.

Parry-Giles, Shawn J. "Mediating Hillary Rodham Clinton: Television News Practices and Image-Making in the Postmodern Age." *Critical Studies in Mass Communication* 17 (2000): 205–226.

Patterson, Thomas. 1994. *Out of Order*. New York: Vintage.

———. 2000. "Doing Well and Doing Good: How Soft News and Critical Journalism Are Shrinking the News Audience and Weakening Democracy —And What News Outlets Can Do About It." The Joan Shorenstein Center on the Press, Politics, and Public Policy.

Paul, David, and Jessi L. Smith. 2008. "Subtle Sexism? Examining Vote Preferences When Women Run Against Men for the Presidency." *Journal of Women, Politics, and Policy* 29, no. 4: 451–476.

Pearson, Rick. 2008. "Clinton Has What? . . . Union Leader Says So." The Swamp, April 30. www.swamppolitics.com/news/politics/blog/2008/04/clinton_has_what_union_leader.html.

Perez, Andrew. 2008. "By Placing Her Name Into Nomination, How Selfish Was Hillary Clinton?" Talking Points Memo, August 28. http://tpmcafe.talkingpointsmemo.com/talk/2008/08/by-placing-her-name-into-nomin.php.

Perez, Jessica. 2008. Telephone interview with the author. May 7.

Pew Research Center for the People and the Press. 2007a. "Public Knowledge of Current Affairs Little Changed by News and Information Revolutions." April 15. http://people-press.org/report/319/public-knowledge-of-current-affairs-little-changed-by-news-and-information-revolutions.

———. 2007b. "A Year Ahead, Republicans Face Tough Political Terrain; Clinton Propelled by Support from Young Women in '08 Test." October 31. http://people-press.org/report/366/a-year-ahead-republicans-face-tough-political-terrain.

———. 2008a. "The Internet and the 2008 Election." June 15. www.pewinternet.org/PPF/r/252/report_display.asp.

———. 2008b. "Men or Women: Who's the Better Leader? A Paradox in Public Attitudes." August 25. http://pewresearch.org/pubs/932/men-or-women-whos-the-better-leader.

———. 2008c. "Obama Inspiring but Inexperienced, Clinton Prepared to Lead but 'Hard to Like.'" February 13. http://people-press.org/report/394/obama-inspiring-but-inexperienced-clinton-prepared-to-lead-but-hard-to-like.

———. 2008d. "Obama Weathers the Wright Storm; Clinton Faces Credibility Problem." March 27. http://pewresearch.org/pubs/779/obama-weathers-the-wright-storm-clinton-faces-credibility-problem.

———. 2008e. "Public Sees Candidates Focusing on Economy; Many

Democrats Say Media Tougher on Clinton than Obama." February 7. http://people-press.org/report/393/public-sees-candidates-focusing-on-economy.

Phillips, Kate. 2008a. "A Country Voice on Rural Voters." *New York Times*, May 20. http://thecaucus.blogs.nytimes.com/2008/05/20/a-country-voice-on-rural-voters.

———. 2008b. "Bill Clinton: 'I Am Not a Racist.'" *New York Times*, August 4. http://thecaucus.blogs.nytimes.com/2008/08/04/bill-clinton-i-am-not-a-racist/index.html?nl=pol&emc=pol.

Pitney, Nico. 2008. "Palin Misquotes Albright: "Place in Hell Reserved for Women Who Don't Support Other Women." *Huffington Post,* October 5. www.huffingtonpost.com/2008/10/05/palin-misquotes-albright_n _131967.html?view=print.

Pogrebin, Letty Cottin. 2008. "The Wife, the Candidate, the Senator, and Her Husband." In Susan Morrison, ed., *Thirty Ways of Looking at Hillary: Reflections by Women Writers*, 104–115. New York: HarperCollins.

Pollitt, Katha. 1994. *Reasonable Creatures: Essays on Women and Feminism.* New York: Alfred A. Knopf.

———. 2008a. "Hillary Rotten." In Susan Morrison, ed., *Thirty Ways of Looking at Hillary: Reflections by Women Writers,* 16–23. New York: HarperCollins.

———. 2008b. "Iron My Skirt." *The Nation*, June 5. www.thenation.com/doc/20080623/pollitt/print.

Popkin, Samuel. 1992. "Information Shortcuts and the Reasoning Voters." In Bernard Grofman, ed., *Information, Participation, and Choice: An Economic Theory of Democracy in Perspective.* Ann Arbor: University of Michigan Press.

———. 1994. *The Reasoning Voter*, 2nd ed. Chicago: University of Chicago Press.

Powers, Madison. 2008. "Media Anxieties Over Campaign Coverage." *CQ Politics*, April 10. www.cqpolitics.com/wmspage.cfm?docID= news-000002701044&cpage=2.

Project for Excellence in Journalism. 2007a. "The Invisible Primary, Invisible No Longer: A First Look at Coverage of the 2008 Presidential Campaign." October 29. www.journalism.org/node/8187.

———. 2007b. "The State of the News Media 2007." No date. www .stateofthenewsmedia.org/2007/narrative_networktv_audience.asp?cat=2& media=5.

———. 2007c. "The Talkers Hammer Hillary Clinton." October 28–November 2. www.journalism.org/print/8433.

———. 2008a. "Character and the Primaries of 2008." May 29. www .journalism.org/node/11266.

———. 2008b. "Media Narrative Vaults Obama into Frontrunner Spot." www.journalism.org/node/9828 (accessed July 23, 2008).

———. 2008c. "Press Takes a Harder Look at Obama—and Itself." February 25–March 2. www.journalism.org/node/10004.

———. 2008d. "Winning the Media Campaign: How the Press Reported the 2008 Presidential General Election." No date given. http://journalism.org/files/WINNING%20THE%20MEDIA%20CAMPAIGN%20FINAL.pdf (accessed October 31, 2008).

Reliable Sources. 2008a. Transcripts. February 10. http://transcripts.cnn.com/TRANSCRIPTS/0802/10/rs.01.html.

———. 2008b. Transcripts. March 9. http://transcripts.cnn.com/TRANSCRIPTS/0803/09/rs.01.html.

———. 2008c. Transcripts. March 16. http://transcripts.cnn.com/TRANSCRIPTS/0803/16/rs.01.html.

———. 2008d. Transcripts. March 30. http://transcripts.cnn.com/TRANSCRIPTS/0803/30/rs.01.html.

———. 2008e. Transcripts. May 4. http://transcripts.cnn.com/TRANSCRIPTS/0805/04/rs.01.html.

———. 2008f. Transcripts. May 18. http://transcripts.cnn.com/TRANSCRIPTS/0805/18/rs.01.html.

Rich, Frank. 2008a. "The Audacity of Hopelessness." *New York Times*, February 24. www.nytimes.com/2008/02/24/opinion/24rich.html.

———. 2008b. "Clinton Women [Love] McCain?" *New York Times*, June 15. www.nytimes.com/2008/06/15/opinion/15rich.html.

———. 2008c. "Hillary's St. Patrick's Day Massacre." *New York Times*, March 30. www.nytimes.com/2008/03/30/opinion/30rich.html?ex=1207540800&en=668f45e460f34063&ei=5070&emc=eta1.

Ritter, Gretchen. 2008. "Gender as a Category of Analysis in American Political Development." In Christina Wolbrecht, Karen Beckweth, and Liza Baldez, eds., *Political Women and American Democracy*, 12–30. Cambridge: Cambridge University Press.

Robertson, Nan. 1992. *The Girls in the Balcony: Women, Men, and the New York Times*. New York: Random House.

Robinson, Michael J., and Margaret A. Sheehan. 1983. *Over the Wire and On TV*. New York: Russell Sage Foundation.

Rodham, Hillary D. 1969. "1969 Student Commencement Speech." Wellesley College, May 31. http://www.wellesley.edu/PublicAffairs/Commencement/1969/053169hillary.html.

Romano, Andrew. 2008. "Obama's 'Sweetie' Challenge." *New York Times*, May 16. www.blog.newsweek.com/blogs/stumper/archive/2008/05/16/Obamas-Sweetie-Challenge-.aspx.

Romano, Lois. 2008. "Clinton Puts Up a New Fight: The Candidate Confronts Sexism on the Trail and Vows To Battle On." *Washington Post,* May 20, C1.

Rose, Melody. 2007. *Safe, Legal, and Unavailable: Abortion Politics in the 21st Century*. Washington, DC: CQ Press.

———. 2008. "Women's 'Double Bind.'" *The Oregonian*, September 7. www.oregonlive.com/commentary/oregonian/index.ssf?/base/editorial/1220651703162390.xml&coll=7.

Rosen, Hilary. 2008. "Why Do We Stick with Her." *Huffington Post*, May 28. www.huffingtonpost.com/hilary-rosen/why-do-we-stick-with-her_b_103861.html.

Rosen, Jay. 2003. "The Master Narrative in Journalism." Pressthink. http://journalism.nyu.edu/pubzone/weblogs/pressthink/2003/09/08/basics_master.html.

Rosen, Jill. 2008. "What To Do NOW?" *Baltimore Sun*. July 20. www.baltimoresun.com/news/opinion/ideas/bal-id.profile20jul20,0,4123319.story.

Rutenberg, Jim. 2008a. "The Battle of Perception Still Wages on Television." *New York Times*, April 23, A18.

———. 2008b. "Pundits Declare the Race Over." *New York Times*, May 8. www.nytimes.com/2008/05/08/us/politics/07cnd-pundits.html?ex= 1210824000&en=fe3c9853f3ddaaea&ei=5070&emc=eta1.

———. 2008c. "Pundits, Like Candidates, Find Themselves in Limbo." *New York Times*, May 22. www.nytimes.com/2008/05/22/us/politics/21cnd pundits.html?nl=pol&emc=pol.

Sanbonmatsu, Kira. 2002. "Gender Stereotypes and Vote Choice." *American Journal of Political Science* 46: 20–34.

———. 2005. "Do Parties Know That Women Win? Party Leader Beliefs About Women's Electability." Paper presented at the American Political Science Association Annual Meeting, Washington, DC.

———. 2006. *Where Women Run: Gender & Party in the American States*. Ann Arbor: University of Michigan Press.

Sanders, Eli. 2007. "Clinton's Gender Politics." *Slog (The Stranger)*. November 2. http://slog.thestranger.com/2007/11/clintons_gender_politics.

———. 2008. "Thoughts on Obama's Speech." *Slog (The Stranger)*, March 13. http://slog.thestranger.com/2008/03/thoughts_on_obamas_speech.

Santora, Marc, and Adam Nagourney. 2008. "On to Michigan, G.O.P. Rivals Turn to the Economy." *New York Times*, January 10, A1.

Sapiro, Virginia. 1982. "If U.S. Senator Baker Were a Woman: An Experimental Study of Candidate Images." *Political Psychology* 3, no. 1-2 (Spring-Summer): 61–83.

Sargent, Greg. 2007. "Did Hillary 'Play the Gender Card'?" *Talking Points Memo*. http://tpmelectioncentral.talkingpointsmemo.com/2007/11/did _hillary_play_the_gender_card.php.

Schlesinger, Joseph A. 1966. *Ambition and Politics: Political Careers in the United States*. Chicago: Rand McNally.

Schnur, Dan. 2008. "Party Rules." *New York Times*, May 7. http:// campaignstops.blogs.nytimes.com/2008/05/07/party-rules/?th&emc=th.

Scott, Joan Wallach. 1988. *Gender and the Politics of History*. New York: Columbia University Press.

———. 1996. "Deconstructing Equality Versus Difference: On the Uses of Post-Structuralist Theory for Feminism." In Kelly Weisberg, ed., *Applications of Feminist Legal Theory to Women's Lives: Sex, Violence, Work, and Reproduction*, 611–623. Philadelphia: Temple University Press.

Seelye, Katharine Q. 2007. "Clinton-Obama Quandary for Many Black Women." *New York Times*, October 14. www.nytimes.com/2007/10/14/us/ politics/14carolina.html.

———. 2008a. "Bill Clinton Accuses Obama Camp of Stirring Race Issue." *New York Times*, January 24. www.nytimes.com/2008/01/24/us/politics/ 24dems.html.

———. 2008b. "Clinton Asked About Veep Role." *New York Times*, February 28. http://thecaucus.blogs.nytimes.com/2008/02/28/clinton-asked-about-veep-role/?nl=pol&emc=pol.

———. 2008c. "In South Carolina, a Bid for Black Women's Votes." *New York Times*, January 15. www.nytimes.com/2008/01/15/us/politics/15carolina .html.

———. 2008d. "On the Road: Clinton's Very Bad Day." *New York Times*, May

24. http://thecaucus.blogs.nytimes.com/2008/05/24/on-the-road-clintons-very-bad-day/?ex=1212465600&en=15e58b09b4d9a19d&ei=5070.

Seelye, Katharine Q., and Julie Bosman. 2008. "Media Charged with Sexism in Clinton Coverage." *New York Times,* June 13. www.nytimes.com/2008/06/13/us/politics/13women.html?th&emc=th.

Shafer, Byron E. 1983. *Quiet Revolution: The Struggle for the Democratic Party and the Shaping of Post-Reform Politics.* New York: Russell Sage Foundation.

Shames, Shauna, and Marion Just. 2008. "A Narrative Overview of the Research." In *Women and News: Expanding the News Audience, Increasing Political Participation, and Informing Citizens.* The Joan Shorenstein Center on the Press, Politics, and Public Policy. www.hks.harvard.edu/presspol/news_events/news_archive/PDFs/Women%20&%20News%20Transcript.pdf.

Shapiro, Walter. 2008a. "Hillary Enters Death-with-Dignity Phase." *Salon.com,* May 12. www.salon.com/news/feature/2008/05/12/end_game.

———. 2008b. "She's Not as Bad as You Think." *Salon.com,* April 18. www.salon.com/news/feature/2008/04/18/clinton/print.html.

Sheehy, Gail. 2008. "Hillaryland at War." *Vanity Fair,* August. www.vanityfair.com/politics/features/2008/08/clinton200808?currentPage=1.

Shriver, Lionel. 2008. "Monarchy in the Making." In Susan Morrison, ed., *Thirty Ways of Looking at Hillary: Reflections by Women Writers,* 47–56. New York: HarperCollins.

Silverstein, Ken. 2008. "The Press and the Campaign: Boosting Obama and McCain." *Harper's,* January 7. http://harpers.org/archive/2008/01/hbc-90002103.

Silverstein, Stuart. 2008. "How to Win a War of Words." *Los Angeles Times,* January 31, 14.

Sinderbrand, Rebecca. 2008. "Ferraro: 'They're Attacking Me Because I'm White.'" CNN, March 11. www.cnn.com/2008/POLITICS/03/11/ferraro.comments.

Skocpol, Theda. 1997. *Boomerang: Health Care Reform and the Turn Against Government,* 2nd ed. New York: W. W. Norton.

Smith, Ben. 2008. "As Campaign Ends, Was Clinton to Blame?" *Politico.com,* June 7. www.politico.com/news/stories/0608/10910.html.

Smith, Ben, and David Paul Kuhn. 2007. "Feminists Split on HRC Sexism Defense." *Politico.com,* November 4. www.politico.com/news/stories/1107/6691.html.

Smith, Eric R. A. N., and Richard L. Fox. 2001. "The Electoral Fortunes of Women Candidates for Congress." *Political Research Quarterly* 54, no. 1 (March): 205–221.

Smith, Jessi L., David Paul, and Rachel Paul. 2007. "No Place for a Woman: Evidence for Gender Bias in Evaluations of Presidential Candidates." *Basic and Applied Social Psychology* 29, no. 3: 225–233.

Smith, Kevin. 1997. "When All's Fair: Signs of Parity in Media Coverage of Female Candidates." *Political Communication* 14: 71–82.

Smith, Sally Bedell. 2007. *For Love of Politics: Bill and Hillary Clinton: The White House Years.* New York: Random House.

Sparrow, Bartholemew H. 1999. *Uncertain Guardians: The News Media as a Political Institution.* Baltimore: The Johns Hopkins University Press.

Stanley, Alessandra. 2008a. "20th Debate: Reality Show or a Spinoff?" *New York Times*, February 27, A1.

———. 2008b. "Clinton Fades Even in a Victory." *New York Times*, May 21. www.nytimes.com/2008/05/21/us/politics/21watch.html?nl=pol&emc=pol.

Steele, Shelby. 2008. "The Obama Bargain." *Wall Street Journal*, March 18, A23.

Stein, Sam. 2008. "Matthews Calls Clinton Press Shop 'Lousy,' 'Kneecappers.'" *Huffington Post*, February 15. www.huffingtonpost.com/2008/02/15/matthews-calls-clinton-pr_n_86812.html.

Steinberg, Jacques. 2008. "On the Press Bus, Some Questions Over Favoritism." *New York Times*, March 1. www.nytimes.com/2008/03/01/us/politics/01press.html?ei=5070&en=b9738d89edc9c249&ex=1205038800&emc=eta1&pagewanted=print.

Steinberg, Jacques, and Janet Elder. 2008. "Analyzing the New Hampshire Surprise." *New York Times,* January 10. www.nytimes.com/2008/01/10/us/politics/10media.html?partner=rssnyt&emc=rss.

Steinem, Gloria. 2008. "Women Are Never Front-Runners." *New York Times*, January 8. www.nytimes.com/2008/01/08/opinion/08steinem.html.

Steinhauer, Jennifer. 2007. "McCain's Children Avoid the Limelight." *Boston Globe*, December 27. www.boston.com/news/nation/articles/2007/12/27/mccains_children_avoid_the_limelight.

Stelter, Brian. 2008a. "Finding Political News Online, the Young Pass It On." *New York Times,* March 27. www.nytimes.com/2008/03/27/us/politics/27voters.html.

———. 2008b. "Super Tuesday: Hallmark Channel Televises Hour-Long Clinton Commercial." *New York Times,* February 4. http://tvdecoder.blogs.nytimes.com/2008/02/04/super-tuesday-hallmark-channel-televises-hour-long-clinton-commercial.

Stephen, Andrew. 2008. "Hating Hillary." *The New Statesman*, May 22. www.newstatesman.com/north-america/2008/05/obama-clinton-vote-usa-media.

Streb, Matthew J., Barbara Burrell, Brian Frederick, and Michael A. Genovese. 2008. "Social Desirability Effects and Support for a Female American President." *Public Opinion Quarterly* 55: 313–330.

Suarez, Fernando. 2008. "N.C. Governor: Hillary Makes Rocky Look like 'Pansy.'" CBS News, April 29. www.cbsnews.com/blogs/2008/04/29/politics/fromtheroad/entry4054429.shtml.

Talk of the Nation. 2008. "Were Clinton's Strengths Also Her Weaknesses? (Interview with Gail Sheehy)." National Public Radio, August 26. www.npr.org/templates/story/story.php?storyId=93987424.

Tanden, Neera. 2008. Personal interview. May 12.

Tannen, Deborah. 2008. "The Hillary Factor." www.youtube.com/watch?v=QfLARzXUwUw.

Tapper, Jake. 2008a. "Bill Clinton: Obama Is Just Like Jesse Jackson." *Huffington Post*, January 26. www.huffingtonpost.com/2008/01/26/bill-clinton-obama-is-ju_n_83406.html.

————. 2008b. "Is Obama Using Sexist Language?" *Political Punch*, February 16. http://blogs.abcnews.com/politicalpunch/2008/02/is-obama-using.html.

————. 2008c. "Obama-Backing Congressman Compares Hillary Clinton to Glenn Close in 'Fatal Attraction.'" ABC News, May 10. http://blogs.abcnews.com/politicalpunch/2008/05/obama-backing-c.html.

Thomas, Evan. 2008a. "Always Their Own Worst Enemies." *Newsweek*, March 17. www.newsweek.com/id/120169.

————. 2008b. "A Perennial Press Opera: Be Serious! Give Us Access! The Roots of the Clinton-Media Tension." *Newsweek*, February 16. www.newsweek.com/id/112842.

Thomas, Sue. 1994. *How Women Legislate*. New York: Oxford University Press.

Thrush, Glenn. 2007. "On Defensive After Debate, Clinton Cites 'All Boys Club.'" *Los Angeles Times*, November 2. http://articles.latimes.com/2007/nov/02/nation/na-clinton2.

Thurman, Judith. 2008. "Fate Is a Feminist Issue." In Susan Morrison, ed., *Thirty Ways of Looking at Hillary: Reflections by Women Writers*, 74–79. New York: HarperCollins.

Time. 1978. "Is a Woman's Place in the House?" November 6. www.time.com/time/magazine/article/0,9171,948265-3,00.html.

Todd, Chuck, and Sheldon Gawiser. 2009. *How Barack Obama Won*. New York: Vintage Books.

Tomasky, Michael. 2007. "Can We Know Her?" *New York Review of Books* 54, no. 12 (July 19). www.nybooks.com/gallery/1566.

Toner, Robin. 2007. "Feminist Pitch by a Democrat Named Obama." *New York Times*, December 2. www.nytimes.com/2007/12/02/us/politics/02women.html.

————. 2008. "Mining the Gender Gap for Answers." *New York Times*, March 2.

Traister, Rebecca. 2007. "Campaigning While Female." *Salon.com*, December 19. www.salon.com/mwt/feature/2007/12/19/wrinkled_hillary.

Tripp, Aili Mari. 2008. "What Does the Rising Tide of Women in Executive Office Mean?" *Politics & Gender* 4, no. 3 (September): 473–474.

Trippi, Joe. 2008. Personal conversation. April 8.

Troy, Gil. 2000. "Mr. and Mrs. President? The Rise and Fall of the Co-Presidency." *The Social Science Journal* 37, no. 4: 591–600.

————. 2006. *Hillary Rodham Clinton: Polarizing First Lady*. Lawrence: University Press of Kansas.

USA Today. 2008. "*USA Today*/Gallup Poll Results." May 4. www.usatoday.com/news/politics/election2008/2008-05-04-polltable_N.htm.

Valbrun, Marjorie. 2008. "Will They Play the Race Card?" *Washington Post*, January 13, B07.

Valdini, Melody E. 2007. *The Strategic Use of Information Shortcuts: The Impact of Electoral Rules on Candidate Selection by Parties*. Paper presented at the Annual Meeting of the Midwest Political Science Association in Chicago, IL, April 12–15.

Vallone, Robert P., Lee Ross, and Mark R. Lepper. 1985. "The Hostile Media

Phenomenon: Biased Perception and Perceptions of Media Bias in Coverage of the 'Beirut Massacre.'" *Journal of Personality and Social Psychology* 49: 577–585.

Vinson, C. Danielle, and William V. Moore. 2007. "The Campaign Disconnect: Media Coverage of the 2000 South Carolina Presidential Primary." *Political Communication* 24, no. 4: 393–413.

Warner, Judith. 2007. "The Clinton Surprise." *New York Times*, October 18.

———. 2008a. "No Ordinary Woman." *New York Times*, October 26. www.nytimes.com/2008/10/26/opinion/26warner-1.html?_r=1&ei=5070&emc=eta1&oref=login.

———. 2008b. "Woman in Charge, Women Who Charge." *New York Times*, June 5. http://warner.blogs.nytimes.com/2008/06/05/woman-in-charge-women-who-charge/?ex=1213416000&en=ecfd6.

Watson, Robert P. 2000. *The Presidents' Wives: Reassessing the Office of First Lady*. Boulder: Lynne Rienner Publishers.

Watson, Robert P., and Ann Gordon, eds. 2003. *Anticipating Madam President*. Boulder: Lynne Rienner Publishers.

Wayne, Stephen J. 2008. *The Road to the White House 2008*, 8th ed. Florence, KY: Thomson Wadsworth.

Weaver, Warren, Jr. 1987. "Schroeder Will Run for President if Her Campaign Can Pay for Itself." *New York Times*, June 20. http://query.nytimes.com/gst/fullpage.html?res=9B0DE7DC1431F933A15755C0A961948260&sec=&spon=.

Welter, Barbara. 1966. "The Cult of True Womanhood: 1820–1860." *American Quarterly* 18, no. 2, part 1 (Summer): 151–174.

"What Went Wrong?" 2008. *New York Times*, June 8, A14.

Whitman, Christine Todd. 2008. "What Went Wrong: Boys on the Bias." *New York Times*, June 8, 14.

Will, George. 2008. "Start of a Marathon." *Washington Post*, January 10. www.realclearpolitics.com/articles/2008/01/long_race_leaves_no_excuse_for.html.

Wills, Garry. 1999. *A Necessary Evil: A History of American Distrust of Government*. New York: Simon and Schuster.

Wiltz, Teresa. 2008. "Obama Has Jay-Z on His Ipod and the Moves to Prove It." *Washington Post*, April 19.

Winter, Nicholas J. G. 2008. *Dangerous Frames: How Ideas About Race and Gender Shape Public Opinion*. Chicago: University of Chicago Press.

Witt, Linda, Karen M. Paget, and Glenna Matthews. 1994. *Running as a Woman: Gender and Power in American Politics*. New York: The Free Press.

Wolcott, James. 2008. "When Democrats Go Post-al." *Vanity Fair*, June. www.vanityfair.com/politics/features/2008/06/wolcott200806.

Women's Media Center. 2008. "Sexism Sells, But We're Not Buying It!" www.womensmediacenter.com/sexism_sells.html.

Woodall, Gina Serignese, and Kim L. Fridkin. 2003. "Shaping Women's Chances: Stereotypes and the Media." In Robert P. Watson and Ann Gordon, eds., *Anticipating Madam President*, 69–86. Boulder: Lynne Rienner Publishers.

Zaller, John R. 1998. "Monica Lewinsky's Contribution to Political Science." *PS: Political Science and Politics* 31, no. 2 (June 1998): 182–189.

Zeisler, Andi. 2007. "The B-Word? You Betcha." *Washington Post*, November 18, B01.

Zeleny, Jeff. 2008a. "Obama Clinches Nomination; First Black Candidate to Lead a Major Party Ticket." *New York Times*, June 4. www.nytimes.com/2008/06/04/us/politics/04elect.html?_r=1&th&emc=th&oref=slogin.

———. 2008b. "Obama, in a Shift, Focuses on McCain Rather Than Clinton." *New York Times*, April 23, A16.

Zernike, Kate. 2008. "She Just Might Be President Someday." *New York Times*, May 18, www.nytimes.com/2008/05/18/weekinreview/18zernike.html?_r=2&hp&oref=slogin&oref=slogin.

Index

About the Book

Senator Hillary Clinton won 18 million votes in 2008—nearly twice that of any presidential nominee in recent history—yet she failed to secure the Democratic nomination. In this compelling look at Clinton's historic candidacy, Regina Lawrence and Melody Rose explore how she came so close to breaking the ultimate glass ceiling in US politics, why she fell short, and what her experience portends for future female candidates in the media-saturated game of presidential politics.

The result is more than just a postmortem of the Clinton campaign. Lawrence and Rose craft a sophisticated argument about the complex mix of gender stereotypes, media routines, and the particulars of individual character and electoral context that will shape the prospects of any woman who competes in the presidential arena.

Regina G. Lawrence is Kevin P. Reilly, Sr., Chair in Political Communication at Louisiana State University. Her publications include *The Politics of Force: Media and the Construction of Police Brutality* and *When the Press Fails: Political Power and the News Media from Iraq to Hurricane Katrina*. **Melody Rose** is associate professor of political science and founding director of the Center for Women, Politics, and Policy at Portland State University. She is author of *Abortion: A Documentary and Reference Guide* and *Safe, Legal, and Unavailable? Abortion Politics in the 21st Century*.